You're Teaching My Child What?

A Physician Exposes the Lies of Sex Education and How They Harm Your Child

Miriam Grossman, M.D.

Regnery Publishing
WASHINGTON, D.C.

Regnery® is a registered trademark and its colophon is a trademark of Salem
Communications Holding Corporation

Cataloging-in-Publication data on file with the Library of Congress

ISBN: 978-1-68451-555-4
Library of Congress Control Number: 2009025268

First trade paperback edition published 2023

Published in the United States by
Regnery Publishing
A Division of Salem Media Group
Washington, D.C.
www.Regnery.com

Manufactured in the United States of America

10 9 8 7 6 5 4 3 2 1

Books are available in quantity for promotional or premium use. For
information on discounts and terms, please visit our website:
www.Regnery.com.

Truth does not become more true by virtue
of the fact that the entire world agrees with it,
nor less so even if the whole world disagrees with it.

—Moses Maimonides, *Guide for the Perplexed*

Table of Contents

♂♀

Preface

YOU'RE TEACHING MY CHILD WHAT? was first published in 2009. How does it feel, fourteen years later, to write the preface to the first paperback edition?

It feels bittersweet—with the emphasis, sadly, on bitter.

Of course, I'm pleased my work will reach a larger audience; there's renewed interest in my analysis of sex education because of my newest book, *Lost in Trans Nation: A Child Psychiatrist's Guide Out of the Madness*.

It's bitter because the red flags I waved those many years ago, alerting parents to the appalling content and dangerous lies of sex ed, did not get the attention they deserved, and too many have, and still are, paying the price.

I warned parents at the time that they were being conned by the sex ed industry, by eminent organizations swelling with government funds, claiming their programs are science based, age-appropriate, and medically accurate. These organizations want parents to believe they know what's best for their kids; moms and dads should trust them, the experts.

I demonstrated how parents were being hoodwinked. Those widely used school curricula and teen-friendly websites were anything but age-appropriate and medically accurate. They were instead steeped in an ideology that promotes graphic material and cradle-to-grave sexual behavior, including sexual deviance, to youth.

I explained how the agendas of what's called "comprehensive" sexuality education undermine the health and safety of children. These groups are dedicated to social change, not health. They seek to eliminate traditional values, not herpes or chlamydia. They distort biology and erase the innate and permanent distinctions between men and women. When a culture celebrates unrestrained sexuality and eliminates male and female, everyone suffers. But girls and women suffer most.

My arguments were supported with forty pages of scientific references. But the book was politically incorrect, so it was largely ignored. Support for my urgent message was limited to some conservative and religious groups.

It's bitter for me to witness the staggering price paid by youth, including those who turn to me for help, for their early sexualization, exposure to pornography, and for believing "boy" or "girl" was randomly "assigned" to them in the delivery room. My gender-distressed patients believe their bodies and minds are mismatched, and they yearn for medical and surgical "alignment." It can be challenging indeed to help them, as they've been indoctrinated to believe anyone who questions their feelings, or urges caution, is the enemy.

In the chapter "Genderland," I warned parents about the tenets of gender ideology, calling them "a dumbfounding departure from reality . . . a recipe for physical and emotional disaster for our kids."

It gives me no pleasure to say I was right, and that this book is more needed now than ever.

Had my alarm been heard and not silenced, some or all of those kids, and their parents, might have been spared their current ordeal. So many moms and dads remark, "You wrote about gender madness *in 2009*? If only I'd known."

I want to mention as well that in the years since the first edition of this book, Dr. Judith Reisman[1] passed away. Dr. Reisman devoted her life to exposing the fraudulent research of Alfred Kinsey, whose degenerate views on sexuality form the cornerstone of modern sex education. She was a fearless warrior on behalf of childhood innocence and was kind and generous to me and many others. Rest in peace, Judith. While the crusade against children has grown bolder, more aggressive, and its proponents more brazen, rest assured—we will fight to the end.

♂♀

Introduction:

Shocked

H AVE YOU EVER CROSSED PATHS with someone momen-
tarily, exchanged a few words, and then discovered you can't
forget their face, or something they said? That's what I'm
going through now. Several months ago, I gave a talk about sexual
health to college students, and a girl in the audience made an astonishing comment. Her words, and her eyes, haunt me to this day.

I'd been invited to speak at a small private college outside
Philadelphia. The auditorium was filled to capacity, with students
sitting in the aisles and leaning against the walls. It was a lively
crowd, but when I stepped up to the podium it fell silent.

They knew I wasn't there with another "safer sex" talk. Why fly me
in from across the country to tell them things they can recite in their
sleep? They invited me because I'm the doctor bringing the science
they'd never heard. The biochemistry of trust and attachment. How
ovulation is affected by a man's scent. Why a young cervix is easily
infected. They'd learn that evening that with or without protection,

sex is a serious matter—especially for girls. That a single encounter can have profound, life-long consequences.

I was there to teach the biology that was omitted from their "safer sex" training. It was a no-nonsense, politically incorrect approach to a subject close to their hearts, and they hung on to each word from start to finish.

Afterwards I asked for questions, and a number of hands shot up.

"What about the HPV vaccine?"

"There's reason to hope it will prevent a great deal of disease," I said, "but it's not a cure-all. Girls," I told them, "you should be vaccinated even if you've already been sexually active."

Next came a complaint:

"You assume everyone is heterosexual. You should be less hetero-normative."

This was not the right time for a discussion about the politically correct notion of "heteronormality," so I just thanked the student for his comment and added that the highest rates of sexually transmitted infections are found in gay men and bisexuals, and the lowest in lesbians.[1]

Then a dark-haired girl in the front row raised her hand.

"I'm a perfect example of what you talked about. I always used condoms, but I got HPV anyway, and it's one of the high-risk types. I had an abnormal Pap test, and next week I'm going to have a culposcopy."

She sounded mellow, but there was panic in her eyes.

I felt a wave of sorrow. This young woman was going in for a biopsy of her cervix because atypical cells were present—a result of infection with a high risk strain of HPV. I knew what that meant: she probably had HPV-16, the type that's most difficult for her body to clear,[2] and most likely to cause malignancy. If the infection persisted, her risk of developing cervical cancer was at least 40 percent.[3]

"But I thought it over," she continued, "and I decided that the pleasure I had with my partners was worth it."

The audience was silent. How does one react to such a declaration? With applause? High fives?

"I hope all goes well next week," I said, "and that you'll never have to worry about this again."

But I knew it wasn't so simple. In a few days she'll lie on a table with her feet in stirrups, a large electronic microscopic inches from her vagina. With a bright light illuminating the site, the gynecologist will examine her cervix. He'll say something like "this might be uncomfortable," then excise abnormal areas with a scalpel. It will hurt. She might have pain and discharge afterwards. Then she'll wait for a call with the results: is she okay, or not?

The way I saw it, her story was a double catastrophe. For a young woman—she couldn't have been over 20—to even *worry* about having cancer was the first catastrophe. At this time in her life, she shouldn't be concerned about anything more serious than finals.

The second catastrophe was her sentiment: "The pleasure I had was worth it."

Worth it? What's she talking about?

Didn't she have the concerns I always hear: *When was I infected, last week or last year?* and *Who was it, Kenny or Ron? Should I tell my current partner, or my future ones? What about Mom and Dad? What does dysplasia mean, anyhow? Could I really get . . .* cancer?

Was this young woman aware, I wondered, of all the possible ramifications? While it's true that most HPV seems to clear, she'll never know—is the virus gone, or just dormant? Had anyone told her that having one sexually transmitted disease (STD) makes her more vulnerable to others, including HIV? That being on the pill could increase her risk, and that pregnancy can re-activate the virus?

All this, yet "the pleasure was worth it"?

I guess she felt that sex trumps everything, even health. It was all about pleasure, even if it ends in disease. Where did this thinking come from?

Back to the Source

According to a 2008 report from the federal Centers for Disease Control, she has plenty of company: one in four adolescent girls in the United States has a sexually transmitted infection.[4] When that fact hit the news, parents were horrified, health experts were shocked, and the CDC called it "a wake-up call."[5]

A statement was issued by the president of the Sexuality Information and Education Council of the United States (SIECUS). The figures, it said, were "staggering" and "disturbing"; they represented an "inexcusable failure."[6]

Their reaction reminded me of a scene in the classic film *Casablanca*. You know, that famous line in which Captain Renault tells Rick he is "shocked—*shocked!*—to find that gambling is going on in here," and then quietly collects his winnings.

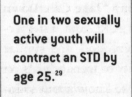

One in two sexually active youth will contract an STD by age 25.[29]

That 3.2[7] million American girls have a sexually transmitted infection should come as no shock, especially to SIECUS and its main cohorts, Advocates For Youth (AFY) and Planned Parenthood. This pandemic is a direct consequence of their vision and ideals.

These groups claim to provide "comprehensive access" to "accurate" sex education. Take a look, though, at their curricula, their guides for teachers and parents, and—most disturbing—the websites to which they direct your kids: you'll see how young people are infused with a grotesque exaggeration of the place of sexuality. Promiscuity, experimentation, and fringe behaviors are encouraged. For them, these are personal choices, and judgments are prohibited. At all ages, sexual freedom is a "right," an issue of social justice. In short, they are dedicated to promoting radical social ideologies, not preventing disease.

That one in four teens has a sexually transmitted infection (STI) is deeply troubling, yes, but it shouldn't come as a surprise. What's

Sex education is comprised of a vast network of programs with Planned Parenthood, Advocates for Youth, and SIECUS at its center. Consequently, every parent should check their child's school curricula for the full picture.

astonishing is the madness called "sexuality education." Until these programs are recognized as irresponsible and dishonest, young people, especially girls, will continue to pay an awful price.

Madness is a strong word, but the more I learn *what* our children are taught, and *when*, the more I stand by that choice.

Parents, have you heard what our kids are told? Have you seen what's put in front of them? I thought it was *illegal* to make indecent material available to minors. You think MTV is vulgar? I suggest you explore the material sex educators have created for kids.

Take a look at Planned Parenthood's revolting "Take Care Down There," and "How Babies are Made."[8] Check out gURL.com, a site recommended to teens by SIECUS, Planned Parenthood, and similar groups that claims to be "the largest community of teenage girls on the web." Their "experts" want your daughter to know about sadomasochism—"being tortured, bound, tickled or having hot wax poured on the body." "Though it may seem painful," your daughter will learn, "those involved find the pleasure outweighs the pain."[9] gURL.com's best selling book for teens, *Deal With It!*, lauded as "a superb reference for young women" by a former president of Planned Parenthood, provides your daughter with instructions on "giving a blow job," "going down on a girl," and features stick figure illustrations of "the three most popular positions" for intercourse.[10] Are you troubled by your teen's language? I direct you to www.positive.org, recommended by both SIECUS and AFY. You'll be horrified. This offensive material is foisted on our kids under the pretence of safeguarding their health and well-being.

When I think of someone exposing my kids to this smut, my eyes narrow and the claws come out. I see red. But what of the many young people who've been raised on this stuff? What effect has it had on their attitudes and behavior? As a physician and a mother, I weep for them.

Hicks vs. Harvard

Objections to today's sex education are hardly new. Some parents have been active in their opposition, taking legal action, even going to jail.[11] But organizations such as SIECUS and Planned Parenthood claim neutrality and successfully portray the conflict as religious right versus medical facts, hicks versus Harvard.

Those hicks must be on to something, because recent discoveries in neurobiology, endocrinology, and histology indicate science is in *their* corner. I contend that it's "comprehensive sexuality education" that's animated by pseudoscience and crackpot ideology. Sexuality educators charge their opposition with censoring medically accurate, up to date science, and argue that kids need more than a "plumbing lesson." Yet the sex ed industry is no less guilty of using science selectively and omitting facts that contradict their agendas. It's time to call foul.

SIECUS and Planned Parenthood have yet to recognize some of the most compelling research of recent years. These organizations are still animated by the philosophies of the infamous sexologist Alfred Kinsey—whose work has been debunked—the birth control and eugenics advocate Margaret Sanger, the feminist Gloria Steinem, and *Playboy* founder Hugh Hefner. These twentieth-century crusaders were passionate about social change, not health. Their goal was a cultural revolution, not the eradication of disease. And the same is true for the sex ed industry. That's why their premises haven't changed in fifty years, even as journals like *Neuropsychiatry* and *The New England Journal of Medicine* have filled with research contradicting them.

Bizarro World

While SIECUS informs kids that culture teaches what it means to be a man or a woman, neuroscientists identify distinct "male brains" or "female brains" while a child is still in the womb. According to the "experts," a girl is a "young woman," ready for "sex play," but gynecologists know the question is not *whether* a sexually active "young woman" will get herpes, HPV, or Chlamydia, it's *which one*. "Respect your teens' decisions," parents are advised; "step aside, and don't judge." But studies show kids do best when parents convey their expectations and stand firm. Give adolescents information, they promise, provide them with condoms and pills, and they'll make smart decisions. But MRIs show that during highly charged moments, teen brains rely on gut feelings, not reason. In other words, it's not ignorance causing all those pregnancies and infections; it's the unfinished wiring between brain cells.

These findings, and more, are excluded from modern sex education. Why? Because they contradict Kinsey, Hefner, and Steinem. They testify against the anything goes, women-are-just-like-men ideology. They announce to the world: Hicks – 1, Harvard – 0.

What Sex Ed Is Really All About

Parents, if you believe that the goals of sexuality education are to prevent pregnancy and disease, you are being hoodwinked. You must understand that these curricula are rooted in an ideology that you probably don't share. This ideology values, above all—health, science, or parental authority—sexual freedom.

According to this philosophy, a successful curriculum encourages students to develop their own values, not blindly accept those of their community. It emphasizes the wisdom they'll gain through open-mindedness and tolerance. "Students . . . become more 'wide awake' and open to multiple perspectives that make the familiar strange and the strange familiar," according to one sex education manual.[12]

If the subject is marine biology or entomology, you might not mind if the "strange" becomes the "familiar" to your child. But when it comes to issues of sexuality, it might be another matter entirely. Do you want instructors, whose personal values might be at odds with yours, to encourage your kids to question what they've been taught at home and at church,[13] and to come up with their own worldview based on taking sexual risks that endanger their health and wellbeing? It seems reasonable to question the ethics of this practice.

What these "experts" are hiding is their goal of bringing about radical social change, one child at a time. Their mission is to mold each student into what is considered "a sexually healthy" adult—as if there was universal agreement on what that is.[14] From a review of many of today's sex ed curricula and websites, it would appear that a "sexually healthy" individual is one who has been "desensitized," who is without any sense of embarrassment or shame (what some might consider "modesty"), whose sexuality is always "positive" and "open," who respects and accepts "diverse" lifestyles, and who practices "safer sex" with every "partner."

This is not about health, folks. This is about indoctrination.

The Madness of "Comprehensive Sex Ed"

Don't wait until children ask questions, parents are told by sex education "experts"; to ensure their healthy future, they need information early. Teach preschoolers that each of us is sexual, from cradle to grave, and that "sexual expression" is one of our basic human needs, like food, water, and shelter. Encourage their "positive body concept," by expanding games such as "Simon Says" to include private parts (*Simon says point to your ear, ankle, penis*).[15] Explain intercourse to preschoolers[16]; tell them they have "body parts that feel good when touched."[17] Inform five-year-olds that "everyone has sexual thoughts and fantasies" and that "people experience sexual pleasure in a number of different ways."[18] Teach kids about HIV before they know their ABCs.[19]

The potential for harm is even greater a few years later when our kids must learn more, we're told, for their own good. Planned Parenthood says 3rd grade is the time to find out about wet dreams, masturbation, rape, and "sex work."[20] Nine- to twelve-year-olds should understand that male and female are not defined solely by chromosomes or genitalia; everyone has an "internal sense" of his or her identity, and that "sense" might not jibe with what they see in the mirror.

As you can imagine, sex educators believe that the "information" teens "need" to know is more explicit and disturbing. But by then, of course, if not earlier, they can go online themselves and check out the sites sexuality educators recommend, like Columbia University's "Go Ask Alice." I urge every adult whose life includes a young person to check out this award-winning site, one that gets over two thousand questions a week, and many more hits. On "Alice," teens find excellent information about drugs, alcohol, diet, depression, and other health issues. But they also learn how to purchase "adult products" by phone,[21] arrange a threesome,[22] and stay "safe" during sadomasochistic "sex play."[23]

Yes, madness—that's the right word.

With messages like this coming from websites recommended to our kids, it should come as no surprise that 34 percent of girls are sexually active by age fifteen. The figure goes up to nearly 80 percent four years later, with more than one-fifth of all fifteen- to nineteen-year-olds reporting two or more partners *in the past year*. Hey, they are exploring their sexuality; it's only "natural."

But in these times, anyone "exploring" sexuality is at risk for some two dozen different bacteria, viruses, parasites, and fungi; and infection is likely to happen soon after sexual debut. Who suffers the most? Girls. One of the many facts withheld by "sex educators" is that teen girls are anatomically more vulnerable to sexually transmitted diseases than boys. They also gloss over the fact that decades of sex education have taken our society from having essentially two sexually transmitted diseases to worry about (syphilis and gonorrhea) to having more than two dozen, including some incurable viruses, and one that's often fatal: HIV. They deem it vital for kids to know there are not one, but *three* types of intercourse; apparently they don't need to know that one of these is so dangerous that a surgeon general warned against it, even *with* a condom.

> **An anonymous survey of 10,000 teen girls found they began having sexual intercourse on average at age 15.**[30]

And this question is never, ever raised: what new bug is out there, spreading undetected, an epidemic in the making?

There are some things you need to know about condoms—what sex educators call "protection." Most teens do not use them correctly and consistently. Even with proper use, both pregnancy and infection can occur. That's why so many health providers have given unwelcome news to young patients who insist, *"But we used a condom, every time!"*

These young victims are angry, because even after following the rules, after being responsible, they're in trouble: using a condom gave them a false sense of security.[24] And need I mention that latex provides no protection against the emotional distress that often follows teen sexual behavior? As many have observed, condoms do not protect the heart, in particular the female heart.[25] That's another thing SIECUS, Planned Parenthood, and Columbia's "Alice" never tell your daughter.

Again, the priority of our nation's sex educators is to promote sexual freedom, not prevent infections and emotional distress. In fact, as the numbers of infections reach ever more mind-numbing levels, these educators argue for more of last century's methods. The solution to the epidemic is to teach *more* kids they are "sexual from womb to tomb," encourage *more* teens to question their families' values, and to send trucks with even *larger* loads of contraceptives to middle schools—to be distributed without parental knowledge. Have they lost their minds?

Wake Up, America!

You might think I'm bashing sex ed because I'm on the other side of the battle. Not exactly. Abstinence education tells kids to wait for marriage, and for many that message rests on moral foundations. As an Orthodox Jew, I share those values—but you won't find me quoting Leviticus in these pages. I'll leave that to parents and pastors. I write as a physician, and my approach is anchored in hard science.

I wrote this book to tell parents they're being conned by the sex education industry. These powerful organizations present themselves as guardians of our children's health and well-being; they claim to provide kids with all the information and skills they need to make healthy choices. They assert they give your child the same message she hears at home: *you're too young—wait until you're older.* They claim their curricula are "science-based," age-appropriate, non-judgmental, up-to-date, and medically accurate. And they believe they know better than you do what's best for your kids, so you should trust them, the "experts," and ignore your gut feelings.

Wake up, America: this is one giant hoax. I know these groups, their values, and curricula. They are *steeped* in ideology, *permeated* with extremism. Non-judgmental? Sure, until they're challenged with scientific facts. Point to the science that discredits their beliefs, and, well, you know the names you'll be called.

They do *not* give young people the same message as parents. Children are inundated from a tender age with a "sex-positive" message; they're taught that sexuality is a life-long adventure, "who they are" from cradle to grave, and that the freedom to explore and express their sexuality is a sacred "right." While teens are told that delaying sexual behavior is an option—and sure, it's the only 100 percent certain way to avoid infections and pregnancy—it is not presented as the healthiest choice, the one recommended by experts. Consider the views of Debra Haffner, a recent SIECUS president who is now a minister. Premarital sex is so essential, the Reverend Haffner appears to believe, that she'd "refuse to marry a couple who told me that they had shared no sexual behaviors at all."[26]

The experts do *not* provide teens with all they need to know to make informed decisions, nor is their information medically accurate. They dismiss fundamentals of child development, and omit critical findings of neurobiology, gynecology, and infectious disease. HIV information is distorted. The psychological distress associated with teen sex, especially when followed by a genital infection, is whitewashed.

The "experts" are wrong, and parents are right. Boys and girls have vast differences, sexual behavior is profound and consequential, and we reap immense benefits from self-restraint. Mom and Dad should trust their common sense, gut feelings, and traditional values. Children raised by parents who are moderately strict and voice clear expectations about delaying sexual activity, are the kids least likely to engage in harmful behaviors. Yes, that throwback excuse works: *"I can't—my parents would kill me!"*

A 911 Emergency

In the course of my practice, your sons and daughters have shared with me what life has brought them—what cards they've been dealt. They reveal their secrets: *I lied to my parents. My girlfriend gave me herpes. My stepfather raped me. I want die.*

The worst part? When something awful happened that was 100 percent preventable. This category includes, but is not limited to, blisters or warts in private places, meaningless, regrettable sex, pre-cancerous conditions, age-related infertility. *If only I'd known . . .*, patients say. *If only someone had told me.*

Parents, there are so many things your children don't know. There are so many things they are not being told.

Here's the bottom line. We have an emergency here, a 911 emergency. Parents, educators, and health providers must convey the same message to kids: *Right now, sexually transmitted diseases are out of control. We've never had a crisis like this. These infections are painful and nasty, they can even be life-threatening, so you want to avoid them at all costs. Girls are particularly vulnerable. Your health and future are precious; don't take a chance of becoming one of the many people who regret putting their entire trust in a vaccine,*[27] *or a piece of latex. Be smart, delay sex until you're an adult, then try to find someone who also waited. The closer you get to that ideal, the better your chances of enjoying a life free of these worries.*

This book will help you do that. I've combed through current medical research, and collected what you need to know when you sit down with your child. If you've got religious values backing you up, you're in even better shape.

> **Almost half of high school students nationwide and about 62 percent of students in the twelfth grade have had sexual intercourse.**[31]

Make no mistake: this is a battle, and the battleground is our kids' minds and values. It's time for sweeping changes in the way we teach them about intimacy; with one in four teen girls carrying a sexually transmitted infection, we've paid the price for telling them "exploration" is beneficial, and a *Sex and the City* lifestyle can be "safe," or even "safer." In providing that message, we have failed our kids.

The sex ed industry cannot be like *Casablana's* Captain Renault, "shocked" about soaring rates of genital infections while crusading for "sexual freedom." It's one or the other. If their priority is our children's health, they must focus on fighting herpes and syphilis, not sexism and homophobia. They must grow up, shed their 1960s mentality, and enter the twenty-first century.

Then they must respond to this catastrophe by declaring war on teen sexual behavior. Yes, *war*—just as we've declared war on smoking, drinking, and transfats. Stop foisting the ill-conceived notion that sexual openness and exploration is healthy. That was never true, and it's surely not true now, with genital bacteria and viruses infecting another young person *every 3.5 seconds.*[28]

How much worse can it get?

It's time to trash the SIECUS and Planned Parenthood curricula, along with the sites they recommend, and start over, from scratch. Sex education in the twenty-first century should have one agenda: to keep kids free of unnecessary physical and emotional distress. It will require straight talk with all the sobering facts. There's much to look forward to, kids will be told, but you've got to play it smart. It will remind them: you are responsible for yourselves; you alone will determine your sexual health; it will convince them that momentary pleasures are definitely *not* "worth it." And it will give them our vote of confidence—we know you can do it.

This book is a tool for parents, health care providers, and teachers to counter the destructive messages that kids are getting—not only from MTV, but from national organizations supported by their tax dollars. It sounds an alarm, delineates the issues, and provides practical solutions.

If only I'd known..., patients tell me. *If only someone had told me.* My hope is that the information in these pages will help spare parents, teachers, health providers—anyone involved in the lives of young people—from hearing that plea in the future.

♂♀

Chapter One

Who's Teaching
Your Children?

THE NATION'S CONFLICT OVER SEX EDUCATION is a battle over your child's mind. How will she understand intimacy, not just its mechanics and risks, but its power and proper place in her life? What was once a discreet conversation between you and your child is now in the hands of educators and politicians.

Parents, beware: the people teaching your child are activists, promoting radical agendas at odds with your values.

They insist they're neutral and free of agendas—promoting healthy sexuality is what they're about. Sounds great, but those claims are bogus. Sex education is about as neutral as a catechism class. And like a catechism, the "information" and "guidance" offered is designed to inculcate particular beliefs in young people.

Sex education is not about health—it's a social movement, a vehicle for changing the world. It happens one child at a time, and it goes on right under your nose.

Take a closer look at the curricula and the websites recommended to teens,[1] and you'll see what I mean. The following questions were posed on websites recommended to teens by prominent sex education organizations.

Question: My boyfriend and I are thinking of having sex. Can I get the pill without my mom knowing?[2]

Answer: Generally, yes. There is no law that requires a parent's permission for the pill...A good place to start is a place that receives money from...Title X funding...they can't tell your mom if you got the pill. You can find a Title X clinic near you through [website provided]...

Question: Is it normal for girls to experiment with sex together when they're not lesbian?[3]

Answer: With young adults, it's always been developmentally common to be less selective about—or to have a wider net of—sexual partners. (And we might also even ask ourselves where people get the idea that sex within the context of romantic love is the best place for it...there's a pretty hardcore political and cultural agenda behind that notion)....When it comes to sexuality...what's important isn't that we are all 'normal,' but that our sexuality feels authentic and good for us...and that whatever we do with others makes us all happy.

Question: What is a girl to do when her boyfriend tells her he likes to be the "slave," and lists the ways he'd like to be punished? *"We're only 15, and I just want to have a fairly normal relationship."*[4]

Answer: 'Normal' is a pretty arbitrary term. The boyfriend's wishes are not abnormal or deviant when practiced consensually...in the right time and place...nearly anything we do can be normal, healthy and empowering....It isn't a particular act or practice that determines normality, well-being and health, but how we practice it.

You could have knocked me over with a feather when I found these Q&A's. "Nearly anything we do can be normal"? "There's a political and cultural agenda behind" the notion that romantic love is the best place for sex? It's "developmentally common" for young adults to have a wide net of sexual partners?

Heather Corinna, Ellen Friedrichs, and other "experts" dish out advice like this to tens of thousands of young readers who visit their sites[5] in search of help with matters small and large: from kissing with braces on their teeth, to abortions and suicidal behavior. Yet in addition to answering teens' questions, Heather and "educators" like her familiarize kids with fringe behaviors, provide links to adult-only sites,[6] and urge their readers to join the fight for "social justice."

As a mother and psychiatrist who has spent years helping kids like these, I had to know: are these individuals qualified to advise teens through complex, life-altering decisions? How would a 13-year-old get to scarleteen and gURL.com, where these questions were posted, anyhow? Why are risky and bizarre behaviors and political agendas endorsed on sites about teen health and sexuality? For that matter, why haven't these sites—in existence for years—been shut down long ago by professional health organizations?

Having read this far, it may not surprise you to learn that these "experts" are not physicians, psychologists, or nurses. Heather, who reassured the 15-year-old about her boyfriend's sexual masochism, describes herself as "a queer, feminist activist, writer, photographer, artist, educator, and Internet publisher and community organizer. . . . She has been considered a pioneer of both online women's and young adult sexuality, having brought inclusive, informative, feminist, original, creative and radical sexuality content to the web and beyond since 1997."

She studied English Literature, Erotic Spirituality and Soci-
ology in college. She ran an alternative Kindergarten in her
early twenties. She sold wheatgrass and sprouts...waited
tables, rang cash registers, taught kickboxing and self-
defense, did political canvassing...

In addition to scarleteen, Heather has two other websites. At Fem-
merotic.com, what she calls her "online home," you'll find this warning: *Portions of this site often contain sexuality, nudity & salty language
and are intended for adult viewers.*

At scarletletters.com, the warning is simpler: "adult themes." From
the homepage: "We break boundaries and bridge gaps, crashing the
genre and gender barricades.... Get ready to look at sexuality, erotica,
creativity and online media in a whole new way.... If you are over 18,
enter HERE."

I'm well over 18, but decided against entering scarletletters or fem-
merotic. I knew enough to conclude that Heather Corinna—the same
Heather to whom SIECUS refers teens in angst about acne, guys, and
parents, is not only without any formal medical or psychological
training—she's a bona fide pornographer.[7]

How Do Teens Get to These Sites?

Simple. They are sent to them, and a host of similar sites, by the
country's largest and most respected sex ed organizations—the Sexuality Information and Education Council of the United States
(SIECUS), Planned Parenthood, and Advocates for Youth. Some of the
sites and organizations maintain presence on Facebook, MySpace, and
Twitter—hoping to connect to even more teens. Furthermore, these
organizations receive funding from the federal Centers for Disease
Control (CDC). So indirectly, our kids access Heather, and other
"experts" like her, with the help of our tax dollars.[8]

SIECUS has been the nation's flagship sex ed organization for nearly fifty years, and is currently the leading advocate for comprehensive sexuality education. This group has "trained hundreds of thousands of educators, worked with thousands of policymakers, appeared in the leading print and broadcast media outlets, and led the effort to advance sexual and reproductive health on six continents," according to their website.[9] SIECUS claims to represent a neutral, ideology-free, common sense approach; it receives federal funding through a cooperative agreement with the Centers for Disease Control and Prevention's Division of Adolescent and School Health.[10]

PLANNED PARENTHOOD FEDERATION is "the nation's leading sexual and reproductive health care advocate and provider."[11] According to its 2007–2008 annual report,[12] Planned Parenthood's "operating and other funds" totaled $1.038 billion, with over a third of that sum ($349.6 million) coming from government grants and contracts. This immense and powerful organization believes "we are sexual from the day we are born until the day we die."[13]

ADVOCATES FOR YOUTH (AFY) is "a bold voice and respected leader in the field of adolescent reproductive and sexual health."[14] They pioneered the movement to establish "reproductive health care clinics" near junior and senior high schools; they also encourage and support "young activists across the country and around the world." Their popular "Life Planning Education" places sex ed in the context of life skills such as communication and decision- making—a great idea, but students learn here that *children are sexual even before birth. Males can have erections while still in the uterus and some boys are born with an erection.*"[15]

AFY describes the nation's sex education debate as being between ideology and science. They think they're on the side of science.

It would be easy to dismiss the unnerving "advice" provided by one Heather Corinna, a dyed-in-the-wool radical "feminist activist," who "lives in Seattle with her partner and cat," and—in between online chats with confused teens—brings erotica to the web. She's just one person. But she has support from eminent organizations, supposedly dedicated to the health and well being of young people. They actually endorse Heather Corinna's anything-goes, agenda-driven website, despite the fact that she promotes a lifestyle that most medical providers—to say nothing of parents—would find alarming.

Over 90 percent of parents want their kids to delay sexual behavior. So why do authorities on the government payroll usher teens to websites[16] where high risk behavior is assumed, and deviant behavior normalized? Why don't they encourage the smartest, healthiest message, and forget all the politics and kinky stuff?

I look forward to an opportunity to pose these questions publicly. In the meantime, I've been to the library. I learned how sex ed—originally called "social hygiene" and "family life education"—was first taught in the last century; about Alfred Kinsey, who introduced a new model of human sexuality in the 1940s and 1950s; and about the institutionalization of this model through SIECUS in the 1960s. I studied the books written for parents and teens, and read biographies, interviews, op-eds, court testimony, and obituaries.

You need to know what I discovered.

The Kinsey Scale of Human Sexuality

To understand how an individual such as Heather Corinna became a recognized teen sexuality instructor, you must understand Alfred Kinsey.

Well, maybe not *understand* him—that would require a team of seasoned psychiatrists. So let's just say, you must be familiar with him. Dr. Kinsey was to sex education what Henry Ford was to the automobile. He was the master architect of a new model of human sexuality—a model based on his conviction that in modern society, traditional morality is irrelevant and destructive. Judeo-Christian teachings have it all wrong. "Sexuality is not an appetite to be curbed," he insisted. He believed that monogamy is unnatural; rather, the "human animal"—a term Kinsey liked to use—is *pansexual*.

Pansexual? Kinsey's authoritative biographer, James Jones, explains the professor's meaning. Kinsey believed that in our natural state—that is, free from social constraints—we humans would become sexually active early in life, enjoy intercourse with both sexes, indulge in a variety of behaviors, and eschew fidelity. Kinsey applauded practically every kind of sexual activity, Jones writes, and he disapproved of sexual abstinence.[17]

So, who exactly was Alfred Kinsey, and how did he reach his conclusions about human sexuality? Kinsey was not a student of human biology or psychology. His training was in the classification of insects. Prior to his scrutiny of human sexual behavior, he collected and classified wasps. Lots of wasps. Like over eight million.[18]

There's more, but I must warn readers that disturbing material lies ahead. In moments you'll wish for a "brain-bleach" to blot out what you have absorbed.

Alfred Kinsey was a bona fide mental case. The American Psychiatric Association will disapprove of my choice of words, but really, what other term adequately describes a man who, throughout his life, experienced pleasure by inserting foreign objects—straws, pipe cleaners, pencils, and toothbrushes—into his penis?[19] Who climbed into a bathtub and removed his foreskin with a pocketknife?[20] Who suspended himself in the air by a rope tied around his scrotum?[21]

"Masochist" falls short, don't you think? Kinsey's pathology went beyond the pursuit of pain and humiliation—his biography describes a man consumed by a grotesque, debilitating, dangerous obsession with sex. The man was a slave—to his insatiable appetite and to his compulsive, self-destructive needs. Through the years, in spite of his professional success and international fame, his self-inflicted brutality only increased: near the end of his life, Kinsey landed in the hospital after traumatizing his genitals, taking months to recover.

> "Kinsey had become a secret reformer in pursuit of the great cause of his life," writes his biographer. "Sex research had given him a way to conduct a public crusade for private reasons, a way to join his outer and inner identities."
>
> — James Jones

Here are some Kinseyian highlights (maybe lowlights would be more accurate):

- He set up a recording studio in his attic to film sexual encounters with his wife and among members of his "inner circle"—staff members, graduate students, and their wives.
- His primary interest was in male sadomasochistic behavior,[22] for which "outsiders" were invited to star in his attic performances.
- He was a sexual exhibitionist: "Kinsey seldom passed up an opportunity to show off his genitals and demonstrate his various masturbatory techniques to staff members."[23]
- Kinsey was all in favor of adult-child sexual contact— what we think of as child molestation—and considered adults who engaged in it "much maligned."
- For his "research," he interviewed jailed pedophiles and sex offenders and trolled the seedier parts of Chicago and New York City, befriending male prostitutes, transvestites, sadists, and masochists.

Why is this macabre tale important to tell? Because modern sex education derives from the personal philosophy of this man—a man enslaved to the urges of a warped mind, who in all probability did not know even one day of healthy sexuality in all his sixty-two miserable years.[24]

He set out to prove to the world, and probably himself, that there really wasn't anything wrong with him; and lo and behold, it turned out that his research on human sexuality did just that. In order to get there, Kinsey and his disciples reduced sexual behavior to a physiological act: emotionless, without context, meaning, or consequences. That's freedom, they said—freedom from judgment, laws, moral restrictions, and religious doctrine. They embraced freedom to be a "human animal."

When the sexually tormented entomologist turned from insects to humans, he wanted to know one thing: what Americans did behind closed doors. Assisted by two colleagues, he interviewed thousands of volunteers about their personal lives. They were asked question such as: Do you masturbate? Engage in homosexuality? Adultery? Bestiality? Then he catalogued their responses, crunched the numbers, and filled two tomes (a report on men in 1948, and one on women in 1953) with statistics, diagrams, and charts. His conclusions: most Americans engaged in some prohibited type[25] of behavior and were living a life of lies; the average mom and dad—think *Leave It to Beaver* sort of folks— were practicing a variety of forbidden sexual activities; no one is truly heterosexual or homosexual; heterosexuality is only "a result of social pressures which tend to force an individual into an exclusive pattern."

Kinsey's findings spawned a revolution and transformed western culture.

The problem is, Kinsey's "research" was fundamentally flawed. His research and findings were questioned at the time by everyone from *Time* magazine,[26] to the distinguished anthropologist Margaret Mead, to one of the country's leading psychiatrists, Lawrence Kubie. Kinsey's samples were too small and the demography was badly skewed. He excluded some populations and focused on others—most notably, imprisoned felons. His subjects were pre-selected, since he relied on volunteers for his data.

When Kinsey's work was published, Margaret Mead said it reduced sexuality "to the category of a simple act of elimination"[27] and "suggests no way of choosing between a woman and a sheep."

Kubie charged that Kinsey's report contained "inaccurate data, wholly unwarranted implications, distortions, errors, exaggerations, errors in sampling, interviewing and treatment of statistics . . . ideas that are patently absurd."

"[I]t is incorrect and misleading to assume," the Yale professor wrote, "that because something is widespread in human behavior it must therefore be regarded as 'normal'. . . this is demonstrably fallacious. In times of epidemic the common cold may afflict more than 50% of the population. This, however, does not make colds normal."[28]

Maybe it made Kinsey feel better about himself to find safety in numbers and to conclude that if everyone was doing it, it must be normal. The problem is, it just isn't true that a behavior or activity can be considered "normal" if it is "common." The time has come to stop talking about normal and abnormal and think about behaviors in terms of whether they promote health or disease.

However normal or abnormal we think Kinsey's views are, in the end, they prevailed. The criticism of his methods just didn't seem to matter. The popular press accepted his conclusions without question, and printing presses ran constantly to keep up with demand for his first book—a three pound, 804-page volume. "Not since *Gone with the Wind* had booksellers seen anything like it," noted *TIME* magazine.[29]

"In father-daughter incest, the daughter's age makes all the difference in the world. The older she is, the likelier it is that the experience will be a positive one. The best sort of incest of all, surprisingly enough, is that between a son and a mother who is really educating him sexually, and who then encourages him to go out with girls."[62]

—Kinsey associate and former SIECUS president Wardell Pomeroy.

Despite the strong and serious objections to his theories and methodology from people who knew what they were talking about, his theories and conclusions took root. Today's sexual mores, sex offender laws, and "safer sex" curricula are founded on his ideology and research.

Scratch the surface of SIECUS, Planned Parenthood, and other groups, and you'll discover that they are essentially mouthpieces for his views. In the upside down world of sex education, the ideology of Alfred Kinsey has been enshrined. Here's how it happened.

Following Kinsey's death in 1956, members of his inner circle— you know, his "close" associates—continued his mission. Paul Gebhard took over the helm at Indiana University's Kinsey Institute. Wardell Pomeroy,[30] who regularly participated, along with his wife, in Kinsey's attic get-togethers—founded the Advanced Institute of Human Sexuality in San Francisco, where thousands have been awarded degrees in "sexology," or become certified to become your child's sex educators. And in the early 1960s, the Kinsey worldview[31] was institutionalized when Mary Calderone established the country's first modern sex education organization, giving it the authoritative-sounding name, Sex Information and Education Council of the United States, or SIECUS.

Calderone, who had been director of Planned Parenthood prior to the creation of SIECUS, was a medical doctor. But the focus of her newly launched organization, which was, by the way, founded with seed money from Hugh Hefner[32] of *Playboy* fame,[33] was not to treat or prevent disease. Like Kinsey, she was crusading for social reform. Her book for parents reads like a primer for his views, and quite a few Kinsey disciples had eminent positions with SIECUS. Calderone—known for her liberal use of four letter words in lectures[34]—believed there was an urgent need to break from traditional ideas about sex, especially the way it was taught to young people. She found fault with the model used in school-based programs because they focused on preventing pregnancy and venereal diseases—as sexually transmitted diseases were called.

Calderone believed that when the negativity of sex educators is added to society's repressive morality, the result is too many *no's.*

They decided it was time for a different approach—one based on *yes's.* They believed sex must be affirmed as positive, natural, and healthy.[35] The time was right: thanks to antibiotics, the most common venereal diseases—gonorrhea and syphilis—were being obliterated.[36] "We have basically wiped out infection in the United States," the surgeon general declared in 1967.[37] Birth control pills had become widely available. With hazardous infections easily cured,[38] and pregnancy preventable, the only obstacles to replacing the *no's* with *yes's* were middle class morality and convention.

At Calderone's side was fellow activist Lester Kirkendall. With A Ph.D. from Columbia University's Teacher's College, Kirkendall was described in *Alternative Lifestyles* as "a pioneer in the study of inti-

Using materials from the Kinsey archives (i.e. films from the attic), a technique called Sexual Attitude Restructuring (SAR) was created. Simply put, this is a multimedia onslaught of pornographic images: films and slides of "a broad range of sexual behavior, with no emotional or relationship elements," projected on multiple large screens simultaneously, with audio, for hours at a time, over the course of two days. The experience—called F-ck-O-Rama in its early days—is followed by small group discussions. Its objective? "To desensitize members of the audience, so they won't be shocked by a wide variety of sexual behavior."[63]

What was SIECUS's stance on this pornographic extravaganza? That's easy: SAR creator Richard Chilgren was on the board in 1972.[64] To Wardell Pomeroy, SAR was "therapeutic." Since its inception, tens of thousands of therapists in training, members of human services professions, and individuals been through SAR. It continues to be offered within the sex ed industry.[65]

macy... his interest in sexuality has focused on alternative avenues to fulfillment in recent years."[39]

Kirkendall came up with a "bill of sexual rights." Inspired, no doubt, by the bi-centennial—the year was 1976—the bill declared, among other things, "The boundaries of human sexuality need to be expanded" and "Physical pleasure has worth as a moral value."[40] In keeping with the Kinsey tradition, what made sense to this SIECUS co-founder was pluralism of lifestyles, such as communes, spouse exchanges, and polygamy.

Together, Calderone and Kirkendall set out, through SIECUS, to transform how American children were taught about sex. Openness, tolerance, and joy were in; church lady and horse needles in the tush—injections of antibiotics to treat venereal diseases—were out. They were fired up and confident. Calderone even wrote to the Pope telling him he should not condemn masturbation, because studies had shown it was not harmful. He didn't answer.[41]

With or without the Vatican's blessing, they embarked on a crusade: to inculcate in American youth what were seen by them as eternal, unquestionable truths. Of course in those early years, Kinsey's personal life, and therefore the depth of his emotional disturbance, was unknown. Still, instead of recognizing that their views were based on the ruminations of one individual, SIECUS promoted—and continues to promote—Kinseyian thinking as if it had been engraved on tablets and revealed while thunder roared and trumpets flared.

"Happy Birthday, Dr. Kinsey."

It's June 23, Alfred Kinsey's birthday. Planned Parenthood's website marks the occasion with a flattering photo of the professor, and a celebration of his achievements.

"[Dr. Kinsey's] groundbreaking scientific investigations...tore through the century-old veils of hypocrisy...." He demonstrated "unheard-of truths," and made "unique contributions"—one of them a "core belief" they hold "dearly": *Sexuality is an essential, life long*

> At a teacher-training conference in New Jersey sponsored by the Network for Family Life Education, a workshop began with this warm-up exercise:
>
> "Turn to the person next to you. Make eye contact. Say 'Hello, penis.' Shake hands and return the greeting: 'Hello, vulva.'"[66]

aspect of being human and should be celebrated with respect, openness, and mutuality.[42]

They worship this guy! Now hold on a minute. Isn't he the same Alfred Kinsey who . . . well, you just read all about him—no need to rehash the gruesome details. Really, how could this depraved individual and his discredited research be the source of anyone's "core belief," let alone a worldwide organization claiming to be "America's most trusted provider of reproductive health care"?[43]

Yet that's the case. When Heather tells kids that "normal is a pretty arbitrary term" and nearly any sexual behavior can be "healthy and empowering," she's spouting his message. When educators encourage kids to question what they've heard at home and church, to be open to the full "range" of sexual expression, and to explore and experiment, they are transmitting Kinsey's legacy.

So, if Kinsey is the idol of the sex ed religion, here are their indisputable articles of faith, the cornerstones of modern sex education.

1. Sexuality is our entire selves, influences us in every way, and encompasses everything.

This is not just self-actualization gobbledygook. This premise provides the rationale for integrating sex education "across the curriculum." Translation: it can be introduced to your daughter in English, Math, and Social Studies, without your consent. Why shouldn't it? It's not about intercourse, it's language arts. How can a parent object to that? In a fourth grade[44] English class, for example, sex ed can be tied in with communication skills. Teachers are instructed, in the SIECUS and Planned Parenthood-recommended book *Teaching About Sexuality and HIV*:

> Effective communication is a key goal of effective sexuality education—a goal shared with language arts programs. Why not, then, teach the concepts and values of sexuality by employing such methodologies as reading books, writing poetry, talking with others—in short, by building upon the components of language arts programs? ... Viewing sexuality as a part of life allows us to teach elementary sexuality education without concern or trepidation.[45]

One prominent New Jersey sex educator came up with a creative way to express this article of faith. She put it this way: "You are not just being sexual by having intercourse. You are being sexual when you throw your arms around your grandpa and give him a hug."[46]

The problem with these views is once kids believe that sexuality is "who they are," "their entire selves" from womb to tomb, the idea that it's an appetite in need of restraint makes little sense. And the notion of waiting years for the right time and person sounds irrational. Why restrain "who you are"? Why wait for "your entire self"? Couldn't that be unhealthy?

2. The more information the better, and the earlier your small children get it, the better.

SIECUS tells parents: "Do not wait until your children ask questions ... be sure your young children know about HIV/AIDS infection and prevention."[47] Even "young children" need to know, they tell parents in their Newsletter "Families Are Talking"; "the only way to help prevent HIV/AIDS among young people is to share accurate, age-appropriate information so that they can protect themselves."[48]

Planned Parenthood claims there is no such thing as too much information[49] and that talking about sex and sexuality is best started from the time the child is born.[50] By age five, they believe children need to know "how a baby 'gets in' and 'gets out' of a woman's body," as well as the basic facts about HIV/AIDS.[51]

Advocates for Youth advises parents: "To help six- to eight-year-old children develop a healthy sexuality, families should: continue to provide information . . . even if a child does not ask for it."[52]

They instruct parents to tell *five-year-olds* about intercourse, though explaining orgasm can wait until he's finished kindergarten.[53] Your six- to eight-year-olds must have "basic information" about abortion, HIV/AIDS, wet dreams, and periods.[54] And of course, there's this universal mandate: adults must use correct anatomical terms, "vulva," "penis," etc.—otherwise kids may get the idea something is "wrong" with these parts of the body.[55] They say failing to discuss your daughter's vulva with her in a calm and comfortable way will not only lead her to seek answers elsewhere, it will lead her into years of therapy.

But this is a bad idea.

A young child's ability to think logically is limited. His understanding of the world is magical and egocentric. Why did his uncle leave? Because little Johnny wished he would. Why is it raining? So Johnny can wear his new boots. He devises his own theories to explain reality, based on his experiences. Providing facts that are beyond his experience—his uncle had a heart attack and went to the hospital; it's raining because ocean water evaporates . . . will likely be ineffective. They will sound bizarre, even impossible, to him. The result: confusion.[56]

The sex ed oligarchy must realize that a young child has his own theories about where babies come from, and he will cling to them regardless of how carefully and deliberately parents follow their instructions. Large amounts of unexpected information that cannot be easily assimilated into previously held beliefs can be distressing to children. Rather than having "the talk"—a frank, detailed monologue about penetration,

Why don't sex educators emphasize that casual sex and multiple partners is a health hazard?

When you have sex with someone, you are having sex
With everyone they have had sex with, and with

Everyone they've had sex with...

Everyone they've had sex with...

Everyone they've had sex with...

Everyone they've had sex with...

Everyone they've had sex with...

> "Sometimes people will have intercourse on their first date.
> Other couples wait until they have dated for months. Some wait
> until they are married. Some never have intercourse. Although
> monogamous relationships are most common, some couples
> will agree to switch partners. Such an arrangement is called
> mate-swapping. Some people engage in group sex, either with
> other couples or other single people or with both. Even people
> who are legally married sometimes have open relationships."
>   —*A Family Resource on Sex and Sexuality*,
>   recommended by sex educators at Rutgers.

sperm, egg, and invisible, deathly viruses—parents should take a child's own theories into account, then slowly introduce him to new facts.[57]

Key word: slowly. It's a process, to be driven by his curiosity, not by what experts say he should know by a certain age. Provide one new item at a time, and make it a dialogue, not a lecture. Limit your response to the question you are asked. "Where do babies come from?"

"Well, what do you think?"

Then,

"I could see why you'd think they come from a store (hospital, the internet), but a baby grows inside his Mommy."

Let the child sit with that, unless he asks for more.

"Where does it grow? In a place mothers have called a uterus/womb."

Resist the temptation to elaborate. That's enough for now. Allow him to absorb it; it will take time. Expect him, every so often, to revert back to believing babies come from a store. Just say calmly, "No, a baby grows inside his mommy."

Later, once he has assimilated that fact, he'll want to know more.

"How does the baby get in/out?"

Again, you ask, "How do you think?"

He'll rely on his experience: by eating/elimination. For him, this is logical. Any other answer will be met with skepticism; it doesn't fit in to anything he already knows. Proceed slowly.

Explain intercourse and HIV to a five-year-old? And expect him to get it? No matter how carefully it's done, he's just not equipped to hear so much, so soon. A penis enters a vagina? Sperm joins egg? "Body fluids" are shared, and maybe a virus that makes you sick? He's never heard anything like it, so the ideas cannot be absorbed. He'll misunderstand, and that's likely to cause worry and distress.

Be prepared, parents, for some surprises if you follow the experts' advice. One writer described a boy who concluded, "If I grew from an egg, I must be a chicken," and a refused to eat his breakfast.[58] "Egg" meant just one thing to him. What if, instead of being born, he'd been made into an omelette?[59]

3. Anything goes.

No judgments are allowed, even of established high risk behavior.

Planned Parenthood tells parents that "the most important lesson we can share with our kids is, 'Being different is normal,'"[60]and their book, *A Family Resource on Sex and Sexuality*,[61] recommended by sex educators at Rutgers, identifies a variety of relationships—monogamous, open, or group sex; long-lasting (months to years) or brief (hours to days).

Go Ask Alice tells teens that "S/M pushes the boundaries between pleasure and pain" and assures them it's "absolutely" normal. She also teaches them about drinking urine, cleaning their whips, and inserting objects into their penises.

Mind you, Planned Parenthood claims to promote "a common sense approach to women's health and well-being" and "Alice" is produced by the Health Services at Columbia University. Wouldn't common sense dictate that kids must understand that some ways of being different are not normal? Wouldn't it emphasize the indisputable fact that casual sex and multiple partners is a health hazard, especially for women? And regarding Alice's celebration of fringe behaviors: shouldn't we expect more from one of the most esteemed medical institutions in the country?

Our kids expect to be bugged by parents and medical providers about eating right, seatbelts, and sunscreen. They worry about second-hand smoke, saturated fats, and genetically engineered vegetables. But thanks to sex educators' belief that "anything goes," the most bizarre, depraved behaviors have become just another thing for them to try.

4. Children have the "right" question their parents' ideas about sex, to explore their sexuality, and to develop their own values. And parents have the duty to support them in their quest.

Again, when it comes to most health issues, it's considered responsible parenting to lay down the law. But with sexuality, parents are told not to lecture or judge. Do not impose your values, they're instructed. Don't interfere with your teen's decisions, unless, of course, you're reminding her about "protection."

Adults who insist their teen lives up to a particular standard or moral framework need a style and attitude adjustment. This is your child's own journey, the experts say; step back while she discovers what works for *her.* Listen calmly, and respect her decision.

This isn't education, folks, this is an ideology. You don't need a Ph.D. to understand its hazards; all you need is common sense. In the chapters ahead, I debunk these sacred beliefs, and indict the sex ed industry of misleading us—promising one thing, and doing another.

♂♀

Chapter Two

Girls and Boys Are Different

A STUDENT ONCE CAME to the counseling center where I worked because she had been unable to get to class for two weeks. Kayla,[1] 18 years old, drank tequila and smoked pot until the morning hours, and then slept the rest of the day. She was vague, at first, about how she'd fallen into this pattern. But our discussion soon turned to David, a guy who lived down the hall. They were friends, and they hung out with the same group. One night they started kissing, and, well, they hooked up—had sex. It was the first of a few casual encounters with him. But after a while, Kayla faced an unwelcome development.

Kayla discovered that the more time she spent with David, the more she needed to be with him. In spite of herself, she had feelings for him, and couldn't help wondering if he cared for her, too. But she didn't ask him—Kayla knew guys don't like high maintenance girls.

So she'd hook up with him and act like it didn't matter. *That's what everyone else is able to do*, she thought, *why can't I?*

But in fact Kayla was always hoping to hear from David: constantly waiting for a text message and compulsively checking her e-mail—longing for some sign of connection, some indication she meant something to him. And it didn't help that he was always around: she'd see him doing laundry or in the cafeteria. Thoughts of David preoccupied Kayla; she couldn't concentrate or sleep well, and so she turned to alcohol and pot to relax. It became increasingly difficult to make it to class, and when she was high, she'd hook up with other guys. But her thoughts always returned to him. "I just can't take it," she told me, holding her head in her hands. "What's wrong with me?"

We formulated a plan. Kayla would contact her professors and also get help for her alcohol and drug abuse. She'd follow my instructions and gradually adjust her sleep schedule back to normal. So far, so good. Then I advised her to refrain from hooking up: no kissing, no sex, no anything in between. Her emotional state was too fragile.

"*Kissing?*" She asked, in disbelief. "I can't *kiss* anyone?"

"Kissing is an intimate behavior," I told her. "It has an effect on you. How about trying it for one week—can you agree to that?"

"Wow," she said, considering my suggestion. "OK, but this is going to mean a big change of lifestyle. I'll need something to remind me."

Something to remind her . . . there was a wide rubber band on my desk; "Take this, and write NO HOOKING UP on it. Put it around your wrist and don't take it off. It will remind you of our conversation. And if anyone gives you a hard time about it," I said with mock authority, "tell them to come and speak to *me* about it!"

For the first time, she laughed. "Thank you, Dr. Grossman."

Telling a patient to wear a rubber band with advice on it is not a therapeutic intervention I learned in my residency. Nor was my abstinence suggestion any more than a stop-gap solution to Kayla's crisis.

But her high-risk behavior was an emergency: she could show up at her next appointment pregnant, or infected with herpes. Stopping these chaotic, meaningless encounters would help stabilize her and perhaps pave the way for some meaningful self-reflection.

Parents might think, what was wrong with this girl? It's tempting to conclude that she must have been immature or unstable, or perhaps not so bright to begin with. That would be a convenient explanation for how she got into this mess.

Not so. Kayla was a smart young woman without a history of emotional problems, and she was no less mature than the average freshman. Furthermore, she always practiced responsible sexual behavior with David. The most popular resource for comprehensive sex education, SIECUS, recommends that sex be consensual, non-exploitative, honest, pleasurable, and protected.[2] Check, check, check, check, and check. Kayla *had* been careful, she *had* played it safe. What went wrong?[3]

The problem wasn't with Kayla; it was with those guidelines for "responsible sexual behavior." They omit the fact that sex, with or without latex, is a serious matter. They fail to mention that even one encounter can have profound, lifelong consequences, and that girls are different from boys—that they are, in fact, monumentally and deeply different. Kayla's female brain, for example, predisposed her to yearn for connection, communication, and approval. Her chemistry promoted attachment and trust of David. Her wiring caused her to minimize his shortcomings, and to take risks. In short, Kayla was ignorant about a girl's unique physiological vulnerability to intimate behavior, because that's a "gender stereotype."

Kayla had asked me, referring to how she'd bonded with David, what was wrong with her. There was *nothing* wrong with her. But there is something wrong when sexuality educators promise comprehensive, accurate, up-to-date medical facts to girls like Kayla, and then fail to deliver the goods.

"Comprehensive" Sex ed—Hardly Comprehensive

I checked Webster's dictionary and "comprehensive" means "covering much; broad; all-inclusive." SIECUS's *Guidelines for Comprehensive Sex Education*[4] appears to be exactly that. Along with contraception, abortion, sexually transmitted infections, and HIV/AIDS, topics include sexual fantasy, masturbation, sexuality and the media, and gender role stereotypes. Downloaded a thousand times a month, in addition to the 100,000 copies that have been distributed, it would seem that if Kayla's schools had followed SIECUS's *Guidelines*, she'd have learned all the up-to-date medical facts she needed to know.

But medically accurate facts are scarce in this publication. In fact, SIECUS's *Guidelines* consist mostly of questionable, agenda-driven material. This curriculum is designed to inculcate students with a specific worldview:

> We are all sexual from cradle to grave.
> We must celebrate the diversity of sexual expression.
> We must speak openly of these issues in the first years of
> life . . .

The only information that makes it into these pages are what supports SIECUS's values and goals. One value, for example, is that "sexuality is a central part of being human."[5] SIECUS expects Kayla and David to "explore their sexuality as a natural process in achieving sexual maturity."[6] Presumably, by doing so, they will learn to "enjoy and express their sexuality throughout life."

Just one minute. A *central part* of being human? What does that mean, precisely? Something that they should *explore as a part of achieving sexual maturity*? Where is the scientific research demonstrating that? With the SIECUS curriculum animated by this ideology, is it any wonder so much emphasis is placed on teen sexual activity, in all its diversity?

The Bikini Approach

SIECUS follows what I term the "bikini approach" in its understanding of male/female differences: men and women are the same, except for some minor physical features that could be covered by a bikini. More influential than biology, SIECUS implies, are "messages" kids get from family, culture, media and society: "Cultures teach what it means to be a man or a woman."[7]

Cultures? What about anatomy, histology, neurology, endocrinology, and physiology? Sure, kids get messages from their environment, but the foundations of maleness and femaleness are rooted in biology, far beyond the reach of Hollywood, *Seventeen* Magazine, or Aunt Sally.

But not according to SIECUS. From the *Guidelines*:

- At age five: "Girls and boys have many similarities and a few differences."
- At age nine, in fourth grade: "The belief that all people of the same gender should behave the same way is called a stereotype"[8] and "[s]ometimes people receive unequal or negative treatment because of their gender."
- In middle school: "Some families and cultures have different expectations and rules about sexual practices for females and males," and "accepting gender role stereotypes can limit a person's life."
- In high school: "Gender role stereotypes can lead to problems for both men and women such as poor body image, low aspirations, low paying jobs, relationship conflict, stress-related illness, anxiety about sexual performance, sexual harassment, and date rape."

From Kindergarten through 12th grade, our kids learn that maleness and femaleness are culturally imposed concepts, and that endorsing them can destroy lives.

This is *comprehensive sex ed*, for sure—comprehensive indoctrination.

Now consider basic biology. You know—cells, organs, hormones, viruses? In spite of the overarching goal of sexual health, and SIECUS's refrain that it provides medically accurate and up-to-date information, the *Guidelines* are noteworthy for their *lack* of technical and cutting edge information. In the entire 112-page document, only a single page, "Reproductive and sexual anatomy and physiology" might be described as biology, and it's anything *but* comprehensive. Instead, it's heavy on the sexual ("Both boys and girls have body parts that feel good when touched") and light on anatomy and physiology.

In fact, what's missing from the *Guidelines* is more important than what's included: research that highlights the differences between male and female brains. Medically accurate? Up to date? It doesn't get any better than this. This science is cutting edge, and comes from the best medical centers in the country. It demonstrates that Kayla's wiring is exquisitely reactive, and distinctly female. A unique female cocktail of estrogen, progesterone, and oxytocin[9] bathe her brain, influencing her perceptions, thoughts, feelings, and dreams. Silently, beneath the radar, her system reacts in a variety of ways to David; it registers and reacts to his scent and touch. Bottom line: that second X chromosome in all[10] her cells creates a distinctly feminine reality.[11] It's a reality of elevated sensitivity and, along with that, increased vulnerability.

SIECUS, there is more to Kayla and David's emotional and sexual functioning than is met with in your philosophy. Your work is animated by dusty themes of social justice, but the idealism is misplaced, the science is outdated, and young people pay dearly. Unlike programs devised in the 1960s and 1970s, sex education in the twenty-first century can and should be based on processes occurring at a cellular and

molecular level. Research conducted over the past two decades provides us with a wealth of insight. Those are objective truths, those are
the facts kids have a right to know, and we have an obligation to provide them.

In this and the following chapters, I provide the science that's omitted from "comprehensive" sex education—science that has confirmed
what common sense always told us: there are more than "a few" differences between girls and boys, and sexual behavior has profound
consequences—with or without contraceptives. It's not a "stereotype,"
it's not a "value," and it's not a "paradigm"; it's what you see under a
microscope. It's information our daughters and sons never hear,
because it challenges the institutionalized ideology and—gasp—confirms traditional values and teachings. The deliberate exclusion of this
science, by those who have our trust—and our dollars—is a crime.

Scent of a Man

The eighteen women who volunteered for a research study[12] at the
University of Pennsylvania thought it was about the scent of a "natural extract,"[13] and its effect on female hormones.

A hormone differs from a pheromone.

The **pheromone** travels by air or water to a different organism of
the same species, be it a frog, an elephant, a goldfish, a moth, or a
roommate. Pheromones are external messengers.

A **hormone** is carried in the blood from one organ to another, for
example the stomach to the brain, signaling satiety; the brain to
the bones, telling them to grow; the testes to the skin, causing hair
growth and acne. Hormones are internal messengers.

In the first month of the study, their morning temperatures were recorded, and urine samples tested, to determine the time of ovulation. The second month, each woman spent twelve hours at a research center, where a drop of the "extract" was applied with a cotton pad every two hours to the area between her upper lip and nose. Some women were daubed with a control substance (like water), while others had the substance that was being tested. Blood was then drawn, and each woman rated her mood. The third month was the same as the first.

The results: the extract—and not the control substance—shortened the subjects' menstrual cycles, causing ovulation to occur sooner. Its scent was also mood-altering: women felt more relaxed after the application.

Now here's the amazing thing. The mystery elixir was neither lavender nor vanilla—it was male perspiration. It was a concoction of the sweat of six men who had shunned deodorant for a month, while wearing cotton pads to collect their underarm secretions. In the lab, an extract was created and disguised. At the end of the study, none of the women could identify its source.

The researchers concluded that a pheromone is produced in the male underarm.[14] Pheromones are molecules that act on the brain but bypass conscious thought, escaping awareness. A woman inhaling this male pheromone, the study indicates, responds in two ways: her reproductive hormones are altered, affecting ovulation, and her level of tension is decreased.

Are you following this? Let's take it back to Kayla and David. His mere closeness—one night together might do it—sends a signal to her brain: relax and prepare for reproduction.

Who would've imagined? Babies were the last thing on Kayla's mind. But don't misunderstand the science. The point is not that David's scent makes conception more likely. Rather, the lesson is that Kayla's female physiology is extraordinarily complex. The intricate processes going on beneath the surface are all but unfathomable. In addition to condom les-

PHEROMONE (fer-oh-mone):

a chemical produced by one individual and perceived by a second individual of the same species, triggering a specific reaction or behavior.[47] These signals have been studied in many species, from yeast to mammals.[48] In animals, there is an accessory organ in the nose[49] that registers these chemicals.

1. **mice:** male pheromones stimulate the female brain during pregnancy in a way that promotes maternal behavior to newborn pups[50]

2. **sheep and goats:** the fleece of a ram or the hair of a buck leads to ovulation in the female[51]

3. **snakes:** females have a pheromone in their skin that makes them attractive to males[52]

4. **goldfish:** a pheromone released by the female elicits large increases in sexual behavior in the male[53]

5. **frogs:** males have a pheromone that attracts females[54]

6. **elephants:** female pheromones inform males how close she is to ovulation; males release pheromones indicating they are in a period of heightened sexual activity[55]

7. **women:** female pheromones alter the timing of ovulation and menstruation in other females,[56] probably leading to the observed menstrual synchrony among roommates

8. **man–woman:** exposure to male pheromones affects female's mood, attention, and ovulation[57]

9. **infant–mother:** smell of infant stimulates mother's attachment[58]

10. **mother–infant:** maternal breast odor attracts infant[59]

11. **father–daughter** : frequent exposure to her biological father delays the sexual maturation of a daughter[60]

sons and assurances she is "safe," or at least "safer," Kayla has the right to know that—notwithstanding pills, patches, diaphragms, and latex—those nights with David may affect her in ways she wouldn't imagine.

This University of Pennsylvania study expanded on previous research that demonstrated significant sex-specific reactions to the substance in question, whose chemical identity still eludes us. Earlier studies had already shown male pheromones to have psychological effects on women,[15] like increased attention and a feeling of well-being.[16]

Compelling business, huh? And the sort of thing Kayla would want to know? I would think so. I don't expect her to understand neuroendocrinology in all its complexity, of course; that's up to the experts. But her sensitivity to pheromones—in particular male pheromones—should be discussed in sexuality education, especially when she's promised "comprehensive" information about sexuality. In the process, Kayla might develop some respect, perhaps even awe, for the elaborate, hardwired circuits that are activated when she gets cozy.

Kayla's Brain

Even before birth, Kayla's brain structure differed from David's.[17] Hers was more skilled at communication, observation, and the processing of emotion. She was adept at gathering information from faces and tone of voice, and unlike him, would infer from this knowledge meaning about her own self-worth. Connecting with others and having their approval were priorities for her female brain from early in life.

Then came puberty. Kayla's brain matured, becoming even more "female";[18] more intuitive, and more averse to interpersonal conflict. When her estrogen surged, she thrived on interpersonal connections: hanging out with friends, chatting with them on the phone for hours, or IMing and texting them throughout the day. This is her special "girl reality."[19]

Testosterone is the hormone controlling sex drive: not for cuddling and connection, but for release—as often, and with as many different people, as possible. When she reached her teens, Kayla's testosterone increased somewhat, but David's soared to twenty-five times higher. As one specialist explains: "Surges of testosterone marinate...boys' brains...sexual pursuit and body parts become pretty much obsessions."[20]

In contrast to David, Kayla's hormones were in constant flux. The structure of her brain was changing from day to day and from week to week.[21] Depending on the phase of her menstrual cycle, she might feel outgoing and self-confident, or irritable and fat. End result of Kayla's intense attachments, dread of dispute, and seesaw of moods? High drama,[22] 24/7.

Are you getting the picture? Are you wondering, as I am, how SIECUS—remember, that stands for *Sexuality Information and Education Council of the United States*—foists its feminist drivel about socially constructed gender differences on kids as young as five? They're stuck in the past. They think it's still 1970. Time to wake up— the bikini approach to male/female differences has no place outside of a history book. In fact, psychiatrists predict that, due to the significant differences in brain structure and function, we'll soon treat depression and schizophrenia differently in men and women.

Kayla has sensitivities that David does not, and we do her—and him—no favor in denying them. To the contrary, being unaware of her vulnerabilities only makes her *more* vulnerable, and the pair more likely to experience misunderstandings and conflict. Better to educate them both, *comprehensively*, about the distinctive wiring of male and female brains. Isn't that what sex education is supposedly all about— making informed decisions about relationships? Our kids must know about pheromones and hormones before they begin to "experiment" with and "explore" their sexuality. They must also know what neuroscience has taught us about the power of touch.

The Female Brain

Okay, guess who gave females this advice: "Don't let a guy hug you unless you plan to trust him."[23] Dr. Laura? Some priest? Try again. The speaker is LouAnn Brizendine, M.D., a neuropsychiatrist at the

University of California, San Francisco. She's discussing the hormones of love and attachment in her bestselling book, *The Female Brain*.

If anyone's an expert on female brains, it's Dr. Brizendine.[24] Fifteen years ago, when few researchers were interested in the neurochemistry of girls and women, she founded the Women's Mood and Hormone Clinic in the Department of Psychiatry at the University of California, San Francisco. She's scrutinized women at every stage of life, from girlhood and adolescence to young adulthood, motherhood, and menopause. And she's used every tool available to do so, from genetic studies to in-depth interviews and questionnaires, body scans, and MRIs. Perhaps more important, this scientist didn't only study pregnancy and the postpartum period, she survived them.

Dr. Brizendine is also a woman of courage. When she learned early in her career of the two-to-one ratio of depression in women compared to men, her explanation for the discrepancy was influenced by feminist thought. As she herself says, "I took the typical 1970's stance that the patriarchy of Western culture must have been the culprit. It must have kept women down and made them less functional than men."[25] But Dr. Brizendine's insights evolved through the years with more research, and now she explains that it's usually hormones, not husbands, wreaking havoc on women's emotions. And she underscores the differences between the male and female experience:

> Because of the fluctuations that begin as early as three months old and last until after menopause, a woman's neurological reality is not as constant as a man's. His is like a mountain that is worn away imperceptibly over the millennia by glaciers, weather, and the deep tectonic movements of the earth. Hers is more like the weather itself—constantly changing and hard to predict.[26]

Kudos to the doctor for describing these politically incorrect truths. She's been attacked for saying these things, but she copes with the backlash. "Some days," she says, "I need ovaries of steel."[27]

Oxytocin: "The Cuddle Hormone"

Again, the brain expert's advice to girls is, "Don't let a guy hug you unless you plan to trust him." Dr. Brizendine is speaking of a serious embrace here: one that's at least twenty seconds long. And in case you're wondering, her recommendation still holds if said hug is consensual, non-exploitative, honest, pleasurable, and "protected." That's because, as with pheromones, practicing "safer sex" is no obstacle to the effects of what some call "the cuddle hormone."

What could be wrong with a hug, even a drawn out one? The doctor's recommendation is based on the power of *oxytocin*, a hormone identified one hundred years ago as a brain substance that facilitates labor, delivery, and nursing. Today we know it has many other functions, and science recognizes that any meaningful examination of sexuality, especially female sexuality,[28] must consider them.

Like pheromones, oxytocin is part of an elaborate structure involving many neuro-chemical messengers, specialized cells and receptors, delicate feedback systems, and other control mechanisms. I promise you, the New York City subway system pales in comparison. It's worthwhile, for a moment, to dwell on this notion: the intricacies of our structure and function exceed our power of observation and understanding, at least for the time being. Nevertheless, while acknowledging the risk of oversimplification, it is possible to focus on a few essential points.

Oxytocin promotes social bonds. We first learned this from a cute little animal called a prairie vole.[29] These mouse-sized rodents, found in the Midwest, caught the attention of scientists because they display an unusual mating pattern: lifelong monogamy. A breeding pair share a nest, sitting side by side most of the time. They attack intruders of either sex. Even after weeks of separation, they prefer their mates to any other companion. When one dies, the widow or widower prairie vole accepts a new mate only about 20 percent of the time.[30] Both male and female are active parents, and newborns crave contact with them. The study of voles in love provided the preliminary data for a new field: the biochemistry of attachment.

In contrast, Montane voles, found in the Rockies, are cousins to prairie voles, but their social lives differ. Montane voles are loners, and when mating time arrives, they play the field. They're not into their kids either: males show little or no interest, and females often abandon their pups within two weeks after birth. The babies don't seem to mind.[31]

What makes one vole loving and the other aloof? It turns out the brains of these cousins differ as much as their behaviors: in monogamous voles, oxytocin (in males, vasopressin[32]) acts powerfully on the reward center, the same area that produces the euphoric effects of drugs like cocaine. The reward center of the montane vole does not respond to oxytocin. Oxytocin (or vasopressin) is released during mating, so the prairie vole, and not the montane vole, experiences a reward when intimate with her mate. This system creates her preference for him, and only him. And it works both ways: sex bonds him to her, too.

Well, okay, but Kayla's not a vole. Nevertheless, these little rodents have provided insights to the way she bonded with David. Like the monogamous vole, intimacy fuels her oxytocin level, lighting up her reward center. For a short time, she feels exhilarated. Intercourse is not necessary; pleasant touch will do the job, especially of her fingers, face, lips, nipples, and genitals. Compared to other areas, these places are rich in touch receptors,[33] cells that send signals to her brain.

That's why I told Kayla kissing is an intimate behavior. It's not like playing golf with someone.

While oxytocin is amping up the reward center and fueling attachment, it's slowing things down elsewhere in Kayla's brain. It is de-activating the centers that mediate negative judgment, caution, and fear.[34] These areas help Kayla assess David's intentions and trustworthiness. I repeat: the chemicals flooding her brain while "hooking up" turn attachment "on" and critical thinking "off."

Think of it like this: with David, Kayla's skin is flooding her brain with a message: This is a different sort of touching. I'm with someone special now; time for attachment and trust. And after a while, her brain may respond to David even without touch—the sight of him in the laundry room or cafeteria may be enough to stir those feelings of attachment.

Kayla's friends realize that David is immature and inconsiderate; he's not even cute. Why doesn't Kayla see that? They needn't bother her with the facts; the information won't register in her brain, because she's become attached to him. Yes, although oxytocin promotes gazing into the eyes of another,[35] love is blind.[36] This phenomenon has been captured on brain scans, but our grandmothers knew it all along.

Oxytocin

Maternal actions:[61]
- Calms mother; lowers her blood pressure
- Promotes maternal attachment
- Promotes mothering behaviors
- Promotes maternal vigilance, if necessary aggression
- Increases mother's appetite; promotes digestion
- Promotes effective storage of mother's nutrients
- Promotes (via prolactin) milk production
- Releases breast milk
- Causes uterus to contract

Other actions:
- Activates brain reward center
- Deactivates networks used for critical assessment, negative emotions (therefore, promotes trust) i.e., love is blind
- Decreases fear
- Increases social intuition
- Facilitates healing and growth

Liquid Trust

Girls who are gaga aren't the only ones who stand to lose from trusting the wrong people. Investors want to be certain their capacity for critical judgment is fully intact. Scientists at Zurich's Institute for Empirical Research in Economics devised an ingenious experiment in which individuals playing a "trust game," involving real monetary stakes, were given a whiff of oxytocin.[37] They then had to decide whether to trust an anonymous trustee, accepting risk levels to which most people are averse. The individuals who had inhaled oxytocin exhibited significantly more trust than those who received the placebo. They took risks most people would avoid.

Conclusion: increased levels of this hormone impact Kayla's decisions *at the moment*. Decisions such as: What do I think of this guy? How far do I want this encounter to go? Also at stake is the bottom line issue, at least to the SIECUS and Planned Parenthood crowd: What about a condom?

Kids are warned all the time about the hazards of combining drugs and alcohol with sexual activity because of the likelihood of poor decisions. Sex educators tell girls: If you make too many trips to the keg, you are more likely to end up making out with that dorky guy from history class because he suddenly is irresistible.[38] So use caution, the warning goes, know that consuming another drink—or taking another hit—will impair your judgment. Yet they don't say that choosing to become intimate with a guy will also impair a girl's judgment; that her own brain produces what can be considered an *internal drug*, one that also affects perceptions, reasoning, and decision-making. They don't tell her that even without a hangover, she can still face the morning after dilemma: *what was I thinking?*

Following the announcement of the Zurich experiment, back in the United States some investors smelled a money-making opportunity. And so "Liquid Trust" was born: bottled oxytocin for sale at

$29.95 for 1/4 ounce. "Apply liquid trust every morning after showering," the ad reads. It is "specially designed to give a boost to the dating and relationship area of your life." A boost, indeed.

The recent breakthroughs about this hormone have been covered with much fanfare by the media. "'Trust me,' says

> **Young women are wise to take their time and investigate a young man's history and character before getting physical. Guidance from elders is strongly advised.**
> — From *The Archives of Common Sense*

cuddle hormone," Reuters reported.[39] "Scientists study 'trust in a bottle'" announced the AP.[40] There were news items by NPR, MSNBC, NBC, National Geographic, and ABC.

But there's no mention of oxytocin in our schools, or should I say, in the "comprehensive, up to date, medically accurate" curricula taught there. Neither is any mention of it found in the books and websites to which our kids are directed for guidance. I searched three[41] of the most popular curricula, five suggested books, and another five recommended websites, and found not a word.[42]

Why don't health and sexuality "experts," who find reason to discuss cross-dressing and sadomasochism with kids, explain that male and female hormones create distinct realities? That because of this, teen boys and girls *do* think and feel differently, in particular about sexuality?[43] That a girl's physiology is so finely tuned, it responds to a boy's scent? That a kiss is, well, not just a kiss?

These biological truths are omitted by the sex ed industry because they fly in the face of the ideology animating their very existence, that's why.

Parents must send a clear message to SIECUS, Planned Parenthood, Advocates for Youth and other sex educators: your approach is dogmatic, reductionist, and out-of-date. It is time to enter the twenty-first century and make some bold changes, starting with reading journals such as *Hormones and Behavior* and *Biology of Reproduction*, and acknowledging the complex findings and insights of hard science.

Attachments

The first thing children should learn about sexuality is *we are hard-wired for close, lasting attachments*.[44]

Attachment is a fitting subject for young children, many of whom are first experiencing—at pre-school and kindergarten—a separation from loved ones. They know about security, trust, good-byes, and yearning. It's a natural time to discuss how some people in our lives are special and we always want them close by. We feel good when they hold us and we believe what they say.

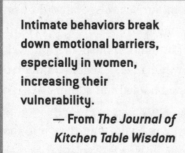

Intimate behaviors break down emotional barriers, especially in women, increasing their vulnerability.
— From *The Journal of Kitchen Table Wisdom*

It's a natural time to point out, in simple terms, how we form these attachments. Planned Parenthood and SIECUS advise we begin sexuality education in the first years of life with, "Each body part has a correct name and function.... Individual bodies are different sizes, shapes, and colors...bodies can feel good when touched...."[45] The message for kids, from the get-go, is: sexuality is about physical pleasure.

Science indicates otherwise. It says that from infancy we have a biological need to form intense, lasting attachments, and that one way we do that is through closeness and touch. Kids must be taught that our bodies are very sensitive to whom we're with. Cuddling with someone, or climbing into their bed, sends silent signals to our brain with the message: *Now I'm with someone special. I can relax and trust this person. I can love him or her.*

In childhood, the sensitivity of boys and girls is similar, but with puberty, a girl's system becomes more finely tuned. Closeness and touch are especially meaningful to her. This difference between girls and boys continues until she's much older.

Anthropologists point out that, from an evolutionary perspective, it makes sense for a human female to be careful about mating: she's the one at risk for what they call the greatest "parental investment burden." In English that means the nausea, heartburn, insomnia and swollen feet; followed by labor, delivery, engorged breasts, etc . . . to say nothing of years of lactation—during which time it's harder for women to reproduce and invest in additional offspring than it is for men—and another dozen years, at least, of mothering. Remember, all men do biologically to reproduce is contribute sperm. So if we're thinking about survival of the fittest, our ancestral sisters who discriminated carefully and chose a mate who hung around for a good while had a distinct advantage. But males didn't need to be so "choosy."[46]

Were those the thumps of falling bodies I heard? Yes, this "sexist" message will cause some to feel dizzy and faint. So be it. Today we know too much to perpetuate the Kinsey-based belief that intimacy is easily separated from attachment, and to tolerate the denial of substantial, inborn differences between male and female.

"Boys and girls receive messages about how they should behave from their families, friends, the media, and society," says SIECUS. Of course they do, and it behooves us to encourage messages that are balanced and fact-based. But the most powerful messages our kids get are not from their environment. They are from their hypothalamus, ovaries, and testes.

Those organizations given the responsibility of providing "comprehensive" sexuality education to our young Kaylas and Davids are obligated to use as their foundation the insights provided by neurobiology and reproductive physiology. To deny these forces of nature in the interest of promoting specific social agendas is an unethical and hazardous blunder.

♂♀

Chapter Three

Red Light, Green Light

ALMOST ALL PARENTS BELIEVE that teens should be encouraged to delay sex until after high school.[1] Abstinence education encourages waiting—ideally until the safety of a monogamous marriage. Where do the "comprehensive" folks stand?

In a 2007 NPR interview, a SIECUS official addressed the issue. "I get a bit flummoxed when I hear constantly that we don't spend enough time in comprehensive programs on abstinence," said Bill Smith, SIECUS's director of public policy. Smith said these allegations were "really silly," and based only on pro-abstinence groups conducting word counts of SIECUS curricula looking for the word "abstinence." "Just sloppy research," he said.[2]

Smith went on:

> There are many, many ways that we need to talk to young people about the importance of abstaining and it doesn't always mean that you use [that word]. It means using words

and concepts like: it's important to wait; it's healthy to wait; it's a good thing to wait—all of those different sorts of ways that we say the same thing that escape this sort of rudimentary word count that makes it sound like comprehensive programs do not support abstinence. It's just simply not true.

The moderator, Margot Adler, then asked: "You would agree that it would be best if kids didn't have sex in high school. Am I right?"

Smith didn't hesitate: "Listen, absolutely. It is better for young people to wait to have sex. There is no question about that."

Oh, *that's* a relief—it's just a vocabulary issue. Educators want kids to wait, just like parents. So in case you were wondering, kids get the same instruction at school as they do at home—teachers just don't use the word "abstinence" is all. "Sex in high school?" they might say. "*Not* a good idea. If you haven't started, don't. If you have, stop." Breathe easy, parents: we're all on the same page.

If only it were so. Unfortunately, the last time SIECUS unequivocally advocated sexual restraint to kids was a half century ago. Perhaps Ms. Adler hadn't done her homework, or maybe she didn't want to put Smith in the hot seat.[3] Either way, she missed an opportunity to reveal the truth.

Bill, she could have said, *if you don't want to use the word "abstinence," that's fine. The point, as you say, is not to use a particular term, but to give teens a clear, no-nonsense message.*

But the message your organization and other "comprehensive" programs teach teens is that "young people explore their sexuality as a natural process."[4] A vast majority of their peers do exactly that, they inform students, while only a small number choose to wait. . . . Becoming sexually active is a decision teens must make for themselves, after examining their "readiness." Adults must provide information, but it's kids who ultimately "decide when the time is right."

So which is it, the NPR hostess might have asked Bill Smith. *"Absolutely" better for kids to wait, as you say on the air, or each teen*

decides when is "the right time," as you write in your curriculum? Red
light or green light? You can't have both.

Ms. Adler might have then discovered that SIECUS's messages differ depending on their audience. Their official position statement on
adolescent sexual health says, "Adolescents should be encouraged to
delay sexual behaviors until they are physically, cognitively, and emotionally ready for mature sexual relationships and their consequences," which to parents sounds like adulthood. But that's not what
SIECUS thinks. Kids who log on to the SIECUS website are directed
to the pamphlet *All About Sex,* and to sites like scarleteen and
gURL.com, which inform kids about their sexual rights, and tell them
only *they* know when they are ready. On many of these sites, 6th
graders learn how natural it is to explore, and find checklists to assess
their readiness; they also are guided to resources for obtaining contraception and abortions without parental consent.

With a bit of investigation, NPR could have exposed the duplicity
of the sex ed industry: in media interviews, a red light; in classrooms
and websites for teens, a green one. NPR could also have learned that's
nothing new—SIECUS has been giving a green light to teen sexual
activity for years.

In 1995, SIECUS released a report containing the consensus of
national sexual health organizations.[5] Policymakers and professionals
were urged to adopt "a new approach to adolescent sexual health."
The report contended that "too much public policy debate has
focused on helping adolescents *abstain* from sexual behavior, especially intercourse, rather than *the complex dimensions of adolescent sex-*
ual development."

These "complex dimensions" were not really so complex. The
report urged recognition of "developmentally appropriate sexual
behavior." It argued that "most young people engage in sexual relationships without negative physical, social, or emotional consequences, and that most teenagers who have intercourse do so
responsibly."[6]

This is the entrenched dogma of sexuality education to this day. To claim otherwise, as Bill Smith did on NPR, is dishonest. NPR may be willing to let the sex ed industry get away with pretending they agree with parents who want their teenagers to delay sex, but if you're not, you can easily find out what they really believe.

From the SIECUS report cited above:

> Responsible adolescent intimate relationships...should be based on shared personal values, and should be consensual; non-exploitative; honest; pleasurable; and protected against unintended pregnancies and sexually transmitted diseases.

Planned Parenthood adds:

> **Guidelines for Sex Partners**
>
> - Have each other's consent.
> - Never use pressure to get consent.
> - Be honest with each other.
> - Treat each other as equals.
> - Be attentive to each other's pleasure.
> - Protect each other against physical and emotional harm.
> - Guard against unintended pregnancy and sexually transmitted infection.
> - Be clear with each other about what you want to do and don't want to do.
> - Respect each other's limits.
> - Accept responsibility for your actions.[7]

Here's what the SIECUS and Advocates for Youth- endorsed website positive.org tells teens:[8]

> There are lots of safe and fun ways to get off, which you probably won't learn in school. You can do many of these

things all by yourself as well as with others, and you can talk about them even if you don't want to do them. Don't feel like you have to do everything on this page, but don't feel like anything is automatically off limits either....

(Parents, there are activities recommended here that you don't even want to *know* about, let alone have your teenagers experimenting with.)

For a description of "readiness skills," log on to any of the Q&A websites SIECUS recommends for teens, and search for "ready."

Planned Parenthood's Teen Talk[9] promises teens the facts about sex so they can "use this information to make [their] own responsible choices." In the article "Am I Ready?" "expert" Elisa Klein—no information is available about her training or credentials—guides teens through the decision of whether to have intercourse "or any other kind of sex play."[10]

The decision, Klein advises, "Requires a lot of thought from you and your partner." Teens must: explore their values ("Do you think that sexual activity needs to be part of an intimate relationship?");

"Choosing What to Do"

Here are some questions to ask yourself before you engage in any sexual behavior.

- Who is your partner?
- Do you feel safe?
- Is it consensual?
- What is your motivation?
- Is it non-exploitative?
- Are you being honest?
- Is it pleasurable?
- Is it protected?
- What does your gut instinct say?

From SIECUS pamphlet for teens called "Talk About Sex"

examine their relationship ("It's important for you and your partner to be on the same page"); and be prepared ("talk about protection *before* . . . don't wait until the heat of the moment"). Ms. Klein reminds kids that "many teens have decided to hold off on having [intercourse and] other kinds of sex play," and concludes: "Am I ready. . . is a question that only you can answer, so take your time and talk things through with your partner if you're thinking of taking this big step."

"A question only you can answer"—again, this is the overriding message given to your child. Adults—not necessarily parents—provide information, teens determine their "ready-or-not" status.[11] Educators describe a range of intimate behaviors,[12] teens decide where to draw the line.

Should parents be uncertain about their role, the "experts" provide guidance: how, when, and what to say to their teen. "Share your values," they say, "and admit your embarrassment, and perhaps, at times, your lack of knowledge. Most important is to face the reality that your daughter will likely have sex earlier than you'd like. Remain calm, listen to her point of view, refrain from judgment, and for heaven's sake: don't use scare tactics!"

Planned Parenthood has a feature on their website[13] called *Ask Dr. Cullins*. It's an opportunity for readers to get an expert answer to their sexual health questions. Vanessa Cullins, MD, is a board-certified

---

Try This:

When faced with a decision try testing your gut instinct. Pick one possible choice and tell yourself it is your final decision. Keep telling yourself that for a few hours or a few days and see how you feel. Then switch to another decision. Do this as many times as there are choices. If you feel differently—whether it's better or worse—that can tell you if you're making the decision that is right for you.

From SIECUS pamphlet for teens called "Talk About Sex"

obstetrician/gynecologist and vice president for medical affairs at
Planned Parenthood Federation of America.

One question for the doctor comes from a worried mom.[14] At what
age, she asks, should she take her daughter to her gynecologist?
They've talked about menstruation and sex, but is it appropriate, she
wonders, to start her on birth control when she gets her period? This
mom gave birth at sixteen and is "scared to death of her going through
the same thing!" Her daughter is twelve.

After providing the guidelines for initial gynecologic exams—
within three years of having vaginal intercourse, or at age twenty-one,
whichever happens first—Dr. Cullins explains that a young woman
may want to consider taking hormonal birth control prior to becoming sexually active, because of health benefits such as lighter periods
and reduced acne. She'll have those benefits, and also be protected
against pregnancy when that becomes a possibility.

Dr. Cullins then warns against mother and daughter sharing the
same gynecologist. With sexual matters, she says, young women are
often more comfortable with their own health care providers. Ask
your daughter if, "now that she is older," she wants her own nurse or
doctor to take care of her. "Respect whatever decision she makes, and
help her to find a caring provider. . . . Regardless of the provider they
choose, young people should be encouraged to have their visits in private—by themselves. They should also be given every assurance that
their confidences will be respected."

Now let me see if I have this right. Here's a twelve-year-old whose
mother is already thinking about birth control for her—that's how
worried she is about a teen pregnancy. Yes, the doctor says, birth control is something your daughter may want to consider. But arrange for
her own provider, mom, and during her appointment, you stay in the
waiting room. Young women get to make their own decisions about
sexuality, and their privacy must be respected.

If anyone needed proof of the war that is being waged over sex ed,
this is it. In my opinion, the advice of Dr. Cullins—a physician at the

most eminent reproductive health organization in the world—is unsuitable and worrisome.

Dr. Cullins, I don't doubt your good intentions, but could we review your advice and discuss it, one doctor to another?

I'm puzzled, first, by your choice of words. You keep referring to "young women." The girl in question is not even a teen, let alone a woman. What's the rush?

Stedman's medical dictionary defines adolescence as beginning with puberty (for a girl, that's marked by the onset of menstruation) and ending with completed growth and physical maturity.[15] For the NIH, anyone under twenty-one is a child.[16] For the World Health Organization, adolescence ends at nineteen.[17] While an older adolescent—seventeen, eighteen, or nineteen—may commonly (but technically incorrectly) be called a "young woman," the individual you're discussing is nowhere near that. She's a *girl*, for heaven's sake; she has yet to enter puberty!

As a gynecologist, you're aware that delaying sexual activity is associated with far-ranging benefits: decreased rates of infection with sexually transmitted diseases, higher academic achievement,[18] decreased rates of out-of-wedlock pregnancy and birth, decreased single parenthood, increased marital stability, decreased maternal and child poverty, decreased abortion, and decreased depression.[19] Yet you don't mention those, and you seem to assume this girl is going to have intercourse sooner or later, regardless of age or maturity. I wonder, do you believe it's healthier for her to abstain, at least until after high school? If yes, why don't you explain those benefits to her mom, and then arm her with strategies that can make a difference?

Naturally, given her experience, this mom's concerns are understandable. She's terrified that her daughter could have a child when she did, and wonders if birth control is the answer. What's astonishing is that you tell her, yes, it is.

How can you do that? Why the automatic reach for a prescription pad? It's a misguided, hazardous strategy. Even if your advice is heeded and this girl is placed on hormonal contraceptives, she is at significant risk of pregnancy and STI's.[20] Why assume she is incapable of being taught to make smart choices? And what of the adults in her life—at home and in the neighborhood, at school, and possibly church—are they completely powerless? Are they utterly inept? Why would you think so? The mere fact that her mom had the wherewithal to seek your advice speaks against that.

At age twelve, what this girl needs isn't pills, Dr. Cullins, it's parenting. There is so much mom can do to keep her on track, and it's critical for her to hear that from you, a medical authority. Sure, I know how much harder it is—to say nothing of time-consuming—to discuss parenting than write a prescription. But Planned Parenthood promises to educate parents about how to protect the health of loved ones,[21] and it claims to have a comprehensive and commonsense approach.[22] I'd say in this instance, you failed to provide that service.

Most of us would agree that parents can have some effect on their teen's behavior, but recent studies overwhelmingly confirm that the impact of parents is profound.[23] They demonstrate that good parenting has a "significant, enduring, and protective influence" on adolescent development. The mom who turned to you needs to know what family factors and parenting style can deter risky behavior, moderate the influence of peers, and optimize her daughter's potential.

I suggest that a "comprehensive and common sense" answer to the query would sound something like this:[24]

> I endorse you for being proactive and seeking advice on protecting your daughter. Rest assured that at twelve, your influence on her is greater than you might imagine.[25] What's critical for your daughter is the parenting she receives. She'll do best if you model good behavior, and you're warm, supportive, and hands-on. She needs you to establish firm rules and high expectations.[26]

Does your daughter's father live at home[27]? Teens[28] from two-parent families are more likely to delay sexual activity. The research findings are robust: the longer a girl lives without her father at home, the more likely she'll engage in early sexual activity and experience a teen pregnancy. According to one study, girls whose fathers lived outside the home from an early age[29] were seven to eight times more likely to have a teen pregnancy.[30]

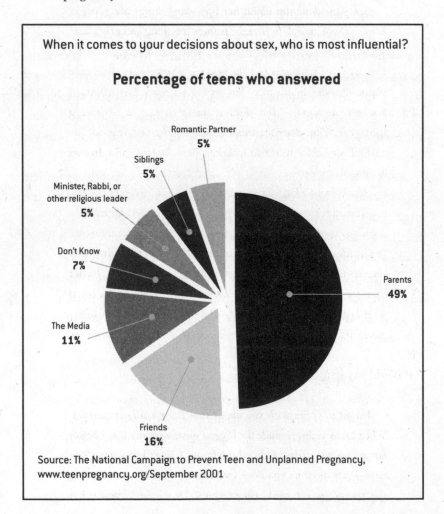

When it comes to your decisions about sex, who is most influential?

Percentage of teens who answered

Romantic Partner
5%

Siblings
5%

Minister, Rabbi, or
other religious leader
5%

Don't Know
7%

The Media
11%

Friends
16%

Parents
49%

Source: The National Campaign to Prevent Teen and Unplanned Pregnancy,
www.teenpregnancy.org/September 2001

Even without dad in the home, your attitude toward teen sex and rules you make about dating can influence your daughter to delay sexual behavior.[31]

But before delving in to those issues, mom, know this: your daughter needs you. Instead of visits to the gynecologist, schedule special time together, just the two of you, and talk. Strengthen your connection with her. She wants a close and confidential relationship[32] with you, not her health care provider.[33]

Ask your daughter about her life—how things are going at home, school, and with friends. Is there anything bothering her? What can you do to help? Find out what she's looking forward to—not years from now (for the next few years she's probably not planning so far in advance) but for her birthday, Christmas, or summer vacation. What does it mean to her to become a teenager? What does she think it will be like in 8th grade, or 11th? Every child wants to feel that their thoughts and dreams are important.

Speak about what you've learned from your own experiences, and communicate your values. It's at least as important as talking about contraceptives, if not more. Affirm that your daughter is precious to you, while explaining why it would have been smarter to give birth to her under different circumstances. It's not that you regret having her—to the contrary!—but if you could do it again, you'd have had her—the same daughter, not different in any way—when you were an adult, married to her father.

You could say something like:

I want to speak with you about something really important. When I was young, I made the biggest mistake in my life. I began having sex too early. I didn't think it out. I didn't know what I do now—that anytime you have intercourse, even if you are using contraception, you could get pregnant. Or maybe I knew it but

did it anyway. Having a baby when you're not ready is like falling
off a cliff. I want you and my grandkids to have an easier time.
So I'm going to keep reminding you: there's a cliff out there. And
I'm going to do all I can to make sure you don't get near it.

Teens often misperceive what adults think and feel; make sure your daughter is certain about your values and expectations—these will impact her behavior. Yes—she may object vigorously, but studies show that high parental expectations are associated with postponing sex.[34]

If your daughter perceives her relationship with you is good, and your disapproval of teen sex is absolutely clear, it can have a powerful effect on her behavior. One study based on data from almost 8,000 mother-teen pairs[35] found that the more liberal teens think their mothers' sexual opinions are, the more likely they are to have had sex and the more sexual partners they are likely to have.[36]

"Girls who reported closer relationships with their mothers were less likely to have had sexual intercourse. They were more likely to report a history of sexual intercourse when their mothers communicated frequently about sexual topics and when daughters perceived their mothers as being more approving of premarital sex. Daughters were less likely to be sexually active when their mothers reported more discussions related to the negative consequences of premarital sex and to delaying sexual intercourse for moral reasons."[37, 38]

If you have religious beliefs about teen sex, mom, you must convey those to your daughter. Even more protective is your daughter's devoutness: religiousness in adolescence is associated not only with lower rates of teen sex, but also lower incidence of binge drinking, marijuana use, and cigarette smoking.[39] Guilt is a powerful variable, in that if a teen believes teen sex is wrong, it limits their behavior significantly.[40] Sex educators who are so big on removing sex from morality remove the guilt factor. But parents should not be afraid of it, as long as the child understands it is the *timing* of sex, not sex itself, that is the issue. For every thing, there is a season.

Monitoring, knowing your daughter's whereabouts, activities, and friends, is critical. Know her friends—aside from you and her father, they have the greatest influence on her sexual decisions. Evidence is overwhelming that monitoring is protective, with benefits persisting into late adolescence.[41] It should come across to her as evidence of your concern and care, not mistrust.

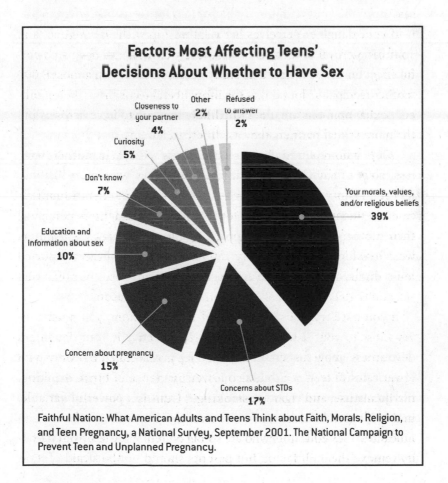

Factors Most Affecting Teens' Decisions About Whether to Have Sex

- Your morals, values, and/or religious beliefs **39%**
- Concerns about STDs **17%**
- Concern about pregnancy **15%**
- Education and Information about sex **10%**
- Don't know **7%**
- Curiosity **5%**
- Closeness to your partner **4%**
- Other **2%**
- Refused to answer **2%**

Faithful Nation: What American Adults and Teens Think about Faith, Morals, Religion, and Teen Pregnancy, a National Survey, September 2001. The National Campaign to Prevent Teen and Unplanned Pregnancy.

A perception of a low-level of monitoring is associated with sexual risk behaviors and, among low-income African American female teens, with getting pregnant, as well as gonorrhea, Chlamydia, and Trichomonas infections.[42] Your daughter should know it's important to you to know where she is, who she's with, and what she's doing.

Newsflash: More unsupervised time, with groups of peers or with a member of the opposite sex, is associated with sexual behavior.[43] Do we really need studies to confirm the obvious? Mom, reduce your daughter's opportunities for sexual encounters. You may want to consider enrolling your daughter in a program for teens that encourages abstinence; some have a proven track record. For example, junior high and middle school-aged girls in the Best Friends program are six and a half times less likely to have sex compared to their peers in D.C. Public Schools.[44]

Dr. Cullins, your advice is contradicted by twenty-five years of research on the teen brain and on parenting. You instruct this mom to step back, but one study after the next tells her to step in. You say you respect your daughter's decisions; they say make your expectations clear and enforce them. You emphasize her relationship with a health provider, but it's her relationship with her mother and her father that's critical. Your approach is based on the notion that parents thwart a child's development—that if kids were left alone, free of our rules and expectations, they'd thrive. But the opposite is true.

The "Facts" of Life

Do you see how this racket works? The experts tell your daughter: If you can answer "yes" to these questions, you may be "ready." They tell you: you may want her to wait, but be realistic: your daughter will probably have sex before she graduates from high school.

When you wince and groan, they reply: Trust us. We've studied adolescent sexuality, and understand your daughter's biological, psy-

chological, and social development. Sure, it's hard for you to
see her growing up so fast. But
it will be harder to see her pregnant. Your job, mom and dad—
even if adolescent sexual
behavior conflicts with your
values—is to share that with
her, and then make sure she
knows about obtaining and
using "protection."[45]

We're not talking only condoms. In her book *Beyond the
Big Talk: Every Parent's Guide to
Raising Sexually Healthy Teens—From Middle School to High School and
Beyond*, former SIECUS president Debra Haffner writes that teens
need to know "that they cannot swallow ejaculate or have oral sex
during menstruation. If these topics seem too embarrassing to discuss,
consider how awkward it would be helping your teen with oral gonorrhea or, worse, HIV."[46]

> **"Children are sexual and think sexual thoughts and do sexual things," Mom and Dad must "accept and honor [their] child's erotic potential."[102]**
> *—Talking With Your Child About Sex: Questions and Answers for Children from Birth to Puberty* **by sex ed matriarch and SIECUS founder Mary Calderone**

Uh . . . okay . . . thanks for sharing! And parents, take note of something else: if you can't stay cool and calm during these explicit talks,
aside from the risk to your child of disease and pregnancy, the experts
warn, you'll pay a hefty price: your child will go elsewhere for help.
That's right, she'll turn to a friend, teacher, or online stranger with her
questions and concerns, and it will be completely beyond your control. Well, that's what you get for foisting your hang-ups on your
child's healthy sexual curiosity.

Wait . . . what was that they were saying about scare tactics?

What should parents do? Have they no choice but to defer to the
"experts"? Are they really the bumbling morons described by educators, the greatest obstacle to their child's healthy sexuality? Is there no

other option but to take a deep breath, squelch their gut feelings, whisper a prayer, and try to speak "openly" with their thirteen-year-old about "sex play" and its accompanying risks?

Yes, parents have a choice. They can reject this madness. They can listen to their gut feelings, because their intuition is correct: No way! This is too much, too soon! We know our daughter, and she's not the self-aware, perfectly rational, disciplined person your model assumes, who already knows who she is and what she wants. She's not a mini adult[47] who can fully analyze a complex decision and consider the risks and consequences. The answer is not "information," it's giving her a chance to grow up. Our obligation is to teach and guide and, yes, sometimes judge her, not to stand by and watch as she determines her own "readiness"! Thanks for your opinions, "experts," but no thanks.

Parents can make that choice and share it with their child. They can calmly but firmly put up a big red light for their sons and daughters regarding sexual behavior during adolescence. And they can rest easy, because they—and not SIECUS, Planned Parenthood, or Advocates for Youth—have the up-to-date, medically-accurate facts on their side.

Newsflash: Teens Are Not Miniature Adults, in Mind or Body

In September 2003, some of the nation's most accomplished developmental neuroscientists gathered in New York City. They met for two days to share their research in a field that did not exist a decade earlier. The conference title: "Adolescent Brain Development: A Period of Vulnerabilities and Opportunities."[48]

Until the mid-1990s, the study of brain development focused on the fetus, infant, and toddler. By age two, the brain reaches close to 80 percent of its adult weight,[49] and so those years were considered the critical periods of development; future maturation was considered almost insignificant. But research was limited, because healthy children could not be ethically examined with x-rays or CT scans, techniques that use radiation.[50] Investigators had to rely on animal studies and cadavers.[51]

Enter magnetic resonance imaging (MRI). This technique, invented in the 1970s, produces "exquisitely accurate"[52] images of brain structure without using radiation. Even more exciting, real-time images of the brain at work—doing a math problem, recalling an event, feeling pleasure or fear—were available with the advent of functional MRI (fMRI). With the elimination of health risks, MRI and fMRI permitted observation of healthy children and teens, revolutionizing the study of brain and behavioral development.

For researchers, the biggest surprise came when they looked inside the heads of adolescents. They discovered that brain maturation does not end in early childhood; it simply pauses for some years, only to restart with vigor at the onset of puberty. During the second decade of life and into the third,

> "Given the pronounced developmental changes occurring in [the adolescent brain] . . . it would be extraordinary if adolescents did not differ from other aged individuals in their behavior."[70]
> — Linda Patia Spear, Ph.D.

a period of "explosive growth and restructuring" takes place. There is a "dramatic metamorphosis of the brain," writes one of the leading developmental psychologists in this young field. "The magnitude of these brain alterations is difficult to fathom."[53]

Think of it as Extreme Makeover: Teen Brain Edition. Due to this massive transformation, adolescence is a period of life with distinct vulnerabilities and opportunities.

We are now certain that the adolescent brain functions differently from an adult's. The importance of this discovery, say some of the country's eminent neurobiologists, should not be understated.[54]

Dr. Jay Giedd, chief of brain imaging in child psychiatry at the National Institute of Mental Health, has used Magnetic Resonance Imaging (MRI)s to peer into the heads of 1,800 kids, gaining a real-time view of the brain at work.[55] He scanned normal volunteers every two years during childhood, adolescence, and sometimes beyond. At first he planned to stop at age eighteen or twenty, but he discovered that was too soon: remodeling of some brain regions continues into the third decade of life. Dr Giedd and others found that an area called the prefrontal cortex (PFC) is the last to mature: it may not completely develop until the mid-twenties. "Avis must have some pretty sophisticated neuroscientists," he jokes, referring to the company's refusal to rent a car to drivers under the age of twenty-five.

The PFC is located behind the forehead, and is responsible for the executive functions of the brain: judging, reasoning, decision-making, self-evaluation, planning, suppression of impulses, and weighing the consequences of one's decisions. "It allows us to act on the basis of reason," explains Daniel Weinberger, Director of the Clinical Brain Disorders Laboratory at the NIH.[57] The PFC is like the Chief Executive Officer (CEO), and it is the final region to mature. Of course, parents don't need to have their kids' brains scanned to know they're capable of goofy and thoughtless behavior, but it's nice when science confirms what moms and dads have always known.

> **AFY tells parents: "Most teens, ages 13 to 17 will: Attain cognitive maturity—the ability to make decisions based on knowledge of options and their consequences."[56]**

If the CEO isn't fully on the job yet, how are adolescents at making decisions, especially ones involving risk? That's a critical question: the rates of death, disability and health problems of teens is *200 percent to 300 percent higher* than in children, due primarily to their poor control of behavior and emotion.[58] A portion of this burden is a consequence of sexual activity: pregnancy, sexually transmitted infections, and emotional turmoil. In devising an effective public health response to this crisis, the process of adolescent decision-making[59] must be examined.

Again, thanks to the new technology, we have a window through which we can observe, measure, and record the brain at work. The "neurobiology of decision making"[60] indicates that making choices relies on at least twelve different brain regions. These areas include cognitive and affective circuits, meaning decisions are based on both thought and emotion.

The PFC is the center of the "thinking" brain, and the amygdala (ah-MIG-di-lah) is a principle structure of the "feeling" brain. These two networks are seen as parallel systems whose integration evolves with time. The emotional system is present early in life; it's fast and mostly automatic—what's often called a gut reaction. The cognitive system develops with age, is slow and deliberate, and sometimes competes with the older system.[61] It has been suggested that because the emotional system is more mature than the cognitive one in teens, it sometimes contributes more to decision-making, resulting in less-than-optimal choices.[62]

Dr. Laurence Steinberg, a nationally recognized expert in adolescent psychology at Temple University, draws a distinction between "cool" and "hot" conditions, referring to the intensity or level of emotion at the time a decision is made.[63] Under "cool" conditions—a hypothetical dilemma in class, for example—a teen might appear to have excellent "executive functions": in making a choice, he engages in deliberate, logical thinking. *Sure,* he might resolve, *being sexually active is a big decision, so I'll take my time and consider the pros and cons. I'll talk it all over with my "partner," and we'll discuss STDs and contraceptives. After we make our decision, at the right time, we'll naturally stop everything and properly put on the condom that I'll have had the forethought to get and carry with me.*

But "cool" conditions are not the real world. Place the same boy in an unexpected situation, say at an unsupervised party,[64] add a cute and

> "The normal adolescent brain is far from mature or operating at full adult capacity. The physiological structure of the adolescent brain is similar therefore to the manifestation of mental disability within an adult brain."[54]
>
> — Daniel Weinberger, MD, NIMH

willing girl to the picture, along with peers who are disappearing together into bedrooms, and it's a different story. Functional MRIs tell us that under "hot conditions"—intense, novel, and highly stimulating—he is more likely to rely on his amygdala, to be shortsighted, emotion-driven, and susceptible to coercion and peer pressure.[65] In real life, his strong emotions and drives can "hijack" his ability for self-control and smart decisions.[66]

Harvard neuropsychologist Deborah Yurgelun-Todd explains, "adolescents are more prone to react with 'gut instinct' when they process emotions but as they mature into early adulthood, they are able to temper their instinctive 'gut reaction' response with rational, reasoned responses". . . . "Adult brains use the frontal lobe to rationalize or apply brakes to emotional responses. Adolescent brains are just beginning to develop that ability."[67]

Hard science is telling us that his response to our bewildered question, *what were you thinking?* should not mystify us. *I don't know*, the teen we love may answer, shaking his head, perhaps with tears of shame and regret. Again, most of us didn't need Ph.D.'s to confirm what common sense told us all along—he *wasn't* thinking.

It's Not Lack of Information—It's Lack of Judgment.

This is the case, Dr. Steinberg states, even when adolescents *know and understand* the risks involved.[68] We can no longer assume that teens make poor choices—drug use, high-speed driving, unprotected sex—because they are uninformed or unclear about the risks. As Dr. Steinberg reiterates, "There is substantial evidence that adolescents engage in dangerous activities *despite* knowing and understanding the risks involved."[69]

There are additional factors that make adolescence a time of increased vulnerability. With the onset of puberty, the brain is flooded with sex hormones. For many teens, this activates strong drives, excitement, and emotional intensity. It's "a natural tinderbox," as one neuroscientist termed the adolescent brain.[71] These hormones appear to alter the levels of dopamine, a neurotransmitter involved in the reward system. The alteration produces what's called a "reward deficiency";[72] in order to experience the same feeling of pleasure from a given activity, whether it's roller-coasters or rock concerts, teens require higher levels of novelty and stimulation. "It is as if they need to drive 70 miles per hour to achieve the same degree of excitement that driving 50 miles per hour had provided previously," said Dr. Steinberg.[73] Subsequently, there is an increased passion for novelty, thrills, and intensity. Add to that the sense of immortality and invulnerability that the average fifteen-year-old has, and you begin to grasp why parents of teens are nervous wrecks.

Dr. Dahl uses a powerful metaphor: an adolescent is like a fully mature car that's turbo-charged, but its driver is unskilled, and his navigational abilities are not yet fully in place.

Professionals in other fields have responded to these findings. The American Bar Association issued an official statement in 2003 urging all state legislatures to ban the death penalty for juveniles. "For social and biological reasons," it read, "teens have increased difficulty making mature decisions and understanding the consequences of their actions."[74] The same year, the Missouri Supreme Court overturned a juvenile death sentence, with the court referring to the volume of studies documenting the "lesser ability of teenagers to reason." The American Psychological Association (APA) followed, with a call for psychologists to "continue to bring forth existing and new data on the limits of adolescent reasoning, judgment and decision-making."[75]

But somehow the APA—or SIECUS, Planned Parenthood, and Advocates for Youth—has yet to acknowledge that this data is relevant to sex education. They're still insisting that deciding about sexual activity is "developmentally appropriate" for teens, that adults just need to "lay it all out there"—the risks and benefits: "Pour it all into teens' minds and watch them process it. They can do it," Planned Parenthood advised.[76]

Yet, the premise for teaching "safe sex" is based entirely on the assumption that teens can think through complex issues, plan ahead, and consider consequences. "Reasoning, judgment and decision-making," the very things they're still developing, are precisely the skills teens must have to determine their "readiness" for a "mature sexual relationship." How, in light of the insights this young century has brought us about teen risk-taking and decision-making, can sex educators still tell kids, "only *you* know when you're ready," and instruct parents to "respect" their teen's decision?

Memo to Debra Haffner, Ms. Klein, and the SIECUS and Planned Parenthood crowd: you know those "skills" you're so keen on adults providing teens, so they can make "informed decisions"? Studying their brains has indicated: it won't work .

You can drill it into them 24/7: *you must think, talk, and plan.* You can talk until you're blue in the face: *HPV, herpes, Chlamydia, and HIV; condoms, diaphragms and birth control pills; Plan B, abortion, or adoption.* And you can role-play all day: communication, negotiation, and assertiveness training.

Sorry, you may have all the good intentions in the world, but even if you provide *all the information*, and teach *all the skills*, you can't bank on producing a sexually responsible teen. The wiring isn't finished. The circuits aren't complete. The driver is unskilled, and only one thing will help: time.

Girls' Bodies Are Not Ready

Girls have another underdeveloped structure that increases their vulnerability, in addition to their prefrontal cortex. The cervix, the entrance to the uterus at the end of the vagina, plays a central role in female sexual health, but few people are aware of how it increases a girl's vulnerability to sexually transmitted infections.

The cervix is the site of two of the most common sexually transmitted infections, HPV and Chlamydia. HPV is necessary for cervical cancer to develop, and Chlamydia can cause chronic pelvic inflammatory disease, ectopic pregnancies, miscarriages, and infertility.

Girls under the age of twenty are being hit hardest[77] by these epidemics.[78] One reason is their immature cervix.[79]

It's critical to understand this. All things being equal,[80] the cervix of an adult is more difficult to infect than the cervix of a teen. The more mature cervix is protected by twenty to thirty layers of cells. In contrast, the cervix of a teen[81] has a central area called the transformation zone. Here the cells are only one layer thick. The transformation zone is largest at puberty, and it slowly shrinks as the cervix matures.[82] The thin folds of fragile, single cells are transformed progressively into a thick, flat shield with many layers. The "T-zone" can be seen during a routine pelvic exam. It makes the cervix look like a bull's eye, which is fitting, because it's exactly where the bugs want to be.

Ask any self-respecting virus or bacteria about his life goal, and he'll tell you: to find a good home where I can be fruitful and multiply. That's the purpose of his existence. To reach that home, the layers of cells must be penetrated. It's difficult, if not impossible, to get through the many layers of the mature cervix.

But penetration of the transformation zone's single layer is a cinch, making this area of the cervix prime real estate for genital infections. This is one of the reasons for our current pandemic of genital infections in teen girls.

Take note, however, that *infection* (the mere presence of an organism, an STI) is not enough to cause *disease* (an STD), which in the case of HPV, would be pre-cancerous changes.[83] The body has mechanisms for eliminating the virus before it causes damage, and for fixing the damage should it occur; it has methods of preventing an infection from developing into a disease. But these strategies are impaired in an HPV-infected T-zone.

Like police forces in a city, the body has specialized units[84] whose job is surveillance and safety. These are cells and organs that take care of "problems." In the cervix, these security guards are called Langerhans cells.[85] They watch out for unfamiliar "visitors." When one is identified, it's taken into headquarters[86] for "questioning," and taken care of—eradicated. In the T zone, compared to the more mature cervix, the number of Langerhans cells is lower,[87] the security is weaker, and dangerous "visitors" like viruses and bacteria may go

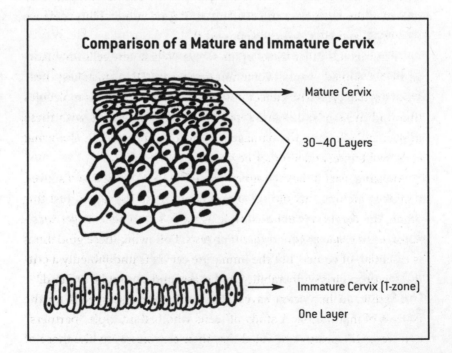

Comparison of a Mature and Immature Cervix

Mature Cervix

30–40 Layers

Immature Cervix (T-zone)

One Layer

unnoticed. Once HPV has settled in, the virus itself can incapacitate[88] Langerhans cell functioning.[89, 90] So aside from having a large area that's vulnerable to invasion, the young cervix also has a weaker "police force" to recognize and deal with the danger.

Also, cells in the T-zone are highly sensitive to estrogen and progesterone.[91] Studies suggest these hormones can enlarge the T-zone, empower HPV, and stimulate cervical cells to rapidly reproduce.[92] That's a hazardous combination. First, it provides bugs with more available "real estate." Because viruses can't replicate by themselves— they must hijack the machinery of the cell "hosting" them, their job is facilitated: hijacking is easier when the cell is working at high gear. So female hormones may boost the power of HPV to cause damage. They may also interfere with the actions of the "police force"—those Langerhans' cells. It's been demonstrated that taking birth control pills containing both estrogen and progesterone for eight to ten years places women at higher risk of cervical cancer. This is thought to be related to the hormones' direct effect on T-zone vulnerability: defense is lowered and HPV power is boosted.[93]

The virus has other tricks up its sleeve. When new cells are made, and DNA copied, errors occur. You don't want DNA mistakes; these are abnormal cells with cancer potential. A healthy cell has molecules that find these mistakes and repair them. HPV interferes with these molecules, allowing the damaged DNA to replicate. The abnormal cells proliferate, and a tumor begins to grow.

Amazing, isn't it, how complex this is? I was surprised to discover, while researching this subject, a number of textbooks about just this organ, the cervix. It's not as simple as we're led to believe: *get vaccinated, use a condom, have regular Pap tests.* Following those guidelines is essential, of course, but the immature cervix is undoubtedly a critical factor in girls' vulnerability to disease, and cannot be omitted.

There is an important caveat: Sexual intercourse speeds up the process of maturation. A study of teens who had multiple "partners" and were HIV-positive revealed that their cervixes were like those of adults—covered by many layers of cells.[94] Something associated with intercourse—the mechanical insult, a substance found in semen, or the presence of an STI—speeds up the process by which the T-zone matures.[95]

So if a girl is having vaginal intercourse, her body "knows" it, and responds by accelerating its defense: a thicker barrier of cells. But here's the problem. When the cells in the T-zone are proliferating rapidly, as they are after sexual debut, their replicating machinery is working overtime. As previously explained, the cell in high gear is the cell that HPV easily takes over. Since girls are likely to be infected with the virus from one of their first partners,[96] this is bad news. The virus is present, and now the machinery through which it does its damage is working overtime. It is now likelier than ever that abnormal cells will get the chance to proliferate. So even though intercourse accelerates cervical maturation, a girl who has just begun having sex is more vulnerable than she was as a virgin, at least to the cancer-causing potential of HPV. This is something she should know, when she comes in for birth control or testing. The awareness of this risk, along with communication skills, may help her to begin saying "no."

Biology Says: Wait!

How long does it take for the cervix to mature? That's what I want to know from every gynecologist I meet. They tell me that everyone is different, but in general, as a girl moves through her teens and into early adulthood, her transformation zone decreases in size. A larger area of the cervix is covered by a thicker, tougher surface.

Now folks, this is big. Based on this finding alone—something gynecologists and pediatricians have known for at least[97] twenty years, girls should be advised to delay sexual behavior. Yes, delay sexual behavior. Not for moral reasons, and not for emotional reasons (although those are significant as well, and we'll get to that in another chapter), but for medical reasons alone.

Question: *why don't we all know about this?* Why aren't pictures of the T-zone found in every sex ed curricula, and displayed on the websites of Planned Parenthood, Teen Talk, and GoAskAlice?[98] Why no pamphlet about the cervix in the waiting rooms of adolescent health providers? What happened to a teens' right to "up-to-date, accurate medical information," and to sex educators' claim of providing it?

I've scoured the resources on this, and read all the Q&A's from girls asking, *"am I ready? How do I know?"* The answer is always, "Only you can decide . . . ."[99] Consider your values, your relationship, and how you feel about it, girls are advised. A responsible sexual relationship is *consensual*; *honest*; *mutually pleasurable*; *protected.* Always included are warnings not to have sex due to peer pressure or coercion. I didn't find a single "expert"—who declared: *you're not ready, take it from me, it's smart to wait* and then explained the immature cervix, and pointed to it as indisputable evidence that *teen sexual activity is high risk, especially for girls.*

How, in 2008, do organizations like SIECUS and Planned Parenthood get away with their 1960s-era mantras about kids being "open," questioning what they learn at home and at church, and telling them, "only-you-can-decide-when-you're-ready," all the while claiming to be based in science? How can they tell parents to "provide information," back off, and respect their teen's decision—the same teen that forgets to bring a pencil to class, and has a meltdown when her sister gets more French fries than her?

In fact, adolescent brain specialists urge the opposite approach to what sex education activists recommend. Dr. Giedd says that parents should "stick around and sort of be the highly developed frontal lobe"—meaning, be involved with the tough decisions facing your teen, even if they resist.[100] Be the CEO—within reasonable limits—until theirs is fully functioning. Dr. Dahl and other neuropsychologists remind us that adolescents need *social scaffolding*—constraints, support, protection, and "most importantly, the rules and behaviors of the adults that provide monitoring and a 'safety net' for adolescents."[101] Are you hearing this? Along with our support and protection, they need our constraints and rules.

This scaffolding, they say, should come from parents, teachers, coaches and other responsible adults and should not weaken until the capacity to self regulate has emerged, and the individual is able to make increasingly independent judgments. "Adult monitoring is all too frequently and too prematurely withdrawn during this vulnerable period, leaving the adolescent to have to navigate situations alone or with peers at a relatively early age . . . [this] plays a part in creating a great deal of vulnerability for youth in our society."

Amen. Teens are not small versions of adults. They need us, along with our rules and limit setting—even though they'll rarely say so. About sex, they must be told: of course you're interested, your urges are natural and healthy, but now is not the time. Trust us, this is not like cigarettes or fast food: one poor choice, *just one,* can affect the rest of your life. Be smart, we expect it of you, and we know you can do it.

Anything less than that is an awful disservice to our kids. We harm them by saying: *only you know*, as if, with all our wisdom and experience, we know nothing. We deprive them of the scaffolding they so need. Why then are we surprised when, like an unsupported building, they wobble and come tumbling down?

Chapter Four

A Doctor's Oath

L IKE ALL PHYSICIANS, Ruth Jacobs took an oath when she graduated from medical school. She stood up, raised her right hand, and swore to prevent disease whenever she could. Since that day, she's treated thousands of patients, learning the hard way that the fight against disease is sometimes lost. Early in her career, in fact, the news she gave many patients was bad; there was little to do but wait for the end. The grief of those left behind was heavy on her heart.

But Dr. Jacobs accepted the fact that some conditions are fatal, and every physician has patients who die. After doing all she could to prolong life, she'd mourn the loss and continue her work with the many others who needed her.

It was difficult, yes, and yet easier in some ways than her current ordeal. Dr. Jacobs is still fighting to prevent disease, but her foe isn't cancer or infection—she's up against her local Board of Education. She, along with other members of a group called Citizens for Responsible Curriculum (CRC), is dueling with school administrators over what teens should be taught about risky sexual activities.[1] This sort of battle is new to Dr. Jacobs; it's fought far from a dying patient's bedside, with lawsuits, not medication. But it's over this struggle, not her earlier ones, that she feels discouraged, sometimes even hopeless, about preventing disease. Why now, nearly thirty years after taking the doctor's oath, does staying true to her promise seem such a formidable task?

Dr. Jacobs is an infectious disease specialist in Montgomery County, Maryland. She was trained at the National Institutes of Health, arriving there in the early eighties—the start of the great plague of our time. AIDS was a mystery during those years. The NIH intensive care unit and immunology division was crowded with young men who should have been healthy and thriving. After being flown in from San Francisco, Los Angeles, and New York for the best in research and advanced care, they all died.

After seven years at the NIH, she worked at the Washington Veterans hospital, where the same scenarios continued. Science was still without an answer. By the time she opened a private practice in the nineties, Dr. Jacobs was more comfortable taking care of patients with HIV than those with the common cold. Like many health professionals who cared for AIDS patients through the eighties, Jacobs saw and experienced much sorrow.

Fast forward to 2005. Dr. Jacobs had been listed as one of DC's best doctors for years. At the request of a concerned mother, she reviewed a video[2] being shown to tenth graders as part of a newly devised Family Life and Human Development course in Montgomery County Public Schools. The video, called "Protect Yourself," stated that condoms provide 98 percent protection against pregnancy and sexually transmitted infections, including HIV. It implied that this nearly perfect level of protection was effective during vaginal, oral, and anal sex.

Dr. Jacobs was alarmed: this was flat-out wrong. First of all, 98 percent protection refers to avoidance of pregnancy, not infection, and is achievable, according to studies, by adult couples with "perfect use"

Terms such as "highly effective," "very good," and "significant" are used by the CDC and other authorities to describe condom effectiveness. While there is no doubt that proper use of condoms prevents some infections to some degree, it appears to me that "significant" sometimes refers to "statistically significant," a level of protection many people would consider unacceptable. It would be ethical to remind people the statistics refer only to vaginal intercourse and to provide the actual numbers so they can make informed decisions about their behavior. Why isn't this done? Maybe because of a fear that people will stop using condoms altogether, losing whatever level of "protection" they do provide.

of condoms. Few individuals manage to use condoms "perfectly"—consistently and correctly. Much more common is "typical use"—the device is not worn for every act, and when worn it's occasionally used incorrectly. With "typical use" by adults, studies show pregnancy prevention falls to 85 percent.[3] Taking into account their immaturity, use of alcohol before sex, and other factors, teens' typical use of condoms could be expected to prevent pregnancy at a much lower rate.

Dr. Jacobs knew that quantifying the degree of protection condoms confer from infection is not a simple matter. Even a panel of 28 experts had a tough time at it. The NIH, CDC, and FDA brought them together in 2001 and asked, "What is the scientific evidence on the effectiveness of latex male condom-use to prevent STD transmission during vaginal intercourse?"[4]

The answer to that question was—and still is—"It depends."[5] Although latex is essentially impermeable to all sexually transmitted organisms, germs and sperm can escape around the edges. At best, protection against HIV has an estimated 80 percent[6] reduction in risk of transmission with perfect use during vaginal intercourse.[7]

Risk reduction for infections transmitted in secretions ranges from 26 percent (chlamydia) to 62 percent (gonorrhea).[8] In one study of sexually active African American teen girls, despite 100 percent condom use, one in five became infected with chlamydia, gonorrhea, or trichomonas within twenty-eight months.[9]

Protection against infections transmitted skin-to-skin is compromised, because sometimes the condom will not provide coverage of the area. Other research indicates perfect condom use only reduces the risk of genital herpes by 25–50 percent.[10] Large studies have found little or no effectiveness of condoms in preventing transmission of HPV.[11]

Again, these numbers refer to correct condom use for every instance of vaginal intercourse.

Jacobs concluded that the "Protect Yourself" video was dangerously misleading. It would give students a false sense of security, and the consequences could be catastrophic. She had evidence in her own practice that even people who use condoms perfectly can be infected with HIV/AIDS. Two of her most recent cases had been patients infected with HIV who were both shocked at the diagnosis. One was a teenager, the other a mature adult. They had used condoms 100 percent of the time and couldn't understand how it had happened. As she later recalled, "They were so angry, it was as if flames were coming out of their heads."

"*This scenario always makes me want to cry,*" she wrote in a letter to a Maryland community newspaper in 2005, "*because if they had only known the risks they were taking, maybe this human tragedy would not be playing out in my office.*"[12]

Pivotal to Dr. Jacobs's objection[13] to "Protect Yourself" was the absence of warnings about the danger of anal intercourse. Students were being told that HIV and other infections are shared through unprotected vaginal, oral, or anal intercourse, as if each activity carries the same risk. Dr. Jacobs wanted students to hear what she told her patients—that due to anatomy and physiology, anal sex has been estimated to be at least 20 times riskier than vaginal.[14] Also missing was the information that condoms are more likely to fail during anal sex[15]—a danger acknowledged on condom wrappers that warn consumers: "Non-vaginal use can increase potential damage to the condom."[16]

This is a subject most people would like to ignore. First of all, it has a high "ick factor." Second, it cannot be discussed honestly in our society without leading to some nasty name-calling. Ruth Jacobs knew that, but she also knew the subject was too important to *not* discuss honestly. So, the fear of being called names didn't stop her. She'd seen too many people fighting these diseases, some of them with AIDS, in their final days, trying to survive another month or week, hoping to see a child graduate or get married. She was not about to sit back and watch as kids were provided dangerously inaccurate information.

If her years of practice had taught her anything, it was that with or without a condom, anal intercourse is high risk behavior, and that kids must be told flat out: Don't do it.

Dr. Jacobs voiced her concerns at a meeting of the school board. She described the anger of her patients who became HIV positive, despite use of condoms 100 percent and following safer sex guidelines. She told the large audience of concerned parents that the video was so misleading it would add new patients to her infectious disease practice.

> **As a result of the distorted information they get from the sex education industry, teens are placed at higher risk for HIV/AIDS and other infections.**

In a letter to the local newspaper, Dr. Jacobs wrote, "Each sexually transmitted disease is a disaster in the life of the individual," she wrote. "We must educate [students] to the dangers and to steps they need to take to have full and productive lives and not spend their lives in a physician's office."[17]

Her concern was for all students, regardless of sexual orientation. A CDC study of over 12,000 people[18] has indicated that by age 19, 11 percent of girls have had anal intercourse, and by 24, almost 30 percent. The rate of condom use during anal sex for those 11 percent of teen girls was only 25 percent. Many teens do not recognize this as risky sexual behavior; one study on urban minority females indicated 41 percent engaged in anal sex to avoid pregnancy, and 20 thought HIV could not be transmitted through anal sex;[19] some don't even consider anal sex "sex."[20] So this is not only about the sexuality of men who are attracted to men. As Dr. Jacobs knew, the hazards of anal intercourse are a matter of anatomy, histology, immunology, and microbiology; and any sex ed program that does not consider what those sciences demonstrate is not medically accurate, let alone comprehensive.

Jacobs' efforts and those of the CRC had no impact on the Board of Education. It was only following a lawsuit and restraining order[21] that the condom video [and another portion of the program] was dropped. The settlement stipulated that Citizens for a Responsible Curriculum[22] would have a seat in the new citizens' advisory committee, charged with establishing a new curriculum and a new condom video for MCPS students.

Dr. Jacobs was amazed at what was passing as sex education in Montgomery County, one of the wealthiest and most educated in the country. She assumed the deficiencies were related to the lack of medical knowledge among school administrators and parents. That could be easily remedied by providing them with some basic facts about infectious disease, she thought, and sharing a few of the harrowing stories of patients in her care. Armed with the facts, they'd certainly understand that vast changes needed to be made.

Whenever the Board of Education meetings were open to the public, Dr. Jacobs would attend and make a presentation.[23] For nine months, she took time away from her practice to speak about the fundamental principles of public health as they related to sexually transmitted infections and HIV/AIDS. Each time, she had two minutes to cover the material—that was Board of Ed protocol. Her talks covered a wide variety of topics including germ theory, the risks of anal and oral sex, and of multiple partners. She provided graphic descriptions of the blisters, warts, discharges, and other medical problems caused by sexually transmitted bacteria and viruses, and explained the inadequate protection provided by condoms. She emphasized to the Board what she knew from medical literature and professional meetings: the patients being seen by clinicians are the tip of the iceberg—most people carrying genital viruses and bacteria don't seek care. They, along with their unsuspecting partners, are unaware of their infections.[24] That even after two decades, HIV/AIDS was still hitting young people hard—half of all new cases were occurring in the 15–24 age group.[25] What we face now, more than ever, is a vast, silent epidemic.

One of her presentations was prompted by a visit to a friend's home, where the babysitter, a MCPS graduate, had proudly announced a unique way of entertaining the kids with a "swirly": have a child place his head in a toilet, then flush the water. What fun! What excitement!

Not so much fun, however, when the child came down with a vomiting illness the following week.

As a specialist in infectious disease, the notion of a "swirly" caught Dr. Jacobs' attention. For her next opportunity at the Board, she'd speak about the dangers of exposure to stool—a topic about which every infectious disease expert could write a book. She designed and printed a handout to supplement her talk, with diagrams and electron microscopic photos of the bacteria and parasites that live in the rectum. Dr. Jacobs practiced before the meeting, so she could summarize the points she considered most critical within 120 seconds.

Fearless of the "ick factor," she explained to the Board and audience of parents that feces are filled with dangerous pathogens: salmonella, shigella, amoeba, hepatitis A, B, and C, giardia, campylobacter, and others. These organisms and others can be transmitted during anal sex or oral-anal contact,[26] she explained, and the consequences can be much more serious than a few days of vomiting. She reminded the Board of their responsibility to include these warnings in the new curriculum.

The doctor's unique mini-course in microbiology, epidemiology, and public health made some difference, but not enough. With time, it was clear that the new curriculum, while improved, would not adequately address the increased danger of anal sex and multiple partners, or the limited efficacy of condoms.[27] Dr. Jacobs concluded that the Board had an agenda, and it had nothing to do with student health. Their priority, it seemed, was to downplay the hazards of high-risk behaviors, anal sex in particular.

"It may not be politically correct to describe ills related to having multiple sexual partners and anal intercourse," Dr. Jacobs wrote in the *Washington Times*.[28] However, it is scientifically correct. "Our tax payer dollars should not be used to encourage or normalize risky sexual behavior or to hide the results of such behavior from youth."

Having hit a wall with the Board, Dr. Jacobs took the issue to her peers—medical doctors. She argued that the new MCPS condom lesson should include these statements:

From the National Institutes of Health:

> HIV/AIDS can be sexually transmitted by anal, penile-vaginal, and oral intercourse. The highest rate of transmission is through anal exposure.[29]

From the Food and Drug Administration:

> Condoms may be more likely to break during anal intercourse than during other types of sex because of the greater amount of friction and other stresses involved.

Even if the condom doesn't break, anal intercourse is very risky because it can cause tissue in the rectum to tear and bleed. These tears allow disease germs to pass more easily from one partner to the other.[30]

And from former Surgeon General C. Everett Koop:

Condoms provide some protection, but anal intercourse is simply too dangerous to practice.[31]

She asked physicians who agreed to sign the following petition:

Health education is important. We the undersigned recognize that anal intercourse (A/I) is a particular high risk sexual practice and it is associated with the highest risk of HIV infection. We further recognize that "although there is strong evidence that condom use generally reduces sexual transmission of HIV, solid data showing the effectiveness of currently available condoms during A/I, a particularly high-risk sexual practice, still are lacking."

As physicians, we are concerned for the health of the students and recommend that the new MCPS condom use lesson must use the Surgeons Generals statement and NIH consensus conference statement to warn students of the risks of anal intercourse and of the risks of condom failure during anal intercourse.[32]

As Jacobs collected signatures, doctors shared their horror stories. A pathologist described the advanced malignant changes in the cervix of a 16-year-old. This was a cancer he would have expected to take six or eight years to develop. Gynecologists reported on anal herpes and warts of the anus—these are due to HPV[33]—in young women. Doctors complained that they're tired of performing LEEPS—a procedure to treat cervical tissue infected with HPV—on girls in high school.

She presented the petition, signed by 70 MDs, to the Board. The response was minimal.

A few months later, she returned with over 270 signatures. I have the list in front of me. It includes family practitioners, neurologists, surgeons, OB/GYNs, gastroenterologists, ER docs, cardiologists, pediatricians, pathologists, urologists, oncologists, endocrinologists—just about every medical specialty. Impressive, right? Not to the Board of Education of Montgomery County. Instead of recognizing her determination and effort—to say nothing of her time and expense—Dr. Jacobs's efforts fell on deaf ears. No changes were made.

Having the FDA, a surgeon general, and over 270 MDs in agreement about the hazards of anal intercourse was not enough, it seems, for the Montgomery County Public School system. Even with all that authority, the words "anal intercourse is simply too dangerous to practice" couldn't get through the schoolhouse doors. Can you believe it? An alien landing in Maryland would conclude that it's not lifelong herpes or deadly HIV that pose the greatest dangers to our kids; instead, we should fear a physician, board certified in internal medicine, infectious disease, and immunology, by the name of Ruth Jacobs.

Messages

In December 2007, a headline on the SIECUS website declared: "Prevalence of Unprotected Anal Sex among Teens Requires New Education Strategies."[34] A study in a recent *Journal of Pediatric and Adolescent Gynecology* was "very disturbing," the site reported, as it indicated teens were not using condoms consistently for vaginal sex, and that they were using them even less consistently for anal sex. SIECUS was worried about the idea teens have that anal sex is somehow "safer" than vaginal sex. This, they said, is "a dangerous misconception"; anal sex is, they reported, "as risky" as vaginal sex, in terms of infections.

Kudos to SIECUS for acknowledging that new strategies are necessary. A good place to start would be in their own backyard.

SIECUS encourages books like *Daddy's Roommate* and *My Dad Has HIV* for kids in early elementary school, in order to begin conversations about sexual orientation. It's vital, they say, to explain to young children that some people are attracted to members of the same sex.

But it's never the right time, it seems, to warn teenagers that the varieties of sexual expression carry vastly different risks, especially for transmission of HIV, and to explain in accurate and up-to-date detail why. They never find it appropriate to instruct kids to avoid behaviors that are high-risk, and to flat-out tell them, "Don't do it."

Instead, SIECUS provides lessons like those in the old MCPS video, the one the lawsuit helped to eliminate. Here's what SIECUS says about anal sex, HIV, and staying safe in their pamphlet for youth, "All About Sex":[35]

> Putting the penis inside a partner's anus is called anal sex. Many couples (both opposite sex and same sex) choose to have anal sex. All STDs can be passed during oral, vaginal, or anal sex with an infected partner. HIV is passed from an infected person through blood, semen, vaginal secretions, and breast milk. It is also very important to use a latex condom during oral, vaginal, or anal sex, or a dental dam during oral sex.

When sex educators teach that HIV can be transmitted by "any exchange of body fluids—blood, semen, vaginal secretions, and breast milk," when they say infection can occur via vaginal, oral, or anal intercourse, and when they claim, "Anyone can get HIV," their message is technically accurate. The problem is, however, that the various "anyones" have vastly different risks—some would say million-fold differences, depending on their behavior.[36] It's like saying, "Lung cancer can be caused by radon, asbestos, tobacco, and air pollution." The statement is correct, but 80 percent of lung cancers are due to tobacco,[37] and a person smoking four packs a day of unfiltered Camels is at much greater risk than someone living in Los Angeles's polluted air, and everyone would agree he needs to know that.

It's as if the smoker is being discriminated against, and, that being unacceptable, all causes of the disease must be portrayed as carrying the same risk. You might call it the equal opportunity approach to epidemiology. It goes like this: All individuals face the same risk of illness, regardless of their genetics, diet, use of nicotine, or drinking habits. It's only fair.

Like the original MCPS curriculum, SIECUS said nothing in "All About Sex" about the highest risk of transmission during anal sex or the increased likelihood of condoms failing. And surely absent is the recommendation to avoid this high-risk act; to the contrary, unsuspecting kids are told, "Many couples (both opposite and same sex) choose to have anal sex."

gURL.COM, a site recommended to teens when they log on to SIECUS, is better. Their "Anal Sex: Fast Facts"[38] warns of the dangers:

> The tissue inside your anus is very delicate and tender, and
> tiny tears or scrapes can happen without you even noticing.

But the warning refers only to the condom-less act. With a condom,

> Both women and men can enjoy giving or receiving anal
> sex, and both women and men can have orgasms from anal
> sex. Likewise, people of any sexual orientation may enjoy
> anal sex.

At Planned Parenthood's site for teens,[39] a reader calling himself "Crazylivedevil" has a question for the experts. He and his girlfriend are going to try anal sex, and she is concerned about safety. What, he asks, are the consequences of anal sex? In their answer, they do not even mention of the 20-fold increased risk *to his girlfriend, not him*, of HIV transmission, or increased risk of condom failure, compared to vaginal sex:

> Like unprotected vaginal intercourse, unprotected anal intercourse is high-risk for many sexually transmitted infections....Use condoms during anal sex to decrease the risk of sexually transmitted infections...it is important to use an artificial water-based lubricant....It is also important to stop if anything hurts and communicate with your partner about how you feel—sex play that is painful or uncomfortable should not continue....Most people do not enjoy anal intercourse. They should not be embarrassed and should not force themselves to accept it. Many people however, do enjoy anal sex and, for them, it's perfectly normal.[40]

Elizabeth Schroeder, chair of SIECUS Board of Directors, is on the medical advisory board[41] that reviews the content of Rutger University's "Sex, Etc."[42] The award-winning site warns teens about the risk of damage to rectal tissue, explaining that tears can make it easier to transmit STDs, including HIV. It also points out that a condom can rip or tear. So far, so good.

Then they turn to the sanitation issue, with the heading, "But, it's nasty!" What follows is this astonishing reassurance, based on the insights of one Jennifer Johnston, identified as an educator at Planned Parenthood of Western Washington.

While there is a possibility of coming into contact with feces, Johnston reassures that "the rectum isn't the main storage area for feces. The colon is. So if a person has had a recent bowel movement and eats healthy food and keeps regular, the rectum can be feces-free, especially if it is washed thoroughly before engaging in anal sex."

Heather Corinna, of Scarleteen, goes further. She not only provides instructions on how to engage in anal sex in her book for teens,[43] she introduces readers to "oral stimulation of the anus or rectum." This, kids learn, is "something people of all genders and orientations may enjoy."[44]

Jennifer and Heather would benefit from Dr. Jacobs's "swirly talk," don't you think? In case you forgot, here are a few of the nasty organisms found in the rectum: salmonella, shigella, amoeba, hepatitis A, B, and C, giardia, and campylobacter, among others.

For Heather, ever the social activist, every subject, even this one, is related to oppression. When "Teenie" wonders why anal sex is "a bad thing," Heather answers:[45]

> It's not a bad thing when it isn't a bad thing for you. . . . But you're right: there are a lot of negative attitudes about anal sex and the anus. For certain, some of that comes down to a basic fear of or disgust about feces. . . . But more of it is often based in homophobia and heteronormativity. . . [unprotected] anal sex does present big HIV risks . . . but the same risks exist with vaginal intercourse . . . you can probably see why homophobia has such a big hand here.

Over at the Columbia's GoAskAlice, a male reader ("well adjusted . . . with a steady girlfriend") finds himself drawn toward trying anal intercourse, on the receiving end.[46] Is he bisexual, he wonders?

Labels, Alice answers, "act like a ball and chain around our desires." Don't feel you need to pigeonhole your sexuality into a comfortable box, she advises. "Alice applauds you for getting in touch with what flies your flag."

That's it. No warnings or suggestions for this reader who is poised to try out something a former surgeon general instructed the country "is simply too dangerous to practice."

> With the rapid emergence of the new sexual mores and permissiveness in our society as well as a greater acceptance and

understanding of sexual deviation by the general public, the sur-
geon is now confronted with new problems in diagnosis and treat-
ment of unusual anorectal injuries.

So began a report called "Social Injuries of the Rectum" in the *American Journal of Surgery,* November 1977.[47] The article described two cases—one a rectal tear with profuse bleeding, the other a laceration of the colon requiring emergency surgery. Both were due to what the authors called "fist fornication"—"the practice of introducing the closed or clenched fist into the rectal ampulla, upper rectum, and sigmoid colon to achieve sexual gratification."

Thirty years later, courtesy of Alice[48] and Heather,[49] teens can easily find guidance—indeed, books are suggested—on how to engage in this behavior and reduce the risk of "social injuries." I suppose some people would consider that progress. Colorectal surgeons are probably not among them.

What Kids Must Know

As mentioned earlier, all self-respecting microbes have one goal: to find a home and reproduce. The same is true for HIV. And there is no doubt, the deadly virus has an easier time doing this in the rectum than anywhere else.[50]

Having receptive anal intercourse with someone who is HIV positive is dangerous; the studies confirming this are voluminous.[51] The reason is biology—actually, to be more precise, histology. Histology is the study of cells, what they do, and how they are organized. To fully understand how HIV is transmitted, and why a "generic" notion of intercourse is dangerously false, a comparison of the histology of the vagina with the histology of the rectum is mandatory.

For infection to occur, keep in mind that HIV must either enter the bloodstream or gain access to deeper tissues. This makes it a relatively difficult bug to pass along. Consider for example the highly contagious viruses that cause conjunctivitis (commonly known as pink eye).[52] They are easily transmitted on your finger, when you touch one eye and then the other. They can also live on inanimate surfaces, like towels or pillows, and infect you from there.

In contrast, HIV must reach a group of cells in the immune system called "target cells." Only here can the virus make a home and reproduce. To reach target cells, the HIV must either bypass or pass through a barrier. For example, the heroin addict sharing a dirty needle infects himself by injecting the virus directly into his bloodstream, bypassing the natural barrier, skin. The same is true for persons infected through blood transfusions. The infant nursed by an HIV positive mother is infected when the virus passes through the lining of the digestive system. So the barrier is important to look at: it is the wall the virus must breach to succeed.

Assuming a girl is healthy—without any STIs or conditions that would weaken her immunity—her vagina has some built-in conditions[53] that are protective from the get-go. In fact, one of the functions of the vaginal lining is protection from infection.[54] The pH is low, which inactivates HIV.[55] Its mucus has anti-HIV proteins.[56] Langerhans cells in the cervix can destroy the virus.[57] The vaginal wall is 20 to 45 cells thick,[58] increasing the distance to be traversed by the virus. Under the wall is a layer in which target cells are found; this area is rich in elastic fibers. Next is a layer of muscle, then more elastic fibers. This architecture allows for significant stretching of the vagina without tears or abrasions. Some researchers believe that HIV is unable to reach target cells in the human vagina under normal circumstances;[59] others disagree.[60]

The rectum has a different structure. As part of the gastrointestinal system, it has a lining whose primary function is absorption, bringing in molecules of food and water. The pH is higher. Most important, the rectal lining—the barrier to be breached—is only one cell thick. Below that delicate lining are blood vessels and target cells. Elastic fibers are absent.

Early in the epidemic, it was assumed that fragility of the rectal barrier accounted for the more common male-to-male transmission. But
later in the eighties came a discovery: infection could occur *without*
disruption of the barrier. Specialized cells on the surface "swallow"
the virus and deliver it unchanged to target cells.[61]

Microfold cells ("M cells") are abundant in a healthy human rectum.[62] Like Langerhans cells in the cervix, M cells are watchdogs that
identify foreign particles and shuttle them over to HQ for manage-
ment by the body's defense system. An M cell *wants* to attract
microbes, so its surface is sticky.[63] When observed with electron
microscopy, M cells appear to reach out, engulf a pathogen, and bring
it into the cell in a pocket.[64] The pocket moves to the other end of the
M cell, to immune cells that process the microbe and determine the
appropriate response: ignore it or rally against it.

Along comes HIV. It subverts the system, turning M cells into an
express lane for invasion. The virus is packaged, transported, and
handed over to immune cells that are one and the same as the target
cells the virus must reach to cause disease. So M cells facilitate the
virus's job; they Fed Ex HIV directly to a lymphocyte—delivery takes
ten minutes.[65, 66]

Remember Dr. Jacobs's talk to the Board of Education: feces are
packed with organisms that can cause disease. The normal gastrointestinal tract, in fact, has the highest recorded bacterial cell density of
any microbial ecosystem.[67] So a host of other bugs, not only HIV, can
gain entry to the body via the M cell shuttle: cholera, shigella, salmonella, and E. coli.[68] No wonder the cell has been called "a potential
Achilles heel" in the GI system's barrier to infection.[69]

There are no M cells in the vagina. This is not to say transmission
of HIV cannot happen there—it can. But for infection to occur, there
must be some weakening of the system—an infection like HPV or herpes, an open sore, trauma, cancerous cells.

As former Surgeon General Koop told the nation, "Condoms provide some protection, but anal intercourse is simply too dangerous to

practice." That's also the message my friend John Potterat told his two sons, his daughter, and their friends.

John has been called "one of the country's leading epidemiologists";[70] he was Director of STD/AIDS Programs in Colorado Springs, CO, for almost thirty years, and has authored, as of this writing, 177 scholarly publications about STDs and HIV/AIDS. Before his kids became sexually active, he told them: The anus is an exit, not an entrance.[71] This is not the Bible, he said; this is science. The anal lining is only one cell thick, there are M cells everywhere, there is no lubrication, so tissue microtears are common, and access to the blood stream is easy. Unlike the vagina, nature put a tight sphincter at the entrance of the anus. It's there for a reason: Keep out!

Few parents are STD experts like John P., but your kids deserve the same insider wisdom as his. Go ahead, tell them: The rectum is an exit, not an entrance. Because you can be sure they won't be hearing that in sex ed class.

The Fight Rages On

Dr. Jacobs is trying to keep the oath she took upon graduating from medical school: to prevent disease whenever she can. But her politically incorrect message isn't welcome, and she's worked, on her own dime, to get life-saving facts to students. If their priority was disease prevention, the Board of Education wouldn't limit Dr. Jacobs' talk to two minutes—they'd give her an entire day. Instead of being ignored, she'd be given her own national radio show, to share her wisdom and experience with the entire country. Instead of legal battles, she'd be publicly honored. It's a sad state of affairs when, due to political correctness and social agendas, a professional with wisdom, experience, and passion must wage war to be heard.

Why promote the untruth that anal and vaginal intercourse are alike? What's behind the notion of "generic" intercourse? It's the preposterous belief that males and females are the same, and their unions are equivalent. It's another example of the indoctrination of children with radical social agendas.

Parents must grasp what's happening in the classroom. The truth of biology—anal sex is too dangerous—is squelched, because it contradicts the ideology of "anything goes—no judgments allowed." As always, when it's health versus sexual freedom, freedom prevails. Kids are encouraged to explore their sexuality, and told precisely how; with the experts' blessings, they go out and play in traffic. Instead of straight talk and hard science, there's a lesson like "Protect Yourself" and discussion of homophobia. *All's well*, goes this thinking, *if kids use latex and there's no name-calling in the halls.*

And then we wonder why, after twenty-five years, HIV is still going strong.

♂♀

Chapter Five

Whitewashing a Plague

IMAGINE THIS: You've been faithfully married for years, you have two kids, and your wife's expecting. One day, you discover a bunch of reddish bumps in your groin. No big deal, you think—it's some sort of rash. But in a while, they really itch and sting. It hurts just to walk or sit down. You miss a day of work, wondering, what the heck is this? When the doctor says herpes, you explain that that's simply impossible. But in a few days the email arrives: your blood test is positive. Yes, you have genital herpes—a sexually transmitted disease. What are you thinking?

No need to imagine—you can hear about the entire ordeal from the unfortunate fellow who lived thru it. Check out the herpes support site racoon.com, his handle is learn2luv, and his first post is "New/Confused/Angry/Lied."

Learn2luv can cope with the blisters, even though they are awful. It's his fury and confusion that got him unglued. All these years his wife kept her infection a secret—and that really burns. For that pain, the doctor didn't have any pills. Whom can he talk to? Learn2luv went online, and spilled his heart out.

> I'm confused, I'm angry, I'm depressed . . . . She tells me her reasons for lying were a fear of losing me . . . . I was hoping that someone could help me understand why she would lie, why she would take no regard for my health or the health of our children . . . . Please help me deal with this news . . . deal with the lies . . . deal with the pain . . . .[1]

He had come to the right place. Members of the site replied within hours, and the online discussion about his situation—a small part of the 52,000 posts here—continued for days.

> "It is hard to think straight when in the middle of an OB [outbreak of blisters]," he was advised.

The Majority of Sexually Active Teens (Age 12–19) Wish They Had Waited Longer Before Beginning Sexual Activity

Wish They Had Waited Longer Before Starting Sexual Activity	All Sexually Active Teens	Sexually Active Boys	Sexually Active Girls
Yes	60%	52%	69%
No	33%	38%	24%

Note: 10% of boys and 8% of girls don't know or refused to answer the question.
Source: National Campaign to Prevent Teen and Unplanned Pregnancy 2007

"If you stick around here at [racoon.com]... you will witness firsthand the anxiety people go through at the thought
of having the herpes discussion with a partner; all tied to the
possibility of losing that person....There are many people
who choose to be celibate and alone because they can't face
telling someone. People let this virus do terrible things to
them emotionally and yes, people lie about having it or at
least withhold the truth...we have all been in her shoes, we
certainly understand how this can happen."

Learn2luv was also reminded that his wife may have been misled by
her doctor: she could have been told the virus is transmitted only during outbreaks:

Your wife might not have lied to you intentionally. Many
doctors as far back as 10 years ago and even today are not
very educated on this virus and your wife may have been misinformed.

Their input was helpful, but learn2luv felt terribly betrayed. He
began to question his wife's fidelity in other matters. His marriage
was in crisis.

I thank you all for your supportive responses....[I] still am
not at ease with lying about an issue that can impact the health
of someone you love. It makes me feel second fiddle that her
shame and image is more important than our relationship.
    In addition to this whopper of a lie, many lies about her
past have been surfacing lately and a whole new person, an
entirely different character, has come out into the light.
    I'm confused and angry how to handle all of this....

From those who've been in learn2luv's shoes—or his wife's, came this
advice:

> Maybe some marriage counseling would be a good idea . . .
> Just keep reminding yourself that your wife is a heck of a lot
> more than herpes. . . . I hope you can find a way to forgive her
> and you can be happy again . . . .The virus itself is not that big
> of a deal. It's the emotional repercussions that are difficult.

Well said. Common sense tells us, and research confirms,[2] that aside from the ordeal of finding sores or warts on your privates, the diagnosis of one of the viral genital infections, usually herpes or HPV is *emotionally* traumatic. *It's the emotional repercussions that are difficult.* For most people, the anger and questions remain long after the blisters heal.

At New York University's STD Clinic, a positive diagnosis of herpes or HPV was often accompanied by feelings of shock, fear, anger, embarrassment, disgust, diminished self worth, and confusion and worry about the future. Nearly half—49 percent—of people with genital warts reported an adverse effect on their overall emotional state.[3] A New Zealand study of HPV showed 75 percent of patients experienced depression and anger at their initial diagnosis, and for one - third of these, the feelings persisted for years.[4] Other research indicates that episodic outbreaks of herpes—most people have at least three to four outbreaks per year[5]—can cause people to feel less sexually desirable, and reduce their enjoyment and frequency of sexual contact. It can cause a "major negative impact on quality of life," greater than the impact of asthma or rheumatoid arthritis.[6]

It's helpful to have the research, but you'd realize all this from simply looking at the handles people chose when they join STD support sites. For example, at HPVsupport.com, the names say it all. A sampling: HatingMyself, NoLuck, worried guy, verysad, givinguphope, scared2death, help-me18, tryingtobestrong, extraordinarilystressed, omg, tiredofthiscrap, FreakedAboutWarts, feelinscrewed, PrayingForACure, and many more—there are 5300 members helping one another out here.

Research also confirms that learn2luv's marital turmoil is typical, and his wife's dilemma is common. To tell, or not to tell? That is the question, especially on the active forums of herpes and HPV online support sites. When you meet someone new, and it's going well, does he need to know? When you're in love and getting serious, will she bolt? On racoon.com, there are 809 topics discussed under the general heading "relationships": Who do you tell?; Grieving, hurting, coming to acceptance; feel like a loser; the talk; first date...when to tell?; I'm panicking! What do I do?; Boyfriend worries each little twinge, he's getting it; guilt; telling him tomorrow, suggestions?; dropping the bomb!

It's harrowing to read these testaments filled with grief and fear. No doubt they are just the tip of the iceburg: for every learn2luv that turns to the Internet for support from strangers, how many others are out there suffering alone?

> With our health insurance crisis, does anyone care to mention the dollar cost of the STD pandemic? It's $15.5 billion per year![63]
> Each infection is a big deal, on both a personal and national level.

As parents, when we learn of dangers like these, we naturally hope that our kids will escape them. We trust that sexuality educators are telling it like it is, emphasizing how devastating—and lasting—the repercussions of an STD diagnosis can be—and how these horror stories can be avoided. After all, isn't protecting our kids the goal of sex education?

I discovered that standard sex-ed curricula spend little time, if any, describing the emotional consequences that often follow a diagnosis of herpes or HPV. Kids don't hear about any of the anguish and drama. Educators often mention the hardships of living in a sexist and homophobic society, but rarely describe how devastating it is to discover blisters "down there," to worry about cervical cancer, and to learn that these viruses might stick around—for a long, long time.

Students don't hear what men like learn2luv have to say, or the voices of women like "scaredjerseychic" or "regretsdonothing." Sure, they're taught about the different bugs that are out there, and how millions of people are infected. They're told the experience "can be annoying."[7] They learn some of the hard facts: transmission, testing, and treatment. But the gist of the message is that genital infections commonly occur, and that most people have one at some point in their lives. The only sure way to avoid them, kids are told, is to abstain from sexual behavior—forever.

That's right: kids are told the only way to completely avoid an STI, is never to have sex. Now, c'mon, who would do that?

The Lie: You Can't Dodge the Bug

Teens are repeatedly taught that STDs are nearly inevitable for any sexually active person. So just decrease the risk, they're advised: use condoms, get tested, and be honest with all your "partners."[8]

Excuse me?

It is a preposterous falsehood that the only way to avoid infection is lifelong celibacy. I've often come across such statements[9] in my review of sexuality education, but they never cease to astonish me. What's implied is that infections are a nearly inevitable consequence of being sexually active. Good grief! Here they go again, assuming that because something is common, it's normal.

We've all heard that the body is regularly host to countless bacteria—germs. While healthy internal organs—the heart, brain, uterus and so on—are free of bacteria, surface areas—like skin, the surface of the eye, mouth, nose, gastro-intestinal tract, vagina and so forth—are colonized by a huge number of them.

The mixture of bugs regularly found at any site is called the *normal flora*, and it's a win-win arrangement. We benefit from the bacteria, and they benefit from us.

However, STIs are not naturally found in the body.

Sexually transmitted infections occur only when an infected person comes in sexual contact with another person. Two uninfected people who are sexually active only with each other will *never* become infected with an STI. End of story.

Students can remain free of genital herpes, HPV, Chlamydia, HIV, and other bugs *without* joining a monastery and sexuality instructors know it. All sexually transmitted viruses and bacteria are *100 percent avoidable* without taking a lifelong vow of chastity. Why do they lead kids to believe they can't dodge these bugs?

As for the advice educators dish out about being honest with partners, I'm afraid that won't help much in staying free of infection.

You see, most people don't know they have an STI,[10] and most transmission of HPV and herpes occurs while the skin looks normal. So in addition to the millions who know they're infected, there's a group at least as large who don't know. To make matters worse, some infections are dormant for months or years before becoming active, as learntoluv discovered. While honest discussions with one's partners are commendable, their utility is limited. Worry instead about the flood of questions that typically follow a diagnosis: *Was it Lisa, Mandy, or someone else? Did it happen last month or last year? Did I pass the virus along to others? Who do I tell, and how? Will this affect having a family?* And perhaps the hardest question of all: *Who will want me now?*

As for the almighty latex, condoms provide varying degrees of protection, from around 80–85 percent for HIV, to zero for HPV. It depends on the bug. HPV, herpes, and syphilis can live on the skin surrounding the genital area—areas a condom doesn't cover.

The medically accurate message is that *all* sexually transmitted infections, and the anguish that accompanies them, *are 100 percent avoidable.* A life free of herpes, warts, chlamydia, and the others is possible. One simply has to delay sexual behavior, find someone who also waited, and then be faithful to one another. Those fortunate enough to do so *never* have to worry about blisters, warts, and discharges; the awkward sharing of "sexual histories"; what to tell and when; doctor's appointments and medications; getting poked, swabbed, stuck, and biopsied; and always wondering: *Am I getting another outbreak? Will blisters ruin my wedding? Will I give warts to my spouse? Will the virus affect my baby?*

To teach kids the cold, dry facts about viral STDs—*40 million people have this one, one in four have the other*—but omit the dire emotional consequences that usually accompany them is a shameful whitewashing of an urgent national catastrophe. For many people, especially teens, the diagnosis is a devastating, life-changing event—the worst thing that's ever happened to them. To pretend that such an event is unavoidable is nothing short of irresponsible.

Perhaps, you might think, sex educators are just trying to downplay all drama? Not at all. SIECUS-endorsed websites—like sexetc.com—are replete with moving anecdotes: Jaclyn's lesbian moms had to wait years to marry[11] (*It is part of the First Amendment*, teens are told, *it's freedom*). Tashina went to Wal-Mart for emergency contraception, only to discover the pharmacist didn't carry it, for moral reasons.[12]

But for every Jaclyn and Tashina, how many more young adults are freaked out about having blisters and warts? How many regret their sexual behavior, and wish they could turn back time? Some studies indicate their numbers are significant.[13]

In a comic on gUrl.com, "The Sex Mission," a girl wants to have sex because she thinks she's the only virgin around.

> "I feel like the last virgin on earth," she tells a friend.
> "I'm pretty sure my sister hasn't had sex yet," the friend responds.
> "She's in training to be a nun," answers the girl. "She lives in a convent. She'll probably never have sex."

Many teens responded to the comic. One girl wrote:

>it's unfortunate but in reality thats how sex is viewed a lot
>of the time. it's like, ok, if i don't do it now i'm some kinda
>loser. i see girls my age all the time going off with random ppl
>just for the experience, just to say "yea, i did him too". it's
>degrading i think. there's a beauty in waiting ...i know i wish
>i had waited . . . [14]

Why would sex educators spotlight one drama and ignore another? The answer is simple: their priority is not disease avoidance. It's to promote a specific worldview—*sex is not an appetite to be restricted*—and rally kids toward social change.

STDs and Depression

While the numbers of cases of sexually transmitted infections have swelled, especially the incurable herpes and HPV viruses, there has been a parallel increase in teen depression and self-injurious behavior, particularly among girls.[15] Isn't it time for sex educators, physicians, and mental health professionals to investigate a link?

Teens should be warned that for many people, the diagnosis of an STD is a nightmare, a complicated and confusing event that can disrupt their lives and return to wreak havoc years later. Learn2luv's discovery came while his wife was pregnant with their third child. They had been together for six years. For a teen, a first outbreak could occur before finals, SATs, or the prom. It can be the curve ball they're not expecting. It can happen at the worst time, and change everything.

"*I really need somebody's advice/help/comfort*" is the title of *all_alone23*'s post. She was diagnosed with HPV over a year ago, but, she reports, "*It's still the only thing I can think about everyday.*" Her warts did not respond to standard treatments; now her doctor says they may be another STD. "I am so confused, and have pretty much lost all hope . . . .I feel like I am going to be alone forever. I guess I just look at myself as 'ruined'....I can't even hang out with friends at the pool or beach because when I wear a bathing suit you can see them."

"Do not underestimate the impact of [a herpes] diagnosis on your patients," advises the medical director of a large STD Center in New York, "They will require extensive, thoughtful counseling...the physical impact of genital herpes is nothing compared to the psychological one."[16]

The scourge of genital infections alone is not to blame for the mental health crisis among teens and young adults. But it surely deserves a seat at the table. In a nationally representative sample of teens aged 15 to 17, the number one concern—expressed by more than 80 percent of them—was sexual health issues.[17] These epidemics are exacting a heavy toll on our youth. Platitudes such as "most people get these viruses at some point" and "usually it goes away" are irresponsible and foolish. For a young person who is already struggling emotionally with other issues, an abnormal Pap or STD diagnosis can lead to suicidal behavior. Where is the SIECUS or Planned Parenthood lesson plan about that?

Gardasil and HPV:
What You Haven't Heard

As much as you've heard about HPV—the human papillomavirus that causes genital warts, abnormal Pap tests, and, very rarely, cervical cancer—you haven't heard it all.

First, the basics: HPV appears to be in many cases benign, it is extremely common in sexually active teen girls,[18] and infection is likely from one of their first "partners."[19] About two out of three people who have sexual contact with a person with warts will also get them.[20] After treatment, warts return in at least 25 percent of cases.[21]

Much of the research about HPV in young people has been done at Washington State University. In one study,[22] female students were followed after becoming sexually active. Of those who used condoms consistently, 37 percent were infected with HPV after one year. The percentage for women who rarely used condoms was 89 percent.[23] Another study at the same school identified a number of factors—such as being on the pill and smoking cigarettes—that placed women at higher risk for infection. Of these, the greatest hazard was having a "partner" with a history of prior sexual activity.[24]

Infection in virgins was rare, but possible. "Any type of non-penetrative sexual contact was associated with an increased risk of HPV infection in virgins." Translation: the virus was sometimes passed along, even *without* intercourse.

A virgin with an STI—you don't hear much about *that* on sex ed websites. With kids being told they are "sexual" from cradle to grave, and provided with lists of "no-risk safer sex play,"[25] it's worth taking note.

To understand why female students at Washington State had such high infection rates, the researchers decided to study male students. Here's some news I bet you never heard. Sixty-two percent of sexually active men[26] had evidence of HPV. It was found both where you'd expect—in their genital region—and where you wouldn't: 32 percent[27] had it under their fingernails.[28]

Yes, you read that right. The DNA of HPV, the virus that causes warts and cervical cancer, was found under young men's fingernails. Not the entire virus, just the DNA. It was "a surprise," said one of the researchers, an epidemiologist.[29] The significance? No one is certain, but it raises the possibility of HPV transmission by finger-to-genital contact.

You won't find news of this "surprise" on Planned Parenthood. They're still telling teens that "outercourse," which includes "mutual masturbation," is a safe alternative to intercourse.[30]

So what *are* the sex ed sites saying about HPV? Columbia's Alice offers some comforting advice: ". . . the only way to be 100 percent certain you don't get any infections is to not have any oral, vaginal or anal sex. Most people eventually decide to take the plunge and explore the joys of sex."

At the website of the American Social Health Organization, a site recommended to young people by SIECUS, readers learn:

> Most men and women are infected with HPV at some time in their lives . . . *anyone* who has ever had sexual relations has a high chance of being exposed to this virus . . . the virus is so common that having only a single lifetime partner does not assure protection.[31]

Reading these, our kids would never know that this infection is 100 percent avoidable—simply by waiting, then being faithful to someone who also waited. The closer they get to that ideal, the better.

But what about the new vaccine, Gardasil?[32] You may already know that your daughter can be significantly protected against HPV if she gets the vaccine before becoming infected. That's probably true, but you need to know the whole story.

There are reasons to be hopeful that Gardasil will prevent a lot of disease, but it's not a done deal. Many critical questions remain. The drug has the potential of preventing disease in females who have not been exposed to four strains of HPV. It targets two of the approximately 19 types of high risk (i.e., associated with high grade cancers) HPV, which together are responsible for 70 percent of cervical cancers. It also targets two of the approximately 12 types of low risk (i.e., associated with warts and lowgrade cancers) HPV, which together are responsible for about 90 percent of warts.

Gardasil is good news, but it's important to remember that it doesn't solve everything. There is much we don't know, and won't know, for decades. How long does protection last? Will the vaccine affect girls' natural immunity against HPV? We also don't know how it will affect pre-adolescent girls—or how it will affect screening practices. Will the vaccine give girls a false sense of security? One Youtube account tells of a pre-teen telling her friends on the playground, "Hey,

I just got that safer sex shot." Will vaccinated girls and women be less likely to go in for Pap tests? There are about 17 other cancer-causing HPV types, so even vaccinated women must continue to be regularly screened. And we don't know if, as a result of the suppression of two of the strains by the vaccine, the other dangerous strains could become more common, or new ones will emerge.

So what's the bottom line? While the vaccine is a welcome development, the most effective way for a girl to avoid cervical cancer is by making smart decisions and delaying sexual activity.

It may not be politically correct. But it's true.

The Compelling Link Between Oral Sex and Oral Cancer

In May 2007, a group of surgeons and cancer specialists reported on the increasing incidence of oral cancers in young adults.[33] Oral tumors used to be considered diseases of people in their 50s and 60s who smoked and drank heavily; young people were at very low risk.[34] But surgeons have been seeing younger patients[35] who are neither smokers nor drinkers.

The risk of oral cancer in these patients was related to their sexual behavior: having more than five oral-sex partners in their lifetime increased their risk a whopping 250 percent. Evidence that the throat cancers—a type found at the base of the tongue and in the tonsils— were caused by HPV was called "compelling." So here's one more way this virus does harm—by traveling from genitals to mouth, and quietly causing deadly cancers in the throat.

This finding is particularly relevant to sex educators, because by ninth grade, that's age 14 or 15, 20 percent of students have had oral sex.[36] Online "sexperts" inundate kids with detailed and graphic information about this activity, portraying it as safe and normal. More than a year after the report, gURL.com's[37] newsletter (delivered right to your daughter's email account) read: "Martina's not afraid of a little man juice"[38] ("... *ewww... it's so sticky... and a little salty....*") But no mention here of HPV-related oral cancer.

Do teens use protection for oral sex? "Never happened, never will," says Lisa, 15. The NCHS [National Center for Health Statistics] study found the same—only nine percent of the teens surveyed reported using condoms for oral sex.

What's the problem here? Why so much unsafe behavior? It's due to abstinence education, says Teen Talk. "Since abstinence-only education doesn't teach about safer sex, many teens may not be aware of how to reduce their risk of infection during oral sex."[39]

What a blunder. I'd say Planned Parenthood, which runs Teen Talk, missed an opportunity here. Instead of trashing the enemy, they need to sound an alarm: *Having oral sex with multiple partners is associated with throat cancer. Don't do it!*

Planned Parenthood is not the only group guilty of ignoring this critical finding: I find no mention of it by SIECUS, on Columbia University's GoAskAlice, or any other of the dozen websites kids are directed to for "medically accurate" sexual health information.

Where are the red flags alerting kids that oral sex can be hazardous? Where are Scarleteen's and Sexetc's activist campaigns urging them to stop? As of this writing, almost two years after the report, they have yet to be seen.

The Number 1 Bug Is Worse Than They Say

Chlamydia is the most common bacterial STD in the United StatesIn 2006, reported infections hit an all-time high—a million new cases, up 5.6 percent from 2005.[40] Usually asymptomatic, chlamydia is notorious for the damage it causes to the female reproductive system: pelvic pain, ectopic pregnancy, and infertility. Girls are instructed: *If you get an annual check-up, chlamydia can be caught. If you take antibiotics, you'll be cured.*

My patient Delia was reassured in that way. She was a graduate student whom I saw while working in UCLA's student counseling center, and I told her story in my 2006 book, *Unprotected*.[41] Delia had chlamydia years before I met her, during her wild freshman year. She and her boyfriend took antibiotics as instructed, and were declared cured. I explained in the book why this was inaccurate and misleading, and I want to explain it again here. Young people, especially women and girls, deserve to know how chlamydia can evade detection and cause persistent problems—even with yearly exams and antibiotic treatment.

Chlamydia's mission is to travel all the way up the genital tract: from the vagina, through the narrow cervical opening, to the uterus, and finally, to enter the fallopian tubes. It might succeed in reaching its destination by hitching a ride on some sperm. In the tubes, the bacteria settle in. The immune system responds to the invasion, and there's probably some swelling and pus. It may cause fever and pain, or it may not.

But the dangerous part isn't the tubal infection, it's what's left when it heals: a scar. The fallopian tubes, where fertilization occurs, are only about one millimeter in diameter. A tiny scar here can cause infertility, or worse.

A fertilized egg—which is much larger than sperm—that's moving toward the uterus can be trapped when its path is narrowed by the scar. Unable to proceed, it will grow in the tube, causing what's called an ectopic pregnancy. Unless discovered at an early stage, the tube will eventually burst, causing sudden, enormous pain and bleeding: a medical emergency.

In *Unprotected*, I wrote:

> Did Delia's infection reach her tubes? There's no way to know now, without doing invasive tests. It's possible she was

treated early, before the bacteria had a chance to travel. That's
the best scenario: the bacteria are gone and her tubes are wide
open.

But what's "early"? Time is of the essence in treating
Chlamydia; we're in a race to get it before it advances. Once
it reaches the tubes, it may be impossible to eradicate.[42]
Women who show up for their yearly check-ups are routinely
screened for Chlamydia, and treated if positive. But what if
they were infected months earlier? How long does it take for
the bacteria to reach the tubes? We don't know. In the female
pig-tailed macaque monkey, it takes about eight weeks.[43]

There's more we don't know. We don't know, for one thing,
how well the screening test identifies cases where the infection is dormant. A negative result does not guarantee the
absence of infection.[44] We're not sure which antibiotic is best,
or how long treatment should last. We don't know if treatment always wipes out the whole infection. It's possible that
in some cases, medication temporarily stops the bacteria from
reproducing, only to be reactivated later.[45] And we don't
understand why women with Chlamydia are more likely to
get cervical cancer.

Chlamydia infection is perilous because it can cause serious damage
without noticeable symptoms: no appreciable pain, fever, or discharge. A woman may be unaware of the infection until years later,
when she tries to conceive. But her delicate fallopian tubes are scarred
and narrowed—sometimes completely blocked. The intricate process
of transporting the egg at the right time to the right place is now
impossible. She's sterile, the doctor tells her, because of this bug she
acquired in her care-free youth.

The experts say that Delia may hear this some day, because
she has some of the risk factors that may lead to Chlamydia

infection: intercourse at an early age, many partners,' and possibly use of oral contraceptives. Having intercourse at an early age was dangerous because—as explained earlier—her immature cervix had a larger transformation zone, containing cells that are more susceptible to infection. These vulnerable cells form a bright red circle in the center of the cervix. Delia's teenage cervix provided a larger target area for infection than if she had waited until she was older.[46]

With each new man in her life, Delia increased the likelihood of infection because men are not screened unless they have symptoms. As a result, there is a huge pool of infected men unknowingly passing the infection along, especially on college campuses.[47] If Delia is like the majority of college students, she's used condoms inconsistently,[10] but even if she had used them correctly and consistently, condoms may not have protected her completely. Finally, there's the pill. It's suspected, but not yet proven, that oral contraceptives may facilitate infection by enlarging the transformation zone,[49] or by decreasing the amount of menstrual blood, which can act to flush the bacteria down and out.

There's more here. Chlamydia infection may lead to fertility problems even when Delia's tubes are wide open and clean as a whistle. Amazing creatures that they are, when white cells recognize Chlamydia as a foreign invader, they memorize the bug's structure, especially that of a protein called hsp. Based on the contours of hsp, the white cells produce weapons to combat it: antibodies. White cells are like mobsters who never forget—they store the memory of Chlamydia HSP, adding it to their hit list, should they cross paths again. And the memory is passed down, to all future generations.

Fast forward ten years: an embryo is growing safely in Delia's uterus. She's finally pregnant. Time to celebrate? Not so fast. The embryo makes a protein, one that happens to be a type of HSP. That's not good. Delia's white cells are unable to tell the difference between the earlier HSP, and the new one. Her defense system concludes: the enemy—Chlamydia—is back. Antibodies are released, and the "invader," the embryo, is destroyed . . . a miscarriage.

Bottom line: Chlamydia infection is a complex issue, about which there are more questions than answers. Following current guidelines is important, of course, but it's not a guarantee that one is out of the woods.

So why tell girls that there's a certain cure for Chlamydia? I've been asking that question ever since I discovered the real dangers of this ravaging bug. I dug up 1994 copies of *American Journal of Obstetrics and Gynecology*[50] and learned how the HSP reaction causes early pregnancy loss and decreased *in vitro* fertilization success years after antibiotic treatment. In a 1997 volume of the medical journal *Human Reproduction*[51] I learned that even after treatment, Chlamydia DNA can be detected in the fallopian tubes, evidence that an earlier infection may not have been cured.

But as of this writing, "comprehensive" sex ed reassures our daughters: just come in for testing, take these tablets, and you'll be fine.

Well, maybe. Hopefully. But maybe not.

Fear-based or Truth-based?

With ten million new STIs every year in young people,[52] no wonder they're fed platitudes: *They're so common. Most people have one at some point.* Telling the truth, sharing stories like learn2luv's or all_alone23's might shake up students. We certainly wouldn't want to frighten them into changing their behavior; that would be what SIECUS and Planned Parenthood call *fear-based* sex education. Scare tactics, of course, have no place in health education.

Or do they?

Think about how other health topics are presented, like alcohol, illicit drugs, tanning beds, trans fats, and—of course—smoking. Subtlety is not the preferred mode of communication.

Consider an ad campaign in New York City called "Nothing Will Ever Be the Same." "Smoking gave me throat cancer at 39," says a poster showing a man named Ronaldo Martinez holding a metal device against his neck. "Now I breathe through a hole in my throat and need this machine to speak."

The TV ad is more disturbing. Kids swim underwater in slow motion and happily splash about in a pool to the sound of a guitar. Mr. Martinez strolls nearby, fully clothed. An eerie, synthesized voice tells us, "I was born on an island where swimming was a way of life. I never thought that anything could keep me from the water. Then I got cancer from smoking cigarettes and lost my voice and have to speak through a hole in my throat. If water gets inside, it will drown me. I used to love swimming."

Scare tactics? You bet. But as a result, says *The New York Times*, thousands of New Yorkers have quit the habit. The campaign, created in Massachusetts, was praised by public health officials in both states. The implication? The ends justify the means.

Educators especially love to warn kids about the dangers of lighting up. Just look at Sexetc.org, a site recommended by Advocates for Youth:

> **Is Smoking Killing You?**[53]
> Smoking wrecks your health from drag one—even if you
> don't notice it . . . .Did you know, for example, that smoking
> can cause:
>
> - Cavities
> - Headaches
> - High blood pressure (which can lead to strokes or heart
>   attacks)
> - Flu
> - Osteoporosis (a bone disease)
> - Stupidity (it can reduce the blood flow to the brain and
>   muddle your mind)

- Raging PMS
- Ulcers
- Wrinkles

It's easy to say I'll stop when I'm sick. But by that time, it may be too late. Be smart. Stay smokeless.

It doesn't appear that Sexetc.org was wary about using scare tactics in this case. Smoking *wrecks* your health from drag one? Cigarettes cause the flu, PMS, *stupidity*?

Don't get me wrong, I agree that smoking is a nasty habit. But let's be honest about the double standard. Educators use scare tactics to influence lifestyle decisions all the time, and no one objects—it's quite the opposite. *Whatever it takes to get kids to stop smoking, drinking, or speeding*, we say: *the ends justify the means*. Only in sex education are so many sobering facts deemed "fear-based," and omitted from the classroom. And these groups call themselves "science-based" and "medically accurate"? Now that's chutzpah.

I submit that when we're dealing with debilitating, lifelong infections, we should tell it like it is—warts and all. But it won't happen, because ideologues are at the helm, And for them, smoking is a loathsome evil, while teen sex is empowering and fun.

Planned Childlessness

With a few subjects, sex educators *are* comprehensive. One of them is pregnancy prevention. Another is reminding teens that should a pregnancy occur, they have choices.

Try this: ask an adolescent to either find France on a map, identify the second president of the United States, or name three types of contraception. I'll bet that to the average kid who's been through years of comprehensive sex education, the choice is a no-brainer: she'll launch into a discussion about condoms (his and hers), birth control pills, and Plan B. If she's listened well, she'll be able to reel off their side effects, cost, and relevant legal issues. You know, it's almost a shame this stuff isn't on the SATs.

But how many young people, especially young women, realize the *limits* of their fertility?

Not all young people look forward to having a family some day, but most do. When freshmen—both women and men—at four-year colleges were asked which life goals were essential or very important, 75 percent said "raising a family."[54] Therefore, one would hope that sex education would include not only instruction about preventing or terminating a pregnancy, but also basic facts about fertility, marriage, and building families.

You may be thinking, *Teens need to know about pregnancy prevention because that's relevant to their lives now. Starting a family will be something that happens later. Why teach them about having babies now?*

For the same reasons, I'd answer, that we teach them about breast self-exam and osteoporosis. Sites like GoAskAlice and gURL.com provide girls with basic facts about these adult conditions. Since most girls want to be moms, shouldn't they know when in their lives it's easiest to conceive and deliver a healthy child?

Sex ed provides kids with pages and pages of information about contraception and abortion, leading them to believe that in a zillion years, when they *do* want to get pregnant, all that's necessary is to stop—stop taking the pill, stop using the diaphragm, and stop wearing a condom. Pull the goalie and let the babies roll. Easy, right?

Try telling that to the hordes of women seeking treatment at fertility centers all over the country. Many of them can't conceive because they waited too long.[55] They've realized a biological truth they wish they'd known earlier: pregnancy doesn't always happen when *you* decide you're ready. There's a window of opportunity, then the window closes.[56]

Young people, especially teen girls, should know about that window, so they can keep it in mind as they make decisions about career and relationships. We're not doing a good job at that; large numbers of women are misinformed about the limits of their fertility. A 2001 survey showed 89 percent of young, high-achieving women believed they would be able to get pregnant into their forties.[57] Another found that women have an excellent understanding of birth control, but they "overestimate the age at which fertility declines."[58] The former director of RESOLVE, a support network for couples coping with infertility, reports: "I can't tell you how many people we've had on our help line, crying and saying they had no idea how much fertility drops as you age."[59]

Here are the facts teens need to know. A woman is born with all the eggs she'll ever have, so when she turns thirty or forty, her eggs do, too. The easiest time for her to conceive and give birth to a healthy child is in her twenties. At around thirty, her fertility begins to decline, and at thirty-five, it begins to decline dramatically. By forty, her chance of conceiving each month has decreased by 75 percent compared to a decade earlier.[60] But what about all those celebrities in their forties and beyond, you may ask, whose gorgeous babies grace the cover of *People* magazine? Many of these older moms have no genetic relationship with their child; adoption or surrogacy had to enable them to achieve their dream of parenthood. *Not that there's anything wrong with that,* but it's something to be aware of.

Teens need to know that using technology to create a child is costly—economically and emotionally—and that some methods are controversial. Many women, troubled by the relentless ticking of their biological clock, pursue extreme measures: spending their nest egg on fertility drugs, using a younger woman's eggs, freezing their own for future use. Next time you're in line at the grocery store, check out the tabloids for photos of middle-aged celebrity mothers. It's unlikely you will come across the following captions: baby on left, born following two years of agonizing treatments costing an arm and a leg; twin girls, right, conceived via *in vitro* fertilization when three embryos implanted, one, another girl, "reduced" in the womb. *People Magazine* can omit these details; it doesn't claim to be medically accurate and comprehensive. Sex education does.

I searched for the word "motherhood" on some of the most popular teen sex ed sites. On Columbia's GoAskAlice.com, no matches were found. On gURL.com, I was asked to check my spelling. On Sex-Etc, a bunch of links about teen mothers came up.

What about Planned Parenthood? Their mission is to offer "accurate and complete information to make childbearing decisions" and to preserve "reproductive freedom—the fundamental right of every individual to decide freely and responsibly when and whether to have a child." Sounds great, but a search of their teen section, Teen Talk, brought up no information about the optimal time to start a family, the whole story about the hazards of Chlamydia, or the regrets of women who always put career first.

It seems fair to ask: does reproductive freedom include the freedom to reproduce?

In *Creating a Life: Professional Women and the Quest for Children*, Sylvia Ann Hewlett explored the lives of highly educated, high earning women as they turned fifty—women who had broken through the glass ceiling. After the tenth interview, she realized that none of them had children. And they all regretted it.

> There is a secret out there, a painful, well-kept secret: At mid-life, between one third and one half of all high-achieving women in America do not have children.[61]...The vast majority of these women did not choose to be childless. Looking back to their early twenties, when they graduated college, only 14 percent said they definitely had not wanted children.
>
> I had assumed that if these accomplished, powerful women were childless, surely they had chosen to be. I was absolutely prepared to understand that the exhilaration and challenge of a megawatt career made it easy to decide not to be a mother. Nothing could be further form the truth. When

> I talked to these women about children, their sense of loss
> was palpable. I could see it in their faces, hear it in their
> voices, and sense it in their words. [62]

Planned Parenthood, SIECUS, and others writing curricula are in an ideal position to prevent some of the future anguish and regret of women discovering that their window of reproductive opportunity has closed. They could, for example, include some of the facts I've mentioned in their classes for twelfth graders. They could suggest students read *Creating a Life*. But don't hold your breath. A unit on fertility would highlight the differences between men and women, and students might realize the value of marriage and families. Who knows what could result? A girl might even—*gasp*—reconsider her plans to become a neurosurgeon. No, it won't happen any time soon.

I see things differently. I believe that authentic feminism *protects* women and girls: their health, their choices, and their dreams. If sex educators genuinely cared about young women having accurate and complete information about childbearing, and about preserving their reproductive freedom, their curricula and websites would include this difficult truth: delaying parenthood indefinitely, especially while living a life of casual sexuality, places your dreams of motherhood at risk. Those who object to this "sexist" message need to accept this reality: biology itself is sexist, and that's unlikely to change—even with threats of legal action from the ACLU or NOW. If you take issue with that, well, don't gripe to me about it. Take your complaints to a higher authority.

♂♀

Chapter Six

Questioning

YOUNG BISEXUAL WOMEN[1] and gay men have the highest rates of genital infections, due in part to early sexual activity. For this reason alone, you'd think educators would target these students with a stern, no-nonsense message of self-restraint. *It's critical that you delay sexual relationships*, you'd expect them to say, *exploring same sex activity can be particularly dangerous*. But even with this vulnerable group, it's the same old story: a green light to early experimentation, detailed how-to instructions, and an assumption of multiple partners.

About their decision to explore same-sex behavior, teens are repeatedly advised, "Do what feels right to you," and, "It's important to always feel good about yourself." But we wouldn't instruct anyone, let alone a teenager, to "do what feels right" regarding other risky behaviors—smoking, drinking, or drug use. These experts seem to neglect how kids will *feel* when they've got open blisters on their genitals or test positive for HIV. For these life and death decisions, how can "educators" recommend kids follow their *feelings?*

You want to see madness? Log on to a few sites[2] recommended by sex educators and search under "LGBTQ"—the acronym for lesbian, gay, bisexual, transgender, and questioning. That should do it.

An enthusiasm for risky liaisons isn't the only problem you'll discover. First of all, the ideology on these sites is suffocating. Instead of sounding an alarm about health risks—the association of oral sex with cancer of the tonsils, for example, or the epidemics of HPV and syphilis among gay men[3]—kids get a hefty dose of leftist indoctrination and recruitment.[4] On these websites, the enemy is not genital infections; it's our oppressive, heterosexist society. Instead of HIV, Republicans are in the crosshairs.

On sites recommended by educators, kids are constantly reminded that the country is permeated by homophobic negativity.[5] Sexual minorities—everyone not strictly heterosexual—are in the same position as African Americans before the civil rights movement: suffering from widespread ignorance, prejudice and unfair legislation. Teens can make a difference—by becoming activists for change.

On Sexetc.org, a site recommended by SIECUS, kids learn about a group called Soulforce, whose mission is "to promote freedom from religious and political oppression for LGBT people." They ride on a "Bus for Equality," visiting Christian schools "with policies that exclude openly LGBT young people from enrolling." If they're allowed on campus, Soulforce members explain how harmful homophobia is. If not, they "find creative ways" to assert their presence off-campus; "This often leads to arrest."[6] The lesson: these kids are to be commended for taking action against injustice.

Advocates for Youth goes a step further—they pay for kids to travel to Washington to participate in four days of Youth Activist Training. The program promises to enhance teens' skills in grassroots, campus, and online organizing as well as media outreach. It includes a day with congressional staff members, who school teens in effective lobbying techniques.

Social agendas drive the discussion of psychological issues too. Contradicting widely accepted principles of emotional development, kids are reassured that confusion about sexual identity is normal[7] and healthy, and that preferences naturally change with time. "Your sexuality is a work in progress," they're instructed, "a life-long adventure."

What? It's *healthy* to be confused, a *lifelong* adventure? Not according to anything I ever learned about human development. I checked a pile of textbooks, as well as online material from the American Academy of Pediatrics, the American Academy of Child and Adolescent Psychiatry, and the Society for Adolescent Medicine, and see nothing of the sort. Instead, it's the *resolution of doubt* that promotes emotional stability—and the sooner the better.

Finally, on many of these sites, every type of intimate behavior—including some you'd rather not know about—is discussed in a breezy manner, sometimes with language and graphics you wouldn't allow in your home.[8]

Question: Are the people at SIECUS, Planned Parenthood, and AFY aware of the dangers they're encouraging kids to fool around with? Do they agree with everything the sites they recommend to kids promote? And if they're not aware of the content of websites and books they're recommending to teens . . . shouldn't they be?

Lucky You

Let's begin by delineating a principle of human development. Each stage of development—infancy, toddlerhood, school age, adolescence and adulthood—is accompanied by specific tasks. For example, infants must gain the skills to sit, stand, and walk; preschoolers must learn to share their toys and visit the toilet. In every case, there is an inner drive—a maturational push—to master the task at hand and move to the next stage.

A task of adolescence is to move toward a firm and cohesive identity.[9] *Who am I? Where do I belong? What do I believe?* To some degree, all teens ask those questions. Am I vegetarian, atheist, "goth," or conservative? Should I join the army, go to college, or get a job? Of course, teens must tolerate some ambiguity while they mature and sort things out, but in time, a consistent and enduring sense of self is achieved. This brings a young person satisfaction and a readiness to take on the tasks of adulthood. This is what growth is all about.

> **Identity:** the sense of self, providing sameness and continuity over time
>
> **Identity crisis:** a state or period of psychological distress, especially in adolescence, when a person seeks a clearer sense of self.

It is axiomatic that people want to know who they are. Confusion and self-doubt therefore implies some degree of distress. Teens might feel mixed-up about almost anything, of course, but identity is a particularly significant issue, and if identity confusion is deep or drawn out, the distress can be significant. In order to face the challenges of adulthood effectively, the adolescent question, "Who am I?" must be answered.

Except, it appears, with sexual orientation. In that case, the educators who claim to be promoting your children's growth and health dump this principle. There's no inner need or drive to clarify this part of yourself, they say; it's imposed on you by society. "There's a lot of pressure to define yourself," explains gURL.com,[10] as if the source is completely external. Restrictive labels may not apply to you, teens are told, but be prepared for everyone else's insistence to place you neatly in one of their boxes.

The bottom line? Kids should resist the pressure, labels, and boxes. They should remain open to all the options, check them out,[11] and feel

good about themselves along the way. In this paradigm, doubt—
"maybe I like boys *and* girls," and exploration—"I'll try it and see"—
represents growth, not crisis.

Where does this come from? Open-mindedness cannot be a goal of
identity development. Otherwise, what does identity even mean, if it's
not a lasting conviction of who you are? And if sexual orientation is
"a fundamental piece"[12] of who we are, "an essential human quality,"[13]
who we are "deep down,"[14] as kids are taught by sex educators,[15] persistent uncertainty about it cannot be healthy.

Columbia University's "GoAskAlice" is an award winning site
manned by "a team of health counselors." When a 12th grader, who has
already had three boyfriends, wonders about relationships with girls,
she's encouraged to "explore" and "experiment." Being willing to do so,
she's told, "will only add to your future well-being and peace of mind."

I am unable to find a study that supports that advice. To the contrary, what's well documented is the many ways this 12th grader would
benefit from *delaying* sex, with boys or girls. In general, the earlier she
begins sexual activity, the greater the number of partners she is likely
to have. Early sexual debut and high numbers of partners are linked
to a variety of negative life outcomes, including increased rates of
infection with sexually transmitted diseases, increased rates of out-of-
wedlock pregnancy and birth, increased single parenthood, decreased
marital stability, increased maternal and child poverty, increased abortion, and yes—increased depression.[16]

Could someone at Columbia direct me to the research showing a
positive association between sexual experimentation by teen girls and
their future peace of mind? "Alice" has no hard data to back her up;
the advice is based on Kinseyan ideology: womb to tomb pansexual-
ity. If this teen's health and peace of mind were the priority of these
health educators, their advice would be the opposite.

Time out, Alice would tell her. *Even with consistent condom use, having so many partners is going to land you in the doctor's office.* There'd be
straight talk with all the sobering facts. Instead, Alice is comfortable

that this girl—not yet out of high school—has already had three sex partners; she appears eager, in fact, for her to add a fourth and fifth.

"If you like women, fantastic," she's told. "If you like sex with both guys and girls, lucky you."[17]

Shades of Lavender

Kids learn from an early age about these discrete categories: gay, straight, lesbian, bisexual. But when they're older, they're informed these sexual orientations exist on a continuum.[18] They're not either/or. Heterosexuality lies at one end, gay or lesbian at the other, and in between lie a multitude of possibilities. Individuals use different labels—er, *descriptions*—of where they fall on this continuum. Ambisexual. Bi-lesbian. Bi-queer. Dyke. Fluid bisexual. Heterosexual with questions. Lesbian who has sex with men. Not straight. Pansexual. Polyfide. Polysexual. Queer. Unlabeled.[19]

"Wherever you are on that continuum," teens learn on outproud.com, "you've got plenty of company...."[20]

"Some argue that there are as many sexual orientations as there are people," teens learn on Columbia's Alice, "everyone defining for themselves their own rules of attraction, fantasy, and relationships."[21]

Gurl.com provides a visual of the spectrum of sexual orientation: twenty-three female silhouettes in shades from dark lavender, representing "totally gay," to white, "totally straight." Click on any of these figures to find quotes from girls and women ages fourteen to forty-one who placed themselves at that point.[22] A sampling:

> "I'm a turbo lesbian! I love women! I had my 1st lesbian experience when I was 11 and would never date a man."
> "...I don't believe in drawing lines. You've got to keep your mind open to possibilities....You can find love in the strangest places!...I'm 100% open to suggestion."

"Today I'm a light lavender. I was more purple in college . . . anything might happen."

"I experience sexuality as a fluid thing . . . I appreciate people who keep things interestingly mixed up and cultivate the
art of ambiguity."

Pay attention, parents. Your child may like the possibility that "anything could happen," or be drawn to "the art of ambiguity," and be
headed for turmoil.

One of the most fundamental premises of psychology is that, in
order to build an acceptable, coherent sense of self, young people
actively seek to answer the question, "Who am I?" Persistent uncertainty about core identity leads to inner turmoil. We're all familiar with
kids who cannot decide on long-term goals, group loyalties, or value
systems. They are pulled in different directions, it causes distress, and
they are pre-occupied—with both the conflict and the distress. There
may be significant anxiety, mood swings, self-doubt, and worry about
the future. It may impair their academic or social functioning.

These kids may have difficulty making decisions or show impul-
sive experimentation. They may "try on" different roles to see what
feels right.[23] A person without a coherent identity is seriously handi-
capped. If the issue remains unresolved, there may be difficulty making commitments to careers or relationships. Friendships and family
relationships may deteriorate. Educational achievement may be lower
than ability.

But while it's self-evident to child development specialists that a
firm identity enhances well-being, sex educators have a different perspective: an uncertain identity, along with "safe" experimenting, is
also fine—not just in adolescence, but any time. In fact, kids learn,
with sexual matters, identity confusion is an identity: you are "questioning"—the Q in LGBTQ. It's as valid a category—perhaps even
more—as the others.

What Am I?

Matt has turned to the experts at Planned Parenthood's site for teens, wondering, "Is it natural to be confused about your sexuality?"[24]

Yes, he's told, it's "normal and very common. Many adults are still figuring it out. Understanding sexual orientation is "a lifelong process,"[25] Matt would learn on positive.org,[26] a site endorsed by SIECUS. Advocates for Youth agrees: Everyone has questions about their sexuality at some time or other, they claim.[27]

Wait a minute. It's *normal* to be confused? *Everyone* has questions? Since when?

Yes, many teens experience brief insecurity about their sexual identity. I won't argue with that. But what's *common* is not necessarily *healthy*. Kinsey used the same logic sixty years ago: his data indicated a high frequency of certain behaviors; therefore, he claimed, those behaviors represent a normal, healthy variant. The logic was faulty then, and it's faulty now. As one of his critics pointed out, if at a given time more people have the flu than not, that doesn't mean that having the flu is normal. Likewise, just because it may be *common* for teens to question their sexual orientation, that doesn't mean it's *healthy* for them to do so.

The claim that confusion is natural and experimenting is healthy, will, for many kids, prolong or intensify an already difficult process. Our job—the job of anyone guiding teens—is to support them through periods of insecurity and caution *against* exploring. Furthermore, experts in child development know that as adolescents seek to define their identity distinct from family, negativism appears—just like in two-year-olds. "I can do it myself . . . Don't tell me how. . . don't tell me what to wear/where to go/who to be friends with . . ."

Adolescent negativism sometimes means taking up behaviors that drive their parents crazy. Teens must announce, "I have a mind of my own," and they may seize on almost any issue to prove that. Once upon a time, that meant sex, drugs, and rock n' roll. Now, in some vulnerable individuals, that struggle may lead to exploring "alternative" sexualities or genders. These kids might get their parents' goat by identifying as non-straight ("Mom, Dad—I'm gay"), or gender-bending ("Mom, Dad, don't call me Robert any more. I'm a girl. Call me Roberta.").

For all these reasons, introducing doubt about sexual orientation ("many homosexual people don't realize it for years," or "who you're most attracted to today might not be the same as who you'll be eyeing five years from now"[28]), and encouraging sexual behavior should be avoided at all cost.

Nevertheless, the oligarchy leads kids to believe that questioning, confusion, doubts, experimentation . . . they're all good.

Exploration

From Columbia's Alice:

> Participating in safe sexual encounters and activity, whether with men, women, or both, can provide wonderful opportunities to learn about your likes and dislikes, passions, and goals. . . . Questioning your sexual orientation or sexual identity is by no means a sign of a problem; . . . . While you may feel confused about your attractions right now, you should know that your feelings are completely normal, as is exploring them. Enjoy! [29]

At scarleteen.com, Hartley has turned to Heather Corinna for guidance. She just turned fifteen, and has come out to family and friends as bisexual. Still, she wonders, is it "because of my hormones" or does she truly like both girls and guys? How can she know for sure?[30]

> "For most people, the teen years are not the time to be 100% in what sexual orientation you are," claims Heather.

"It's not just okay not to be sure at your age, it's totally normal, and no one is required to identify as any one orientation
and stick with it for the whole of their lives....The only self
we know is who we are right now....If something changes for
you later on, that's okay: not only do people GET to change,
we SHOULD change—we call that personal growth, and it's
what we should all aim for."

But these intensive efforts to redefine social norms and reassure
mixed-up kids—*it's "natural," you're "normal," just relax and be "who
you are"*—don't appear to work. Teens still flock to the experts in
angst, asking, *what am I?*

On Teen Talk: *I love my best friend. Am I lesbian?*
On scarleteen: *I fantasize about guys. Am I gay?*
On gURL.com: *I like kissing girls and guys. Am I bi?*
And on Alice, a young woman is in distress: *"I'm engaged
to a man, but I like lesbian porn. Am I out of my mind?"*

These readers don't experience their doubts as "natural." They are
troubled by their questions. They don't like the uncertainty.

What's an expert to do? They've provided reassurances ad nau-
seam—"It's OK to not know!" and "As long as you feel comfortable
with your sexuality, there is no need to compare yourself to a
norm"[31]—they've come up with all sorts of ways for teens to find support and accept themselves,[32] but these kids keep pestering them:
Help! Who am I?

The "experts" have a brilliant solution: have kids consult with their
peers—other teens who are also confused. Kids have just as much
wisdom as adults, right? Maybe even more. Here's how it works.

A teen girl turns to the expert on gURL.com. She sometimes fan-
tasizes about women when she's with her boyfriend, she admits. *Am
I a lesbian?* She wants to know. *Is this normal?*

Of course you are normal, she's told. But it will take time for you to sort it all out. In the meantime, check out the "confused and curious" folder on the "when girls like girls" board. There are lots of other gURLs on that board who can give you advice and additional support.

As a parent, being curious myself, I ventured over to the "confused and curious" folder on gURL.com.

Talk about the blind following the blind—this is a cyber café for very lost souls. Can the experts at this SIECUS-recommended site be aware of what goes on here? These girls, some as young as thirteen, speak openly of their depression and self injury; a few provide the dates of their last cut or burn. Their questions abound: Who am I? How do I know? How do I pick up a girl? There's no end to the vulgarities. A poll, presumably devised by a teen, asks, among other things: Your favorite part of a woman's body? Do you like butch girls or femmes? Which do you prefer, beer or hard liquor? Have you ever given or received a lap dance? Which do you prefer, the taste of p***y or sushi?

I'm not making this up, folks. This is where the authorities entrusted with our kids' well-being and health send teens to sort things out. You can check it out yourself.

Similarly, Advocates For Youth refers "questioning" teens to a site they host called youthresource.com., where trained peer educators,[33] ranging in age from thirteen to twenty-four, will help with their questions and concerns.[34] Who are these peer educators?

Devin is a peer educator of undisclosed age. He writes,

> As someone who might fall under the bisexual umbrella but rejected the label, as someone who once questioned his gender identity but realized the complexity and fluidity of male and female, as someone who now understands himself to be a two-spirited male....I open my arms and doors to anyone that has questions about sexual orientation....Consider me an ear.[35]

Jae is getting a Masters in Gender and Sexuality Studies. She is passionate about "diversity in gender and sexual expression."

> I love to talk to people and help them to know themselves....I have made my own gender and sexuality journey and continue to be on it. I identify as a lesbian, gay, queer, gender queer and as a king....[I] would like to be a supportive person to you!

Another peer educator, Theodora, came out as a lesbian when she was fourteen. But now, she admits,

> I've never really known for sure what I am in terms of sexual orientation, so I've stopped labeling myself...although I am not born in the wrong body, I am male, not female. However, for personal reasons, I guess I'm not male enough to give up my womanhood, so I don't deny my vagina....I'd love to answer any questions.[36]

These are some of the "trained" peer educators that kids struggling with identity issues are referred to by a leading sex ed organization. I wonder, before writing that check out to Advocates for Youth, did anyone in Washington consider the dangers of confused kids consulting with even *more* confused kids?

As a final example, Sexetc.org[37] offers this pearl:

The only way to know if you are gay or bisexual "is to experience it and reflect carefully on the feelings that come up as a result of the experience."[38]

Whose wisdom was that? Was it Devin's or Jae's? No, this gem came from a national authority. Elizabeth Schroeder is a human sexuality professor at Montclair State University and executive director of Rutgers University's ANSWER, a national organization that promotes comprehensive sex education.[39] She's also at SIECUS—the chair of their board of directors.[40]

With Ms. Schroeder's tip, readers can learn about teens who have followed it.

> Seventeen-year-old Natasha Gutierrez, of New York City, reflected on her sexual identity after experimenting with both guys and girls. She first realized she was a lesbian in eighth grade.... Juliet, 15, of South Plainfield, NJ, is also still exploring her sexual identity. She is currently experimenting with another girl. "We've always been pretty close and we always used to kiss on the cheek. One day we missed, and it's been kisses on the lips [ever since]. One day we decided to take it a step further. We just felt comfortable around each other. It kind of comes naturally."[41]

So there it is, folks, guidance from a head honcho, supported with testimonials from Natasha and Juliet: *Boys and girls, you hear so much about sexuality, and you're wondering where you fit in. Do you like girls? Boys? Perhaps... girls and boys? You won't know 'til you try. Afterwards, think about the encounter. Contemplate how you felt. You'll know.*

> I kissed a girl and I liked it
> The taste of her cherry chapstick
> I kissed a girl just to try it
> I hope my boyfriend don't mind it
> It felt so wrong
> It felt so right
> Don't mean I'm in love tonight
> —Excerpt from "I Kissed a Girl,"
> Lukas Gottwald, Max Martin,
> and Katy Perry

This is unnerving. While parents worry about the anything-goes message on *Gossip Girl*, their kids are hearing the same thing from a credentialed professional—from SIECUS's board of directors to boot.

It shouldn't come as a surprise. No doubt Schroeder's touchstone is Kinsey's philosophy—*"sexuality is not an appetite to be curbed"*—so how could her suggestion to teens be any different? Her counseling is consistent with Kinsey's legacy and in the same spirit as books written for adolescents by an earlier SIECUS official, Wardell Pomeroy.[42]

But Pomeroy was writing in the 1970s, before herpes, warts, HPV, and chlamydia became household words. Most importantly, it was pre-HIV and AIDS. Natasha and Juliet live in a different world. When Ms. Schroeder encourages today's teens to experiment with same sex behavior, she's sending them to play in a minefield.

The Minefield

Teens and young adults with persistent, same-sex attraction face unique challenges. They are more likely to feel confused and isolated. Their families, schools, friends, and religious organizations may reinforce negative stereotypes. Coming out may be followed by rejection, discrimination, and even violence.

The last thing these young people need is more worry, shame, and stress. The last thing they need to hear is they've got herpes, HPV, syphilis, gonorrhea, or HIV. Yet each year,[43] more and more of them[44] hear exactly that.

Sex educators[45] blame homophobia. Due to bias and victimization, they argue, non-heterosexual teens have less access to accurate health information and supportive medical care. Rejection by family and friends may lead to depression, substance abuse and runaway behavior. These young people can become homeless and engage in prostitution as a matter of survival. The remedy is to fight prejudice, improve these kids' circumstances, help them feel better about themselves, and—of course—provide ample "safer sex"[46] information.

Worthy goals, but when the strategy includes giving the impression that all encounters—boys with girls, boys with boys, girls with girls,

girls with boys *and* with girls—carry an equal risk of infection, it's ill-advised. And dishonest.

The objective, I assume, is to level the playing field. Educators want all students to feel good about their families, themselves, and their sexual choices, and that's facilitated by teaching that everyone faces the same risks. Straight, gay, lesbian, bisexual—everyone's in the same boat.

This equal-opportunity approach to infection sounds fair—all orientations face the same risk—so both teacher and student feel good. You might say that sex educators have, for fairness sake, rewritten the principles of virology, bacteriology, and epidemiology. The hard truth is that the playing field is not level, and in the long run, denying that reality has catastrophic results for the very population it was designed to help. Teens embarking on same sex experimentation are on a road more perilous than their sexually active "straight" peers, and they need to know it.

The worst news first: as many as 50 percent of new HIV infections in the USA occur in persons under the age of twenty-five,[47] and gay, lesbian, and bisexual adolescents[48] are disproportionately represented among those with new infections.

Despite decades of comprehensive sex education, billions of dollars toward safer sex programs, free condoms, and testing, the incidence of HIV in thirteen- to twenty-four-year-old gays and bisexual women is increasing. Says the CDC, "This age group has more recently initiated high-risk behaviors."[49]

The behaviors placing them at higher risk than heterosexuals include:[50] earlier age of sexual intercourse debut,[51] more lifetime and recent sexual partners,[52] equal or greater levels of unprotected intercourse,[53] and drug and alcohol[54] use.

"Safer sex" doctrine calls upon teens to share their histories before commencing intimate behavior. Even if teens follow that advice—and usually they don't—the value of those histories could be moot. In the worst case scenario, they provide a false sense of security, because many young gay and bisexual men are carrying HIV unknowingly. In one study of men who have sex with men aged 15–29, 77 percent were unaware of their infection, and of these, 51 percent had unprotected anal intercourse.[55] The researchers conclude: "The HIV epidemic among MSM [men having sex with men] in the United States continues unabated, in part, because many young HIV-infected MSM are unaware of their infection and unknowingly expose their partners to HIV."

Some of these unsuspecting partners are girls and women. You are probably aware that girls are not getting HIV from sex with other girls; female-to-female HIV transmission is extremely rare. They're getting it the same way straight girls do: from HIV positive boys. Lesbian and bisexual girls and women are as likely as heterosexuals to report experiences with males.[56] Most significantly in terms of HIV risk, they are more likely to report sex with a gay or bisexual man[57] and more likely to engage in unprotected intercourse.[58]

This is worth repeating. Females who are not exclusively heterosexual are more likely to have unprotected intercourse with a gay or bisexual male. Those males,[59] in turn, are at high risk not only for HIV, but for HPV, herpes, syphilis,[61] and gonorrhea.

Do you see why I call it a minefield?

"Bisexual College Women at Greatest Risk for STDs" was the headline of an article reporting the results of a study of 30,000 sexually active women on 117 campuses.[62] Students who described themselves as bisexual were 60 percent more likely to report an STD than their heterosexual counterparts,[63] perhaps because of the number of their partners: women who reported having sex with only men or only women reported an average of two partners in the past year, while women having sex with both men and women reported an average of five partners in the same period.

Individuals who identify as gay, lesbian, or bisexual report more problems with mental health too: higher rates of anxiety, depression, substance abuse, and suicidal thoughts.[64] While I'm sure that for some people, societal bias contributes to their distress, the entire onus for these difficulties—emotional and physical—cannot be placed at the feet of a "heterosexist" society. It's just not intellectually honest.

The Netherlands is probably the world's most open-minded and sexually tolerant country in the world. At the vanguard of homosexual rights for decades, gay marriage was legalized there in 2001, with over 75 percent of the population supporting the bill.[65] A 1998 study examining sexual attitudes in 24 countries asked the question, "Is homosexual sex wrong?" Only 26 percent of U.S. respondents indicated "not wrong at all" or "only sometimes wrong"; the corresponding number in the Netherlands was 77 percent.[66]

> **The prevalence of HPV among men having sex with men is alarming: 93% in HIV positive men and 73% in HIV negative men.[60]**

In light of that country's stance, it is worth noting that, as in the United States, young gay, lesbian, and bisexual individuals in the Netherlands report more high risk sexual behaviors, higher rates of infection with HIV, syphilis, and gonorrhea,[67] and more mental health problems[68] than their heterosexual counterparts. In these studies, younger age was not protective; even as Dutch society became more accepting of sexual minorities, the health disparities persisted. Clearly, societal bias is not to blame for the disproportionately higher numbers in the homosexual populations in the Netherlands.

I'll be called names for bringing attention to this data, because it doesn't jibe with the ideology of the activists seeking to change our country by indoctrinating the next generation. But who suffers the most when members of "sexual minorities" are always portrayed as victims? Who suffers when society—a force they can't control—is blamed for all their ills? They do, of course. And how can they be helped if we're afraid of the truth? The consequences of same-sex experimentation are not as rosy as kids are led to believe, and society's intolerance of gays, lesbians, and bisexuals is just one of many reasons why.

When Alice tells her curious twelfth grader, "If you like sex with both guys and girls, lucky you,"[69] she's turning a blind eye to a mountain of evidence that says the opposite. When Ms. Schroeder justifies experimenting with the same sex, she is, as I said, encouraging our most vulnerable teens to play in a minefield. How does this advice go unchallenged, even while the numbers of young casualties swell?

If their priority was teen health, sex educators would not be focused on recruiting kids to become mouthpieces for their social agendas. They'd be telling them hard truths about hazardous behavior and epidemiology, truths that have nothing to do with lobbying skills or riding the Bus for Equality. Same-sex behavior[70] in adolescence is more dangerous than heterosexual behavior, they'd explain. The playing field is not level. While it's smart for all teens to delay sex, it's particularly important for you.

The "Right" Information

Educators teach teens they have the right to complete, accurate, and up-to-date information. What could be wrong with that? When you look closer, though, you'll see they mean the right to an uncensored, encyclopedic knowledge of sexuality—including, but not limited to: instructions on how to masturbate,[71] kiss, perform oral[72] and anal sex[73] arrange a *ménage à trois* ("household of three," or "threesome"),[74] get birth control and an abortion without parental knowledge,[75] purchase and care for "toys," and set up a sadomasochistic "scene."[76]

It would appear, however, that it's okay to deny teens' rights to information in some instances. As discussed earlier, when research highlights the differences between male and female—the immature cervix, the actions of oxytocin and pheromones—it's banned. It's taboo. So while your daughter can easily gain expertise in sexual practices, I guarantee she'll remain ignorant of the most compelling research about sexual orientation ever conducted. A landmark study, probably the most significant ever on female sexuality, is being ignored because its findings fly in the face of entrenched dogma.

Your daughter could sit through years of comprehensive sex ed, read every word about being gay or lesbian on Teen Talk, Scarleteen, SIECUS, Advocates for Youth, Outproud, Sexetc, gURL.com and Alice, and research every website, book, or video they recommend. This is what she'll know: some men are gay, and some women are lesbian—as if it's the same phenomenon, two sides of the same coin. But it's not.

Lesbian until Graduation

"I don't know when it happened exactly, but it seems I no longer have the easy certainty of pinning my sexual desire to one gender and never the other."[77]

The confession was that of Anna Montrose, 22, writing in *The McGill Daily.* She was sharing with the world how hard it is to "keep your rigid heterosexuality intact" while going through university, studying philosophy and gender, and "watching *The L-Word.*"

While being interviewed on a radio talk show,[78] she explained that prior to arriving on campus at age eighteen, her "rigid heterosexuality" was intact, and she was unaware of any sexual attraction to women. Now, after a few years on campus, and sexual experiences with both men and women, she believes society's preference for male-female bonding is "wrong in that it limits other possibilities, which are equally good."

Is Anna Montrose unusual? Can a campus environment, or studying gender theory, influence a young woman's sexual desires and behavior? Social scientists have been examining the question for decades, and they have an answer.

Meet Dr. Lisa M. Diamond, associate professor of psychology and gender studies at the University of Utah. After studying women like Anna Montrose for years, she introduced a model of female love and sexuality[79] that challenges previous assumptions. The revelations in her book, *Sexual Fluidity: Understanding Women's Love and Desire*,[80] will astonish you.

Diamond followed almost 100 lesbian, bisexual and "unlabeled"[81] young women for a decade, focusing on the development of their sexual identities. This study was the first to follow women's sexual transitions as they occurred over an extended period of time.[82] Her findings not only contradicted existing models, they contradicted them, in Diamond's words, "strongly and consistently."[83]

To begin, most of her subjects were like Anna Montrose; before consciously questioning their sexuality, they had no awareness of attraction to other women.[84] In contrast to the prevailing model of homosexual identity, early attractions to girls did *not* predict lesbian orientation later in life.

Their sexual identities were characterized by change, not stability. Two-thirds changed their identity at least once during the study,[85] and one-third two or more times.[86] The identity change was most commonly in the direction of opposite-sex behaviors.[87] The rate of change did not decrease over time. "Coming out" did not as a rule bring increased certainty and stability. As years passed, they acknowledged *more* fluidity, not less.[88]

Some findings to illustrate the point: Of the women in Diamond's study who initially identified as lesbian, 60 percent had sexual contact with men during the next ten years, and 40 percent did so within the first two years. Even among those who identified as lesbian for the entire ten years, more than 50 percent had some sexual contact[89] with a man.[90]

Her findings would be remarkable if they ended here. But this is only the beginning. Diamond's study showed that female fluidity does not just happen—it can be "triggered." One facilitating factor may be heightened physical closeness and contact. Some girls and women have the potential of being profoundly influenced, in both thought and behavior, by their environment: a class on feminism, joining a political organization, attending an all-girls school. (In fact, students at Smith College joke that the college motto should be "Queer in a year or your money back.")[91] And, for girls, awareness of same sex attraction often *follows* questioning instead of preceding it. That is, *girls don't question because they feel attracted to their friend; they feel attracted to their friend as a result of questioning.*

There's been information out there about female fluidity for a long time. An article from 1984 in *The Journal of Sex Research* described how women lured into "swinging" by their husbands ended up bisexual. A landmark book in the 1990s reported that a college education increased women's likelihood of becoming lesbian by a factor of nine.[92] Apparently, Anna has a lot of company.

But Diamond's study was the first to follow girls and women long-term, and her findings suggest that once girls enter the anything-goes "questioning" world, they could find it difficult to reach resolution and closure.

In other words, the openness and experimentation SIECUS, Planned Parenthood, Advocates for Youth and the entire sex ed network celebrates may well add to a girl's confusion and distress.[93]

This information is vital to young women like Anna. Where, if not in sex ed class, and on sites like gURL.com, can they learn it? Who, if not people like Schroeder and organizations such as SIECUS and Planned Parenthood, are responsible for conveying it? Girls need to know about the G-spot, but not this? Diamond publicized her findings regularly, in 1998, 2000, 2003, 2005, and finally in February 2008, with publication by Harvard University Press of her book. Why then, in 2009, are Planned Parenthood, SIECUS, and the rest still telling girls that their sexual orientation is innate—"who you are deep down," something you "just know," a "true inner feeling"—as if these were indisputable truths?

Ask yourself this: Are you right-handed? At some point back when you were a baby, you instinctively started picking things up with one hand or the other. Now ask yourself, are you straight? Like being right-handed, sexual orientation starts very, very young—usually before puberty and before people start having sex.[94]

This simply is not true.[95] For some girls, experimenting may lead to confusion over sexual orientation. It's not always the other way around.

If the women in Diamond's study were sensitive to "facilitating factors," it seems reasonable to conclude that some girls and teens, who turn to sites like Teen Talk, scarleteen, and gURL.com, are even more sensitive to "triggers" in their relationships and environment. Their thoughts and sexual behavior are no doubt very prone to influence. I remind you, as well, that all girls (and boys) go through a period in which the opposite sex is considered "yucky," and that during this preadolescent period, and after, many girls have particularly intense same sex friendships. For example, a study of eleventh and twelfth grade girls found that they are much more comfortable and engaged with their female friends than with their male friends. And yes, lesbian relationships often have their beginnings in those comfortable female friendships.[96]

> "I lived through the McCarthy era and the Hollywood witch hunts and, as abominable as these were, there was not the insidious sense of intellectual intimidation that currently exists under political correctness."
> — Nicholas A. Cummings Ph.D., former President, American Psychological Association[113]

What happens when a girl with this vulnerability takes Ms. Schroeder's advice "to experience [same sex intimacy] and reflect carefully on the feelings that come up as a result of the experience"?[97] Let's be honest: She's likely to experience same-sex feelings, at least temporarily.

Is there a problem with that? There could be. In addition to all the other identity challenges of adolescence, she'll need to cope with this one too. And as Diamond has shown, her identity may shift for years. She may not have closure for a long time. Is that likely to promote, or obstruct, establishing a stable, committed relationship with one person, something most people want very much?

To glamorize the questioning of sexual orientation and promote experimentation with same sex intimacy is hazardous to our children, and it must stop. It introduces doubt to young minds that are especially sensitive and vulnerable to influence. For those kids who are genuinely confused, reassurance should be provided, but so should reminders that sexual activity—especially with both sexes—is dangerous and won't necessarily help sort things out. If preoccupation with the issue is significant, counseling may be needed. Otherwise, these kids need to get the same advice: delay sexual behavior.

Once again, the ideologues have it all wrong. They value, most of all, for kids to question themselves and the world. They wish to cultivate openness to all possibilities. But their goal should be to help teens achieve a firm and enduring sense of self, so that they know without a doubt who they are and can move on to the challenges of adulthood.

As a psychiatrist, I know that one source of help in reaching that goal is therapy. But here, once again, we are treading on dangerous ground, ground that the vast majority of those directing our children's sex education have marked as forbidden territory.

Educators at places like SIECUS and Advocates for Youth teach kids that sexual orientation changes. Then, as if it's a done deal, they discredit any claim of successful *intentional* change.[98] Even Dr. Diamond, whose research overwhelmingly indicates a "quirky and mercurial"[99] quality to female sexual attraction, insists that intentional change is impossible—and violates "APA [American Psychological Association] ethics."

Are you following this? Orientation can *change*, says sex ed, but it cannot *be changed*. The distinction may sound like splitting hairs, but I warn you—it's a serious matter with real-life consequences.

If a certain relationship, environment, or class can trigger an awareness of authentic *homosexual* attractions for women, why can't the experience of psychotherapy[100]—which also provides a unique relationship, setting, and opportunity to learn—trigger *heterosexual* ones?

And what about men? Is there a role for therapy (known as "reparative") in helping those who are struggling with their own feelings about sexual identity? A small, respectable group of professionals called NARTH (National Association for Research and Therapy of Homosexuality) believes there is. They contend that men who struggle against same sex attraction do so because of personal issues, not societal, and should be respected. In fact, they say, clients who are highly motivated can decrease and even eliminate same sex attraction.

Robert Spitzer, MD, a Columbia University researcher,[101] studied a group of 200 men and women like Malik, a patient I once had—young, religious, and distressed with their sexual inclination. He found that following reparative therapy, a majority reported significant change.[102] But this kind of information is extremely controversial, highly politically charged, and either completely ignored or strongly condemned by psychological and educational establishments. The American Psychological Association even tried to pass a resolution (rejected by a very small margin) condemning reparative therapy and requiring the disciplining of any therapist who offered it.

I Don't Want to Be How I Am

Malik was an international student from Malaysia studying architecture. At the urgent request of one of our social workers, I squeezed him into my schedule. This was a true emergency, Karen explained;

earlier today, he had considered jumping from the window of his apartment.

I don't want to be how I am, Malik explained, avoiding my eyes. *I am attracted to men, but I can't accept it. I want to be different. In my country people are whipped and jailed for this. My family expects me to come home when I graduate and get married. This isn't me . . . I want to change. Why would God do this to me?*

What a dreadful situation. Malik described how he'd struggled for years, never sharing his secret, and now he was hopeless. His parents had given him everything, and now he'd disappoint them. After a sleepless night, he had opened the window of his ninth floor apartment, intending to jump. But he hesitated, and, suddenly frightened, walked over to see us.

I listened carefully. This was a red-hot issue, the question of whether unwanted same sex attraction can be decreased or eliminated. The position of major psychological organizations was that change is impossible and people making the claim are deceiving themselves. Furthermore, they say, trying to change can be harmful. Malik's anguish was a result of intolerance: he had "internalized" society's homophobia; he'd become intolerant of himself. Proper treatment is to affirm his homosexuality and help him accept it. My colleagues sided with the establishment, affirming therapy is the only valid approach—and assumed I did too—of that I had no doubt.

That's what flashed through my mind as Malik sat in silence, head down. Forget politics, I resolved. Here was a life at risk. Hospitalization was not an option, because he'd agreed, at least for the time being, not to harm himself. What could I do? In a few minutes he'd leave, and I knew what I said now could make a difference.

"Malik," I said, "I can prescribe medication so you'll feel calmer, sleep, and get some work done. You also need therapy. The therapy we provide here may help you accept yourself, and figure out how you want to deal with friends and family."

"No," he interrupted, "I could never tell anyone. I will never, ever tell my family. You don't understand! This is not who I am!"

"There is another kind of therapy," I continued, "that would support you in struggling against your attraction to men." I decided to tell him, because it was the right thing to do.

"What?" he asked. "I never heard about that. Does it really work? Can I do it here?"

I shared what I knew, and suggested he research it on his own. I mentioned NARTH's[103] website as a good place to start. And I explained that, no, reparative therapy is not available at our center. It was his decision; if he was interested in learning more, I'd help him with the next step.

I wrote a prescription, and we discussed the proper use of medication. We arranged a follow-up appointment; he thanked me and left.

The door closed, and though I knew I had done the right thing for Malik, I couldn't help wondering what the reaction would be from my colleagues. Word would spread: *Miriam referred a student to the NARTH website.* I could just as well have announced my membership in the KKK.

Was there even *one* other person on our large staff, I wondered, who shared my views—that Malik should be told about *both* options, and allowed to choose his own path? If so, they'd never publicized their opinion. But considering how worried I was about my own deviation from the party line, I could understand their silence.

Inner and Outer Battles

Malik soon felt better on medication, and his suicidal thoughts receded. He decided against therapy of any kind; he only wanted medication. With the crisis over, he was back to his routine, and would, he said, work out the sexuality issue on his own. For a while I'd see him every so often, but then his name disappeared from my schedule. My calls to him were not returned.

I wondered, though, about the people who go against the tide and choose to fight their same sex attraction. They must have some interesting stories to tell. I discovered a support group for men in reparative therapy that meets monthly in a Los Angeles home. The twenty members of this "Circle of Men," as they call themselves, consider the meetings a lifeline, essential to their mental health.

They welcomed me as a guest one evening, and I asked: what is your message to the mental health profession?

They were eager to be heard. Adam said, "I am angry that I didn't know about this therapy for seventeen years. When I discovered it, it was such a liberating sense of relief. In six years I have changed beyond my wildest dreams."

"Therapists told me for years that this is my identity and I should embrace it," a middle-aged man with a wedding band said, "But that never felt right to me. Now I consider it just one part of me—a part I don't have to accept."

"I have chosen the long, hard way instead of the short, easy way," a young man named Greg told me, "and that choice is right for me."

And there was this from Hector: "The old warrior went out and fought battles for land or power. The new warrior fights a bigger battle—the battle within. This is our choice. What gives you the right to take it away?"

I had an idea: Invite these remarkable men to come and speak to my colleagues at the counseling center. Have them describe their journeys to therapists who are convinced that therapy for unwanted same sex attraction is wrong and dangerous. Here's a chance for open discussion of an urgent topic. The men were all for it; "Just tell us when and where—we'll be there," they promised. What a great plan!

Boy, was I naïve. "Sounds fascinating," the director told me. "But the University wouldn't go for it."

Well, so much for being open-minded. So much for celebrating intellectual debate, diversity, tolerance, and multi-culturalism. And so much for a patient's right to self-determination.

Educators and therapists, with their intolerance of diverse views, harm students like Malik in the following ways:

- By neglecting to inform them that alternatives to gay-affirming therapy exist, thereby depriving them of the right to self-determination
- By imposing their Western liberal values: your culture is homophobic and repressive. Our approach is better.
- By depriving them of a source of hope, thereby worsening their emotional distress

Like the University, sex educators want students to believe that men like Adam, Greg, and Hector don't exist and that efforts to change sexual orientation are futile.

I doubt Debra Haffner has had the opportunity to speak with men such as these. Otherwise, how could she declare, "Therapy cannot change one's sexual orientation"?[104] Homosexuality is not an illness, the reasoning goes on sites like AFY, so the idea of a "cure" is meaningless. Does anyone speak about a cure for *heterosexuality*, they demand?

John is sixteen. He has turned for advice to Dr. Savin-Williams, a psychologist, on the Human Rights Campaign (HRC) Foundation[105] ("Working for Lesbian, Gay, Bisexual and Transgender Equal Rights") website.

After finding out he's gay, John writes, his father wants him to see a Christian psychiatrist. "He doesn't believe I was born this way... he insists that I can change....I really don't know what to do."[106]

A year after Robert Spitzer published his research on the efficacy of reparative therapy, the psychologist replied:

> "As scientists, we know that it is impossible to change your sexual orientation... back off these kinds of "discussions." Avoid arguments....It is not your job to convince him....If your

> father loves you unconditionally... he will come around....
> Never agree to go to a therapist that he selects....Will your
> father let you select your own therapist? "

Then he tells John how to locate a "gay-positive" therapist, and recommends some websites and books.

Interestingly, one of the organizations recommended by Savin-Williams was Young Gay America. This group—whose mission is "to promote community, information, and empowerment by and for gay youth"[107]—was founded in 2001 by Michael Glatze and his boyfriend. But, oops, Mr. Glatze has identified as ex-gay since 2007. Could both the HRC and Dr. Savin-Williams be unaware of that development, when the news was given prominent coverage by leading gay news websites?[108] Unlikely. Yet the answer to John, still featured on the site as of this writing, remains unchanged. As far as they are concerned, the change in Glatze's orientation never happened.

Troubling, no? For starters, psychologists are expected to refrain from undermining parents. Dr. Savin-Williams should have told John that his attraction to other boys may be temporary,[109] and for this reason alone he'd be wise to delay sexual behavior. Boys who self-label as gay in high school are more likely to use drugs and alcohol,[110] be infected with an STD, and become HIV positive.[111] It would have been appropriate, too, as a "scientist" to tell John about Spitzer's research, and about organizations like NARTH and Parents and Friends of Ex-Gays[112] ("PFOX").

There's also a deeper issue, one that really hit home for me after meeting the Circle of Men. Educators and therapists must recognize that not everyone worships at the shrine of self-love and acceptance. Some people wish to struggle against their natures. While many choose to define themselves by their desires, others discover who they are in their struggle *against* those desires.

Professionals must understand that in this struggle, success is not measured by outcome. One person has better results, the other worse;

what confers meaning is the daily effort to live in a manner consistent with one's values.

But how can educators recognize these truths, when doing so would bring down their house of cards? Their worldview is based on *rejecting* moral restrictions and struggles. Their aim is to replace the no's with yes's, remember? How can they, heirs to Kinsey's model of sexuality, and after decades of crusading for the *expansion* of sexual expression, admit that for some people, the exact opposite is best? The patriarch would turn over in his grave.

♂♀

Chapter Seven

Genderland

PARENTS, FASTEN YOUR SEAT BELTS. If what you've learned so far about sex education horrifies you, and you believe it can't get any worse, I caution you. it can and it does.

Remember *Alice in Wonderland*? How Alice followed the White Rabbit into Wonderland, and each new adventure was more impossible than the last? A cat that vanishes into thin air, leaving only its smile behind. A tea party that never ends, because time has stopped. A queen making loony decrees, such as, "Sentence first—verdict afterwards."[1]

Well, welcome to Genderland, where the madness of sex education reaches a peak, and everything you know is turned on its head.

If you're like most people, you assume someone with a Y chromosome and affiliated genitals is male, and the rest of us, with two X chromosomes, are female. You are certain that girls become women and boys become men. Can anything be more obvious than that? But for sex educators, this is a thorny subject requiring pages of clarification.

There's more to male or female than DNA and anatomy, they explain to kids. There's also gender.

Sex, gender—is there a difference? You bet, and you need to know what it is. Ditto for distinguishing a cross dresser from a transsexual, and knowing why our "bipolar gender system"[2] is flawed.

Genderland is a dumbfounding departure from reality. Here, male and female are arbitrary identities based on feelings, not biology. Here it's normal for, say, your adolescent son to wonder what he is—a boy, a girl, or neither? That's right, in Genderland the idea that he must be one or the other is an arbitrary, oppressive paradigm—another noxious "ism," like racism. Citizens of Genderland reject that model—some insist they're male *and* female, others claim they're neither. Hence words such as "ze" (another option aside from "he" and "she"), and "hir" (an alternative to the oppressive "his" and "her").

Have I already lost you? It's okay. Trust me, I've been there.

What's the difference, you wonder, between *sexual* identity and *gender* identity? The former refers to the sort of person you're attracted to. The latter refers to whether you experience yourself as male or female (more on what that means later). Sex ed dogma claims the two are unrelated; in other words, gender identity does not necessarily determine sexual identity.

Yes, Genderland sure is a peculiar place. I discovered it on websites and in books recommended to teens. With each visit, I feel like Alice lost in Wonderland—confused and disoriented. My jaw drops, my eyes open wide. *What the heck is this?* I keep asking, as I inspect what experts teach our kids.

Every parent needs to visit Genderland, ahead of his child, and carefully observe the landscape. Many will feel, as Alice did, like they've fallen down a black hole and landed in a truly bewildering place.

We Are All Hermaphrodites

We owe it all to psychologist John Money, who in 1955 introduced the concept that humans develop an internal sense of maleness or femaleness, separate from chromosomes and anatomy.[3] Infants are born gender-neutral, he claimed, without a predisposition to think, feel, or behave in a masculine or feminine manner. "[M]en impregnate," Money wrote, "women menstruate, ovulate, gestate, and lactate."[4] All other distinctions are due to socialization.

According to Money's scheme, while Baby Jill has two X chromosomes, she has the potential to feel like a man. Little Jack has a penis, but if he's dressed in pink, given Barbies, surgery, and estrogen, he'll do fine as Jacquelyn. Jack and Jill's gender identity will depend on messages they receive in the first years of life from family, friends, school, religion, and media. Money taught that until two and a half to three years of age, gender remains vulnerable to environmental influence. After that, the feeling is fixed.

You should not be surprised to discover that, like Alfred Kinsey, John Money had some—well—unconventional views. This is not a 1960s version of Dr. Phil we're talking about. For one thing, like the good Dr. Kinsey, John Money believed sex between adults and children could be beneficial.[5] He was a proponent of adult–child love,[6] even incest.[7] For another, Money crusaded against traditional morality, arguing that ancient taboos were destructive.

Kinsey and Money appear to have been kindred souls in another way: from John Money's writings about childhood and abuse at the hands of his father, we see evidence of deep emotional wounds and (you guessed it) gender issues.

"I suffered from the guilt of being male," he wrote. "I wore the mark of man's vile sexuality. . . . I wondered if the world might really be a better place for women if not only farm animals but human males also were gelded (neutered) at birth."[8] That's troubling, isn't it, coming from someone who ended up advising parents to have their sons castrated?

Money was fascinated by hermaphrodism[9]—a rare medical disorder in which a baby is born with both male and female reproductive organs. And he dedicated his life to proving to the world that psychologically, we are all hermaphrodites.

For real hermaphrodites, and their parents, the condition is not some ideal psychological state, but a serious dilemma. Boy or girl? That's the first of many urgent questions that follow the birth of these unfortunate children. Blue blanket or pink? What about a name, and what should parents tell family and friends? Money's Ph.D. thesis, completed in 1952, was on this medical condition and its treatment. Afterward, he pioneered the work in "sex assignment"—the complex decision of whether to raise a particular hermaphrodite as male or female. He established the country's first clinic for hermaphrodites' surgeries at Johns Hopkins University. Money's clinic later became the first in the United States to provide sex-change surgery for adults.

Money didn't confine himself to deciding the sex of hermaphrodites. Bruce Reimer, Money's most famous patient, was born a full-fledged boy, with an identical twin named Brian. In a ghastly medical accident when he was eight months old, Bruce's penis was destroyed. Bruce's parents heard Money holding forth on TV about how all it took was a little estrogen, a few Barbie dolls, and some surgery to make a boy into a girl, and they turned to him in their desperation over their son's plight. At twenty-two months of age, Bruce was castrated, renamed Brenda, and dressed in frilly clothes. He would be raised alongside his twin, who would be given trucks and GI Joes instead of Barbies, as the perfect test case for Money to prove to the world that nurture, not nature, determines gender identity.

The twins' story became a landmark case, widely cited as proof that the sense of male or female is learned, not inborn. Money's theories were accepted and taught as dogma; because of them, parents all over the world facing similar circumstances—due to trauma or a medical condition—were advised to castrate their sons and raise them as girls.[10]

Fast forward to 1996. Dr. Money had not seen or heard from the twins for about twenty years; nevertheless, he republished *Man & Woman, Boy & Girl*, in which he described the experiment as a complete success.

But a year later, "Brenda" came forward and revealed that "she" was now David,[11] a janitor in a slaughterhouse, married and father to three adopted children.

The public learned that the whole thing was a hoax,[12] and a fiasco ensued. Contrary to Money's published results, far from accepting the gender reassignment, David had fought against it tooth and nail from the very beginning—refusing to play with dolls, preferring wrestling over cooking, and even urinating standing up whenever possible. She was teased relentlessly for the boyish way she moved, spoke, walked, and gestured. Kids called her "cavewoman." In second grade she wanted to be a garbage man, and in eighth, an auto mechanic.[13]

In short, Bruce/Brenda/David endured years of agony, exacerbated by the "therapy" Money put him and his twin brother through. During their yearly visits,[14] Money firmly, loudly, and angrily told the children to take off their clothes, look at each other's genitalia, and act out sexual intercourse.[15]

After years of this nightmare—not only for Brenda but for the whole family[16]—Brenda's psychiatrist urged her parents to reveal the truth: Brenda was male. Despite Money's warning never to do so, they gave in.

The twins were 14 when "Brenda" was told that she'd been born a boy. His reaction? "I was *relieved*. Suddenly it all made sense why I felt the way I did. I wasn't some sort of weirdo. I wasn't *crazy*."[17]

And how did Dr. Money respond? He didn't. The esteemed professor simply stopped mentioning and writing about the case.[18]

So while the pretense ended, the misery did not. The damage had been done. Both David and his twin eventually were lost to suicide.

Apparently, David's story—and the doubts it raises about Money's gender theory—hasn't penetrated the hearts and minds of today's sex educators; they remain loyal to that theory. In the same matter-of-fact way your daughter is taught multiplication or geography, she's told a girl's preference for pink, her interest in dolls, and her tendency to empathize are due to cultural messages she's received about how a girl is supposed to feel, think, look, and behave.

> Advocates for Youth: Gender is the collection of behaviors, dress, attitudes, etc., culturally assigned to people according to their biological sex.[19]
>
> Scarleteen: Gender is a man-made set of concepts and ideas about how men and women are supposed to look, act, relate, and interrelate, based on their sex.[20] What our mind is like—the way we think, what we think about, what we like, what skills we have—really is not, so far as data has shown us so far—about our gender or biological sex, period.[21]
>
> Planned Parenthood: All people are "gendered beings" by virtue of the fact that we are socialized into a heavily gendered culture. . . .[22] Cultures teach what it means to be a man or a woman.[23]

What cultures teach about gender, your daughter learns early on, is wrong and harmful. Most cultures endorse "gender stereotypes" and expect everyone to fit them. Like racial and ethnic stereotypes, she learns, gender stereotypes are unsubstantiated and destructive. They prevent people from being who they really are.

According to gURL.com, society expects females to be "emotional, delicate, domestic, nurturing, creative, introspective, meterialistic (sic), patient, moody, concerned with looks, not assertive, catty."[24]

If she fails to meet these expectations, your daughter learns, the consequences can be grave. Chances are she'll be scorned and called names: dyke, butch, or tomboy. She might be assaulted and raped. She could even be murdered. That's what happened to Brandon Teena, a woman who chose to live as a man.[25] If your daughter wants to know more about gender, instructs gURL.com, she should check out Brandon's story in the film *Boys Don't Cry*.

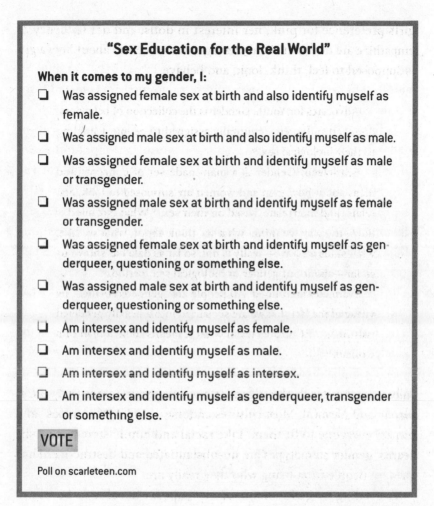

"Sex Education for the Real World"

When it comes to my gender, I:

❑ Was assigned female sex at birth and also identify myself as female.

❑ Was assigned male sex at birth and also identify myself as male.

❑ Was assigned female sex at birth and identify myself as male or transgender.

❑ Was assigned male sex at birth and identify myself as female or transgender.

❑ Was assigned female sex at birth and identify myself as genderqueer, questioning or something else.

❑ Was assigned male sex at birth and identify myself as genderqueer, questioning or something else.

❑ Am intersex and identify myself as female.

❑ Am intersex and identify myself as male.

❑ Am intersex and identify myself as intersex.

❑ Am intersex and identify myself as genderqueer, transgender or something else.

VOTE

Poll on scarleteen.com

Outdated

In the 1960s Money's theory of infant gender neutrality may have been plausible, given what was known at that time, but in this century it is not. Fifty years ago, the predominant view was that the Y chromosome[26] carried little important information; aside from the genes for male genitalia, it was considered a "genetic wasteland." If males and females essentially had the same genetic endowment, went the thinking of that time, differences between them must be due to society's messages and expectations.

That was before the biotechnology revolution. Now we can scrutinize DNA and carefully map out each twist and turn. Today we know the Y chromosome is teeming with units of DNA that are unique to males.[27] There are distinct male and female blueprints created from the moment of conception.

"The striking quantity and diversity of sex-related influences on brain function indicate that the still widespread assumption that sex influences are negligible cannot be justified, and probably retards progress in our field,"[28] reports Dr. Larry Cahill from the University of California, Irvine's Center for the Neurobiology of Learning and Memory. "There has been a renewed emphasis on the direct actions of the X and Y chromosomes in bringing about sex differences," state a team of neuroscientists at the Isis Fund for Sex Differences Research; "Cutting-edge discoveries are revolutionizing our concepts of what makes a male or female brain."[29]

Consider a boy's preference for rough play with other boys, and for vehicles and building toys. According to Money—currently echoed by SIECUS, Planned Parenthood, Heather, and the rest—these result from messages received from his environment, starting with the blue blanket. *You are a boy. Boys like blue, they are active and physical, they love construction, trains, cars.* So when a boy picks a Thomas the tank engine instead of a Barbie, they claim, he's conforming, albeit unknowingly, to those expectations.

Rubbish, says neurobiology.[30] He goes for the truck primarily because of his boy-brain. The toy provides an opportunity for movement, something he's predisposed to enjoy. Sure, it's socially reinforced, but his masculine brain circuits precede any cultural messages. For similar reasons, he's partial to competition and rough-and-tumble play, but unlikely to be drawn to babies. He'll have a stronger sex drive, and be less likely than a girl to change his sexual preferences during his lifetime. To explain these differences, and others, neuroscience leads us away from social cues like blue blankets. His boy-brain existed long before birth, due to a very different sort of message.

It comes from a gene that instructs the testicles to produce and secrete testosterone.[31] Unless directed otherwise, the prenatal brain grows in a female direction. If testosterone is released during critical periods of development, that changes. The hormone travels through the blood, targeting cells whose surfaces have matching receptors. Like a key in a lock, when a hormone molecule fits a surface receptor, a "door" opens, allowing entry. The hormone makes a b-line for the control center. In the nucleus it instructs the DNA: turn these activities on, and those off.

Think of each cell as a factory. A hormone breaks through security, finds the foreman, and directs him to change the work orders. Make hats instead of shoes, it demands. The machines grind to a stop and change course. When the order comes from the top, everyone complies.

Testosterone inhibits the development of a feminine brain, with larger centers for communication and emotional memory, and establishes a masculine course—more brain space devoted to centers for action, aggression, and sex drive.[32]

The cascade of hormonal effects are global and permanent. Although some manifestations will not be seen for years, such as the changes that come with puberty, the boy-brain trajectory is set at eight weeks, when the gene directs the testes: get to work![33]

Not eight weeks after birth; eight weeks after *conception*—seven months before the pink or blue blanket. That's right, a fetus has a boy-brain or girl-brain before some women are even aware they're pregnant—when it is the size of a kidney bean.

The research supporting that fact is voluminous, but to SIECUS and all the rest of them, it doesn't exist. *Gender is man-made*, they still insist in 2009; *cultures teach what it means to be a man or a woman*. Are they stuck in a time warp like the March Hare—at a tea party where clocks stand still? Instead of force-feeding kids 1960s ideology, modern sex ed curricula should describe studies done in *this* century—on infants in their first day of life, on Japanese kindergarteners, and on juvenile monkeys.

These studies indicate that genetics and pre-natal hormones pre-dispose boys and girls to have—among other things—specific toy preferences, play styles and activities, and peer relationships.[34] Simply put, science in the twenty-first century supports the stereotypes SIECUS, Planned Parenthood, and other sex educators are telling kids to reject.

What Crayons Can Tell Us

Let's discuss babies first, then their blankets. Abundant research indicates that sex differences in social behaviors—girls' and women's increased sensitivity to emotional nuance, for example—are related to early brain development. At one day of age, presumably before the child has received any messages about conforming to a gender stereo-type, boys look longer at a mobile, while girls show a stronger inter-est in the face.[35] At one year, girls are drawn to a video of a face moving; boys to a video of cars moving.[36] And at both one and two years of age, girls make more eye contact with their mothers than boys. Remarkably, the amount of contact is inversely correlated with the prenatal level of testosterone. The higher the testosterone level was before birth, the lower the amount of eye contact.[37]

Now what about those blankets? gURL.com considers them part of "gendering," a message for the baby about social expectations based on identity. Color preference, they insist, is a result of socialization.[38]

The color pink is mainly associated with females, says gURL.com. *If a boy painted his room pink, people might think it was a little weird.*[39]

But those people would be right; it *is* weird to find a boy who prefers pink, and not only because of what others might think. How do I know? I read about it in the medical journal *Hormones and Behav-ior.*

Researchers in Japan examined the drawings of 252 kindergarten-ers.[40] They found significant differences between the drawings of girls and boys. Among them: boys drew a moving object twenty times more than girls. Girls included a flower or butterfly seven times more than boys. Then they examined the crayons each child had used over the course of six months, measuring how much of each color remained. Overall, girls decidedly preferred pink and flesh colors. Boys used two colors more than girls: grey and blue.

Okay, you're thinking, but girls are supposed to like flowers, butterflies, and pink; boys are dressed in blue and expected to enjoy things that move. These preferences aren't innate, they were learned.

To control for that, the researchers analyzed the drawings of a third group—eight girls with congenital adrenal hyperplasia. CAH is a genetic disorder in which the fetal brain was flooded with high levels of male hormones. Girls with CAH may have an enlarged clitoris; they may even be identified at birth as males. They are treated medically and surgically, and raised female. In the nature/nurture debate, these girls are intriguing, because nature signaled "you're a boy" to the fetus, but nurture has been saying "you're a girl" since birth.

Clearly, the people over at gURL.com aren't reading *Hormones and Behavior*. Otherwise they'd know the astonishing results: CAH girls drew cars and buses, not butterflies. And the cars and buses were blue, not pink.

Gender is *culturally* assigned? I don't think so. And neither can any person who follows neuroscience in this century.

In a radio interview in 2000,[41] David Reimer laid bare the horrors of the years spent as Brenda. "I was betrayed by the medical profession . . . they put my life on the line so that they could hold onto their theories." David has since been lost to suicide, but the betrayal continues. Other lives are on the line, but hard science is scorned, and phony theories canonized.

The educators who have enshrined Money's gender theory and now foist it on our youth need to understand that John Money's preoccupation with hermaphrodites and sexual reassignment was related to his own inner struggles. His belief in gender plasticity was wishful thinking. Gender identity is separate from anatomy and chromosomes? It's based on feelings, learned from experiences? Baloney. In what's probably just the tip of the iceberg, twenty-first century science indicates that the tendencies to typical boy or girl behaviors—yes, gender stereotypes—are innate. We're not psychological hermaphrodites at birth, potentially masculine or feminine—we are wired for one or the other in the womb.

Different Worlds

"Step on to any playground anywhere on the planet and you will see boys and girls playing in different worlds. They differ in what they are doing, with whom they are doing it, and how they are doing it."

So begins a chapter in a 2008 book by an international group of experts, *Sex Differences in the Brain: From Genes to Behavior*.[42] We learn here that "across cultures, girls more than boys are interested in and engage with dolls and doll accessories, arts and crafts, kitchen toys, fashion, and make-up, whereas boys more than girls are interested in and engage with transportation toys, electronics, blocks (especially complex building sets), and sports."[43] These preferences are pervasive and consistent.[44] They begin to emerge at nine months,[45] and are stable by eighteen months.

Yet we're suppose to believe that when a two-year-old girl passes up the set of Hot Wheels, choosing the Dora the Explorer doll instead, it is because of cultural expectations—because she has learned girls play with dolls, not cars? This is what gender theory would have us believe, and what your child learns, but it's unlikely. You see, at that age, she doesn't know she's a girl. That awareness comes later.[46]

Until at least two and a half years of age, children are unable to consistently label themselves—or discriminate between—male and female. That's a year or more *after* showing a preference for the doll or the truck. How can children choose particular toys based on what's expected of them as a girl or boy, before grasping the *concept* of girl or boy?

That's a problem for those who argue that kids are socialized to pre-fer one toy or activity over the other. A more likely explanation, con-sistent with data collected in the past two decades, is that preferences relate to the toy's use or function. Prenatal hormones wire a girl's brain to be interested in nurturing, and a boy's to enjoy motion. Children then choose the doll or the car for the opportunities they provide for the respective activity.[47]

In support of this theory, girls with CAH show increased preference for male playmates and toys typically preferred by boys.[48]

Studies conducted on young male and female monkeys produce similar results. Juvenile male monkeys, both rhesus and vervet, pre-fer playing with balls and vehicles. Female monkeys like dolls and pots.[49] . . . *Pots?* Researchers suggest the female monkeys' increased interest in them was due to their red color. The faces of infant vervets are reddish-pink, so the color may act as a cue signaling an opportunity

The female monkey chose a doll while the male chose a truck.

for nurturance. Are animals oppressed by gender stereotypes too? The author of one study, a psychologist, notes: "They are not subject to advertising. They are not subject to parental encouragement, they are not subject to peer chastisement."[50]

Over the Edge

I wish this were the end of the story, but the principles of Genderland have gone far beyond Money's pseudoscience—*we are born gender-neutral; cultures teach what it means to be a man or a woman*. That's old. Like an angry adolescent testing limits, pushing the envelope harder each day, the agendas have become increasingly radical. But how radical can you get, how far from the truth can you move, before falling over the edge and losing touch with reality?

In step with Money, sex ed curricula define gender as separate from biology. They take his theory a step further, however. When gender and biology don't "align"—you've got boy genitals but feel like a girl, or the opposite—they say that's normal. "Being transgender is as normal as being alive," kids are told by Advocates for Youth.[51] "It's not uncommon for a person to identify strongly with the other gender," says Planned Parenthood's teen site. "Many people, including teens, have non-traditional feelings about gender roles and sexual identities and that is normal, too."[52]

Let's say the experts are right, and it's "normal" for a boy to insist he's a girl. It's a "variant" that he loathes his genitals and wears dresses. What about other cases of "misaligned" identity? Are they "variants" as well?

Consider a rare condition called Body Integrity Identity Disorder. Its victims, according to a recent *Newsweek* article,[53] have "an overwhelming desire to amputate one or more healthy limbs or become paraplegic.... They describe a persistent, tortuous chasm between their mind's image of their own body, and the physical body they inhabit." Only after they're disabled—by self-inflicted mutilation, or with the help of an underground surgeon—do they feel complete.

The similarity of their condition to that of transgenders is apparent. The "amputee wannabees" also suffer with a "misaligned identity." What causes this strange affliction? Some speculate it's due to an abnormality of the area of the brain involved in constructing a coherent body image.[54]

These people need our understanding, support, and help. Should that include extreme measures, like amputation of a healthy limb, or sex reassignment surgery? I'm not sure.

I am sure however, that a boy who persistently and intensely feels he's a girl, like someone distressed about having two healthy legs, has an illness. The goal should be to help him find relief. Normalizing transgenderism—called Gender Identity Disorder by mental health professionals—is, again, based on an ideology that wishes to blur the distinctions between male and female. Having this disorder is not "as normal as being alive," as Advocates for Youth want young people to believe.

I wonder, do those who teach our kids that being male and female is subjective and changeable apply that approach to other aspects of identity? Does the individual who yearns for his legs to be severed represent a "normal variant"? It seems a fair question to pose.

The Gender Binary

As extreme as it may be, even the idea of transgenderism is nevertheless consistent with the premise that there are two, and only two, possible identities, male or female. It's blue or pink, Jack or Jill, one box marked "M," another marked "F."

But in Genderland this model, the gender binary, is considered false and oppressive. It stands in the way of the right to what's called gender expression. Instead, authorities say, male and female are on a continuum, with many genders in between. There are endless shades between blue and pink, and a whole bunch of boxes on the application. At different times in life, kids learn, you may feel male, female, both, or neither. And that's just fine.

As Heather Corinna says on scarleteen:

> Like most aspects of identity, as you continue into and through your adult life you'll likely find that your personal gender identity…changes and grows, and becomes more clear (and more murky!) with time and life experience. Likely, you'll find that the older you get…you realize that gender isn't anything close to binary, but like most things, is a wide, diverse spectrum, a varied, veritable genderpalooza.[55]

Let's examine this one point at a time.

1. *As you go thru life,* says Heather, *your gender identity changes and grows.*

Now where did *that* come from? Not from John Money: he taught that gender identity ("I am a boy") is fixed by age three. Not from child development experts: they explain that gender identity is followed about a year later with gender stability ("I will grow up to be a man"), and by age seven at most, by the more sophisticated idea of gender permanence ("I cannot become a girl, even if I wear a dress and lipstick"). As one authoritative psychiatry textbook explains, "Children know that nobody can change gender…[a boy] knows that he will always be a boy until he becomes a man."[56] And not from the eminent psychiatrists, psychologists, and social workers who authored the *Diagnostic and Statistical Manual of Mental Disorders.* As mentioned above, according to the current edition, a child with a strong and persistent gender dysphoria—the desire to be, or insistence one is, the other sex—is given the diagnosis Gender Identity Disorder.[57] It's seen as an emotional disorder.

No matter. Heather rejects these conventions, in company with SIECUS[58] and Planned Parenthood.[59] "Our gender identity may shift and evolve over time," says Planned Parenthood. "It may change over the course of your lifetime," agrees SIECUS. And Advocates for Youth adds: "People can realize their . . . gender identity at any point during their lives."[60]

Gender identity, Heather states with authority, *changes and grows, sometimes it's clear, sometimes murky.*

What do they mean? That while your daughter insists "I'm a girl" at age five, she might also insist "I'm a boy" at fifteen? And you have no reason for concern? Isn't identity by definition a stable sense of self? Stable—you know, as in, stays the same?

This is absurd. It's one thing to propose that boys climb trees because of social expectations; that's a somewhat plausible theory, even though current science has disproved it. It's altogether another to state that often boys yearn persistently to *be* girls—not to play dress-up or help in the kitchen, but to *be* a girl. To have breasts, periods, the whole shebang. And to assert this is nothing to worry about.

The "experts" want teens to think that there's nothing unusual about all this; to the contrary, it's another struggle for freedom and basic personal rights. It's about being yourself, free from arbitrary, unnecessary restrictions. Society dictates strict gender roles, kids are reminded, and some people are dissatisfied with that.[61] The gender expressions[62] of these individuals "vary from common social expectations;"[63] they don't conform to social norms and want to "redefine traditional notions."[64] They're no different from you or me, it seems, except for feeling uncomfortable with the sex they were "assigned" at birth—as if the "assignment" was a hit or miss process—and this is in reference to genetically, developmentally, and endocrinologically normal children.

To be dissatisfied with society's expectations . . . to fight against norms and restrictions . . . to join with others in the struggle for freedom and rights . . . do you see why young people, especially troubled ones, might be drawn in to gender-bending?

This has real-life consequences. "Luke" Woodward arrived at Brown University a "masculine-appearing lesbian," with no plans to change his sex. It was not until a trip to Cuba, he reports—where people were shocked to discover he was female—that he began to wonder: Am I a woman? Returning to the United States, he met several transsexuals, and realized there were other options. The summer before his senior year she/he underwent a double mastectomy. No testosterone for Luke yet—he can't afford it. And what about more surgery—as Luke puts it, "down there"? He hasn't decided.[65]

In my experience as a campus counselor, I know of students like Luke, undergoing dangerous hormone treatments and irreversible surgeries[66] after being introduced to the notion of fluid gender on campus or elsewhere. But kids hear about these far-out ideas long before college.

> *I hate being a girl, a* thirteen year old calling herself "abnormal" tells Heather. *Is there something wrong with me wanting to be a boy?*[67]
>
> Heather replies: *There's nothing patently abnormal or wrong about being uncomfortable with your own sex or your gender. . . . Gender dysphoria is especially common at the age you're at right now . . . .It's really typical to feel this way . . . .*

Just a moment, Heather. That's not true. If you're going to use technical terms, use them correctly. Gender dysphoria, defined as "a persistent aversion toward some or all of those physical characteristics or social roles that connote one's own biological sex,"[68] isn't just some pesky matter teens must tolerate, like oily skin or annoying siblings. We're not speaking here of, for example, a girl envying boys because they have more athletic opportunities, or don't need to diet or shave their legs. Gender dysphoria is a girl's yearning for a double mastectomy. It's wanting testosterone injections to lower her voice and allow her to grow a mustache. Gender dysphoria is a disturbance in a child's view of herself. And it's not "really typical"[69] at *any* age.[70]

Heather is in no position to counsel thirteen year old "abnormal" about her gender identity—a complex matter that can involve genetic and medical disorders, as well as psychosocial factors. While Heather touches on these in her reply, she's clearly in over her head; the gist of her advice rests on Genderland ideology—it's all about what feels right to you.

What's most important isn't having a gender identity that "matches" your biological sex, or one which everyone else thinks is best, but having one that feels best to YOU and most authentic for you.

2. As you get older, it's likely you'll realize that gender isn't anything close to binary...

Now that's interesting. In a binary, there are only two possibilities. On or off. Positive or negative. Left or right. Yet Heather's saying gender isn't binary? We're not either male or female?

Nope. That's another falsehood foisted on us by society, says Heather. Like the incorrect assumption that everyone who "menstruates, ovulates, gestates, and lactates" feels like a woman. This view is restrictive, intolerant, and must be challenged.

Reject the binary, kids are told. Gender is "a wide, diverse spectrum."[71]

Says SIECUS: People "have an internal sense that they are female, male, or a variation of these."[72]

Gender Isn't Just Either/Or, claims a brochure[73] students might find in the nurse's office.

"The truth is....Not everyone looks or feels like one sex or the other," Advocates for Youth says. "Traditionally, gender has meant either 'male' or 'female'.... However, there is really a range of genders, including male and female, but also including genderqueer[74] or gender ambiguous, butch (man or woman), femme (man or woman), transgender... and many others."[75] And according to gURL.com, the spectrum of gender includes transgender, transsexual, transvestite, and pangender, the latter signifying *people who do not identify with the term male or female. The person may feel they are a mix of either genders, genderless or another gender altogether.*[76]

Did you get that? "A mix of either genders, genderless or another gender altogether." This is what I mean when I say these people are going over the edge. Some people do suffer from a disorder in gender identity; they deserve understanding, compassion, and treatment. But this goes beyond Roberta becoming Robert. *Another gender altogether* is about becoming someone that's neither Roberta *nor* Robert.

As gURL.com states on the hazards of the gender binary:

> When we place people into very strict categories... it makes it hard for people to truly be themselves. And by placing people into categories of "this" vs. "that," it doesn't leave much wiggle room. And when a lot of people do not fit into either or more than one... that can be lonely. It can be isolating. And, as in the Brandon Teena case, it can result in harmful incidents.

A summary of today's lesson on being male or female: your identity is based on how you feel; those feelings may shift and evolve; there are more than two genders; assuming otherwise is oppressive and sometimes dangerous.

How Many Genders Are There?

If anyone is *another gender altogether*, it's Kate Bornstein. When teens go online with questions about being a boy or a girl, they're referred not to *The Female Brain* (2006), not to *As Nature Made Him* (2000), the book about David Reimer, but to Bornstein's *My Gender*

Workbook[77] (1998). In fact, Heather recommended the book to "abnormal," the troubled thirteen year old.

> *You might also want to hop over to your local bookstore or*
> *library and check out some books on gender identity.... Kate*
> *Bornstein's* My Gender Workbook *is one I'd very enthusiasti-*
> *cally recommend.*

With such a rave review, how could I resist? I hopped over to Amazon, and bought the book. That's how *My Gender Workbook* became our final adventure in Genderland.

Like the Cheshire Cat who vanishes and reappears—as a floating head, or just a grin hanging in the air—Kate Bornstein has had many incarnations.

Read carefully, because this is tricky. Kate (formerly Al) was born male and raised as a boy. In adulthood, he "became a woman" for a few years, then "stopped being a woman and settled into being neither." His (her?) lover, Catherine, decided to "become a man," David. Kate and David stayed together as a "heterosexual couple." Their relationship ended when David found "his gay male side."[78]

Kate asks, "What a whacky world, huh?"

Given Kate's extraordinary journey, it's not surprising that the subtitle of her (his?) 300-page manifesto is, *How to Become a Real Man, a Real Woman, the Real You, or Something Else Entirely.* Now firmly established in her identity as *something else entirely*, Kate hopes to "dismantle the 'gender system' on the planet as we know it."[79]

On the front line of her attack are pronouns. She, he, his, and her don't work: they support the gender binary. The English language needs gender-neutral pronouns. Instead of "he" and "she," we have "ze" (pronounced zee). In place of "his" and "her" there's "hir" (pronounced here).

Please take this seriously. The culture your child is in certainly does, especially the campus culture, where students who identify as neither male nor female contribute to campus diversity. Gender neutral housing and bathrooms are available on a growing number of campuses. The health clinic at Wesleyan University no longer requires students to check off M or F; instead they are asked to "describe [their] gender identity history." Applications to Harvard's business school allow prospective students to identify themselves as one of three genders.[80] Smith, an all women's college since the nineteenth century, now has some male alumni—they enrolled as women and graduated as men. Accordingly, students on that campus voted to eliminate female pronouns from the student constitution.[81] Pronouns such as "she" and "her" were replaced with the phrase "the student."[82] At four campuses of the University of California,[83] hormones and surgical sex re-assignment are covered by student insurance plans.[84] The education at Sarah Lawrence includes the Gender F—k Symposium— "a week long series of programming to challenge gender assumptions, roles and stereotypes."[85] And at the University of Massachusetts, the assumption that everyone is either male or female constitutes "transphobia."[86]

The sooner you grasp this, the better: there's nothing radical about gender bending at our colleges and universities. To the contrary, Kate Bornstein's speaking calendar is packed with college events: Brown, Emory, SUNY, Yale, Northeastern, University of Minnesota,[87] and University of South Florida. Her signature lecture is called "On Men, Women, and the Rest of Us."

What's Kate's message to young people? In addition to the need for new pronouns, they learn that the gender system has a "deathgrip" on them, and that identifying as a boy or girl "is neither natural nor essential."[88]

> I think we create our identities . . . with a similar purpose
> that a crab excretes the substance that eventually hardens into
> a shell, its armor. It's safe having an identity, it's secure. It's safe
> having a gender. But there's a price for safety and security

within some hard shell. We can't grow any more. Our identities become so hard and so restrictive that we can no longer stretch and explore, we can't find new ways of experiencing the world, new ways to delight ourselves....We're frozen in that shell.[89]

Do you see how enticing this argument is to "abnormal" and other troubled souls? I can't think of a better way to recruit kids. Who wants to live in a shell, unable to grow, stretch, and explore? Sounds like living with parents, doesn't it? Unlike Mom and Dad, Kate understands being suffocated by stupid rules and restrictions.

Stupid rules—like having to do homework or mow the grass. *Stupid restrictions*—like imposing the gender binary.

> I know I'm not a man...and I've come to the conclusion that I'm probably not a woman, either.... The trouble is, we're living in a world that insists we be one or the other.[90]

You see, it's the world's fault. Kate is a victim. The crime? All cultures, legal systems, and major world religions assume people are either male or female, making her an outsider. "This has made her life, "sad and frightening," and made her feel "alone," as one of her friends put it.[91] It's certainly not too much to demand they all change, right now, to accommodate her.

This is upside-down. These two individuals, "Abnormal" and Kate, are unsure who they are. Abnormal, thirteen years old, concludes: something's wrong with me, I need help. That's healthy. Kate, sixty years old, concludes, everyone is to blame *except* me; she embarks on creating a world to suit her needs, a world that denies biological truths. That's a departure from reality. And the authorities, the eminent organizations with government funding, send the girl to Kate, saying, she's the one to help you through this.

Don't say I didn't warn you: Genderland is bewildering.

I want to be clear: my grievance is not with Kate Bornstein. She is free to be a "gender outlaw," as she calls herself, and spread her way-out beliefs—although I believe she'd be more effective if she cleaned up her language. My outrage is directed at the sex ed oligarchy for directing naïve, vulnerable kids to her preposterous, debased philosophy.

Kate is right: it is a wacky world. It's wacky for adolescents, who need stability, order, and limits, to be led into anarchy. It's wacky for kids striving to determine their identity to be schooled in an anti-identity philosophy. Adolescents yearn to consolidate their identity; Kate seeks to unravel it. They wish to stabilize their sense of self; "she" hopes to undermine it. Their goal is to solve the mystery of "Who am I?" and progress to adulthood; "she," well into middle age, is still wondering:

> The sadness that comes from being a freak is compounded by the fact that as gender outlaws....We leave one identity behind, and take up another... we change identities over and over again, searching for "the one that's going to work," or "the real me."...For nearly fifty years, I've been acquiring identities and abandoning them....I think it's identity itself I want to quit now.

Celebrate Who You Are?

There's another issue to consider, that of intellectual honesty. If there's one overarching rule of Genderland, it's this: don't let anyone tell you who you are. Especially not your parents. It's your right, kids are told, to make that decision. Celebrate who you are, whether the world likes it or not.

Sounds great, until you look closer. There's one group without that right. They know who they are—they're *certain*—but it doesn't matter.

Take, for example, the hypothetical case of Roberta. She feels trapped in the wrong body. Her sex and gender are not aligned. She wants bilateral mastectomies, testosterone shots, and other irreversible procedures for relief of her distress. Educators have compassion for Roberta's plight. Chromosomes don't matter, they say, it's Roberta's *sense of herself* that counts. She is to be called Robert, and her right to self-determination is respected. Even if she's only thirteen.

Now remember Hector, from the Circle of Men? He's attracted to members of the same sex, but it doesn't feel right. It's not who he really is. He chooses to struggle against the attraction, and work toward what feels genuine.

But Hector is told he's in denial. *You're just refusing to accept who you really are,* he is told. *You must recognize your true identity, and stop trying to change the unchangeable. Trust us, we know.* This is the proper response, say educators, even if Hector is forty years old.

Is this a bad dream? Will we wake up, like Alice did from her afternoon nap, and realize Genderland was just a curious, made-up adventure?

I'm afraid not. It's more likely we'll wake up and see Barbara Walters fawning over Thomas Beatie, the "man" having a second child. Or maybe not. Maybe we got used to seeing "him" the first time around. Is it still a big deal?

I think it is. Because Thomas's image—the goatee, the flat chest, and pregnant belly, looks us in the eye and declares: Hi there. You thought I was an impossibility, didn't you? Well, say good-bye to what you held as true. My existence creates a new reality.

Why do the sex education gurus choose to teach that "reality," based on John Money, over the hard science of sex differences: newborns who prefer looking at a face instead of a mobile; monkeys who play with trucks and red pots?

They cling to Money for the same reason they cling to Kinsey: they like his thinking—that society places undue restrictions on our freedom of sexual expression. This has come to mean the freedom to be male, female, or—as Kate would say—something else entirely. If that's the case, well, then anything goes. And that's a recipe for physical and emotional disaster for our kids.

At least one leading expert recognizes this, and has the courage to say so. Dr. Paul McHugh took over as chief psychiatrist at Johns Hopkins in 1975, remaining in that position for over twenty years. After initiating a study of men who had undergone sex reassignment, Dr. McHugh shut down Money's clinic, concluding that "sexual identity is mostly built into our constitution by the genes we inherit and the embryogenesis we undergo." Dr. McHugh writes: "We psychiatrists . . . would do better to concentrate on trying to fix their minds and not their genitalia."[92]

Science has confirmed that judgment. But so blindly devoted are these sex educators to radical beliefs, so zealous are they about "sexual freedom," that instead of heeding authorities such as McHugh, they embrace the ideals of people like "gender outlaw" Kate/Al, sending vulnerable teens to absorb her—or is it hir?—wacky convictions. Even the Mad Hatter would be scratching his head.

⚥

Conclusion

Sex Education for the Twenty-first Century

I T'S BEEN ALMOST FIFTY YEARS since we embarked on an adventure called sexuality education, all fired up about change and the new world it would bring: open, positive, and free. Where did it get us? From rare instances of teen infections to nine million new cases a year. From two bugs to two dozen. It got us to babies having babies, sixth graders on the pill,[1] teens with cervical cancer, and to HIV and AIDS.

Some new world, huh?

Yet the lessons for your kids are the same, as if nothing's changed since the sixties: you're sexual from cradle to grave. Be free to decide when, how, and with whom to get it on. Explore and experiment; take a walk on the wild side. It's a lifelong journey—"safe" travels!

You know that this philosophy can harm your kids, inside and out. Don't allow it to go unchallenged, permitting the sex crusaders to commandeer your authority. Make it clear that in your home, you see things differently. Grab the wheel, Mom and Dad. It's time for a U-turn.

What Parents Can Do

What can you do to optimize your child's chance for a life of healthy sexuality?

First, beware the "hicks versus Harvard" tactic. Don't be intimidated, because you *do* know what's best for your kids. If your instincts say, "No, not for my child," they're probably right. Follow them, not someone who happens to have a website or a bunch of diplomas. Diplomas represent years in graduate school, not wisdom.

Value your child's innocence. Protect her, as much as possible, from things she cannot grasp. She is not a miniature adult. She does not understand the world the same way you do.

Be "authoritative" parents with your teens, combining warmth and support with firm rules and high expectations. When you speak to your child, stay grounded in your love and common sense. Your opinions count more than you think. Tell him that sexuality is not a recreational activity, but an appetite. Healthy, of course, and wonderful, but like all appetites, only if restrained. He understands the benefits of self-discipline in many areas: sports, diet, drugs, and alcohol. Tell him sexuality is one more area—a major one—where his discipline will be well rewarded.

Teach your child that the highest goal in life is not the satisfaction of his urges. In your own lives, live by that value.

Many sex educators refer to "sex play," and use comics, cartoons, and slang to teach young people. But you want your child to know sex is a serious matter. A single act can change her life forever. While sexuality may, as educators insist, be "central" to being human, so are many other things that have no place in the life of an adolescent.

Remember that even if he's taking AP Math and Physics, your teen's brain is immature. There's an extreme makeover going on, and until the paint is dry and the fixtures secured, he could have poor judgment. Under "hot" conditions, he may rely on his "feeling"—not his "thinking"—brain. Monitor his activities, whereabouts, and friends. He's a work in progress, and you are his scaffolding, providing support and structure. He benefits from your rules and supervision when they come from care, not distrust.

By all means, find out what your child will be taught at school. This is a daunting task, but it can be done. Recognize that there is a difference between sex ed, and HIV/AIDS prevention, and that the school may need your consent for one but not the other. Ask to see the curriculum. Where does it come from, and who will be teaching? Will material such as pamphlets, condoms, or lists of recommended websites be distributed? Check them out ahead of your child.

Take note of material related to sexual orientation and gender. There is widespread confusion about these matters, and young people who turn to sex ed authorities may end up more perplexed, not less. They may seize upon faulty ideas that can be hard for parents to refute. Remind teens struggling with these issues of the vital importance of delaying sexual activity. Proceed thoughtfully, with patience and compassion.

While acknowledging it's not easily achieved, give your kids an ideal to strive toward. Tell them to delay sexual experiences until adulthood, and to try to keep their lifetime partners as close to one as possible. Tell them "exploring" is likely to be followed, sooner or later, by regret, while "waiting" has only benefits.

Emphasize that although certain beliefs and behaviors may be common, it's no indication they are healthy.

Is your teen in need of a strong dose of reality? Google "STD support," and read the posts together. Scary? Yes. Disgusting? You bet. Remind her that those characters on *Sex and the City* and *Grey's Anatomy* are fiction. In real life, Carrie Bradshaw would have herpes. In real life, Meredith would be worried about cervical cancer. In this century, you cannot have that many "partners" without paying a price, especially if you are female.

Your child's sex education must be grounded in biological truths. These are the indisputable findings from hard science that simply aren't up for debate—what this book is all about. Whether popular or not, they must form the foundation for sex education in the twenty-first century.

Ignoring these biological truths has done more than cause soaring rates of distress and disease: our youth cannot appreciate or experience the depth and power of genuine intimacy. They may understand the plumbing, but they do not grasp the big picture—that sexuality is like fire. Depending on the circumstances, fire can sustain or destroy. Therefore, you don't play with it.

Responsible adults desperately want to communicate this message. They want to articulate to young people what we've forever known, but has been lost in the madness: when sexuality is about fleeting urges and attractions, it is hazardous. When its place in our lives is exaggerated, it is destructive. But with the right person and at the proper time, it is transcendent and life-affirming. Those are truths our kids have the right to hear, and we an obligation to convey.

Acknowledgements

PEOPLE SAY WRITING A BOOK is like having a baby. If that's the case, this one was a high risk pregnancy complicated by prolonged labor and an emergency C-section.

My heartfelt thanks to everyone who helped. First, all the wonderful people at Eagle Publishing: Marji Ross, Karen Woodard, Harry Crocker, Kathleen Sweetapple, Sally Brock, John Lalor, Alex Novak, Jeanne Crotty, Christian Tappe, Mary Beth Baker, Emily Thiessen, Amanda Larsen, Amber Colleran, and Sekayi Brunson. Special recognition goes to my editor, Anneke Green, whose painstaking work and long hours are deeply appreciated.

Being a fellow at the Clare Booth Luce Policy Institute allowed me to take a break from practicing medicine, and to focus on research, writing, and speaking. I owe Michelle Easton and the other "Luce ladies"—in particular the multi-talented Jessica Cantelon and Kathleen McCann—gratitude for their generosity, creativity, enthusiasm, and warmth. Katie Collins was the ideal assistant—exceptionally bright, good natured, and principled. Katie, you've set the gold standard for any help I might have in the future.

"Questioning" is dedicated to the memory of Hector Roybal. Hector was a warrior and a leader of men. His life story continues to inspire me and countless others.

My work has benefitted from the research and writing of so many, including Joe MacIlhaney, LouAnn Brizendine, John Potterat, James Jones, John Colapinto, Anne Bernstein, Ruth Jacobs, Judith Reisman, Gerianne Alexander, Selma Freiberg, Jay Giedd, Laurence Steinberg, Ronald Dahl, Anna-Barbara Moscicki, Sylvia Ann Hewlett, Lisa M. Diamond, and Paul R. McHugh.

I also acknowledge the awesome work of the thousands of abstinence educators around the country working in small communities and on the national level to promote the healthiest choice for teens. Valerie Huber, Leslee Unruh, all the people at the Medical Institute for Sexual Health, and many others have devoted their lives to this cause.

I am beholden to Naomi Decter, who is brilliant, professional, and high-speed. Boy was I lucky to find you!

I'm also grateful to, in no particular order, Ashley Herzog, Leah Klein, Molly Resnick, Elizabeth Christy, Charles Paternina, Tim Flanigan, Sue Schmidt-Lackner, Victor Grossman, and Adina Rimmon. Thank you Tova Pollen for your friendship and hospitality, in good times and bad. The Bendik-Rimmon household is my favorite place to eat, drink, debate, and be merry. Angela Villatoro makes my life easier.

Tanya, you've been so forgiving about my piles of work all over the place. Now we can use the dining room table for eating. You—along with Shuki, Chasida, and Ruchama, of course—are what life is all about.

Notes

Preface

1. "Remembering Dr. Judith Reisman on the One Year Anniversary of Her Death," The Reisman Institute, https://www.thereismaninstitute.org/home.

Introduction

1. I pointed out this refers only to the minority of lesbians who have never been sexually active with males.
2. H. Trottier and F. L. Franco, "The epidemiology of genital human papillomavirus infection." Vaccine 24, Suppl 1 (March 2006): S4–15.
3. "Managing HPV: A New Era in Patient Care," Association of Reproductive Health Professionals (January 2009) http://www.arhp.org/publications-and-resources/quick-reference-guide-for-clinicians/managing-hpv.
4. Press release, 2008 National STD Prevention Conference, March 11, 2008; available online at: http://www.cdc.gov/stdconference/2008/media/release-11march2008.htm.
5. Dr. John Douglas, in an interview on The Early Show, CBS News, March 12, 2008.
6. Statement of SIECUS President Joseph DiNorcia Jr. on New Data on Teen STD Rates, www.siecus.org/media/press/press0166.html.
7. Victoria Stagg Elliott, "Plans sought to curb teen girls' high STD rate," amednews.com, April 14, 2008; available online at: http://www.ama-assn.org/amednews/2008/04/14/hlsa0414.htm.
8. "Teen Talk: Pregnancy," Planned Parenthood; available online at: http://www.teenwire.com/interactive/movies/do-070213-pregnancy.php.
9. "Fast Facts: S&M," gURL.com; available online at: http://www.gurl.com/findout/fastfacts/articles/0,,605386_708158,00.html.

10.   Esther Drill, Heather McDonald, and Rebecca Odes, *Deal With It! A whole new approach to your body, brain, and life as a gURL* (New York: Pocket Books, 1999), 87–90.
11.   For example, David Parker, see www.massresistance.org.
12.   Patricia Barthalow Koch, quoting M. Greene, *Landscapes of Learning* (New York: Teachers College Press, 1978) in "Integrating Cognitive, Affective, and Behavioral Approaches into Learning Experiences for Sexuality Education," in James T. Sears, ed., *Sexuality and the Curriculum: The Politics and Practices of Sexuality Education* (New York: Teachers College Press, 1992), 255.
13.   SIECUS, "Guidelines for Comprehensive Sexuality Education," touts itself as providing "an opportunity for young people to question, explore and assess their own and their community's attitudes about society, gender, and sexuality," 19; available online at: http://www.siecus.org/_data/global/images/guidelines.pdf.
14.   See David Elkind, *The Hurried Child: Growing Up Too Fast Too Soon* (Reading, MA: Addison-Wesley, 1988).
15.   Patricia Barthalow Koch , "Integrating Cognitive, Affective, and Behavioral Approaches Into Learning Experiences for Sexuality Education," chapter in James T. Sears, ed., *Sexuality and the Curriculum: The Politics and Practices of Sexuality Education* (New York: Teachers College Press, 1992), 258.
16.   "Growth and Development, Ages Four to Five—What Parents Need to Know," Advocates for Youth; available online at: http://www.advocatesforyouth.org/storage/advfy/documents/4_5.pdf.
17.   SIECUS, "Guidelines for Comprehensive Sexuality Education," 3rd edition, 25; available online at: http://www.siecus.org/_data/global/images/guidelines.pdf..
18.   Planned Parenthood, "Human Sexuality—What Children Need to Know and When," October 29, 2008; available online at: http://www.plannedparenthood.org/parents/human-sexuality-what-children-need-know-when-they-need-know-it-4421.htm.
19.   Early Childhood Sexuality Education Task Force, *Right From the Start: Guidelines for Sexuality Issues, Birth to Five Years* (SIECUS, 1998), 53; available online at: http://img.thebody.com/siecus/pdfs/RightFromTheStart.pdf.
20.   Planned Parenthood, "Human Sexuality—What Children Need to Know and When," October 29, 2008; available online at: http://www.plannedparenthood.org/parents/human-sexuality-what-children-need-know-when-they-need-know-it-4421.htm.
21.   "I want to buy a vibrator but ..." Go Ask Alice! September 8, 2000; available online at: http://www.goaskalice.columbia.edu/1757.html
22.   "Menage a Trois?" Go Ask Alice! July 5, 2002; available online at: http://www.goaskalice.columbia.edu/2184.html.
23.   "S/M Role-Playing," Go Ask Alice! May 12, 1995; available online at: http://www.goaskalice.columbia.edu/0646.html.

24. One recent study of adult women found that the probabilities of contraceptive failure for withdrawal (18 percent) and condom (17 percent) are similar: Kathryn Kost, Susheela Singh, Barbara Vaughan, James Trussell, and Akinrinola Bankole, "Estimates of contraceptive failure from the 2002 National Survey of Family Growth," *Contraception* 77, no.1 (January 2008): 10–21. Guttmacher Institute, "Get 'In the Know': Questions about Pregnancy, Contraception and Abortion," reports the percentage of women who will become pregnant in their first year of use of male condoms is 2 percent for "perfect use" and 15 percent for "typical use." They also report that of women who had an abortion following proper condom use, 42 percent, had said it slipped out of place. Available online at: http://www.guttmacher.org/in-the-know/prevention.html. Also see Rachel K. Jones, Jacqueline E. Darroch, and Stanley K. Henshaw, "Contraceptive Use Among U.S. Women Having Abortions in 2000-2001," *Perspectives on Sexual and Reproductive Health* 34, no.6 (2002): 294–303; on inconsistent condom use in adults, see Bruce Jancin, "Despite Guidelines, U.S. Condom Use Still Low," *Clinical Psychiatry News* (January 2004): 66; and in college students, see "American College Health Association—National College Health Assessment (ACHA-NCHA) Spring 2004 Reference Group Data Report," *Journal of American College Health* 54, no.4 (2004): 207.

    On limited efficiency of condoms in preventing HPV transmission: "Using condoms ('rubbers') can lower the chance of HPV infection, but they cannot completely prevent infection," in American Cancer Association, "Can Penile Cancer Be Prevented?" available online at: http://www.cancer.org/docroot/CRI/content/CRI_2_4_2X_Can_penile_cancer_be_prevented_35.a sp?sitearea=; Lisa A. Manhart and Laura A. Koutsky, "Do Condoms Prevent Genital HPV Infection, External Genital Warts, or Cervical Neoplasia?" *Sexually Transmitted Diseases* 29, no.11 (2002): 725–35; Rachel L. Winer et al, "Genital Human Papillomavirus Infection: Incidence and Risk Factors in a Cohort of Female University Students," *American Journal of Epidemiology* 157, no.3 (2003): 218–26.

25. Joseph J. Sabia and Daniel I. Rees, "The effect of adolescent virginity status on psychological well-being," *Journal of Health Economics* 27, no.5 (2008): 1368–81.

26. Debra Haffner, "Telling Teens Not to French Kiss," RH Reality Check, September 13, 2006; available online at: http://www.rhrealitycheck.org//blog/2006/09/12/telling-teens-not-to-french-kiss (Haffner, in her book for parents, *Beyond the Big Talk: Every Parent's Guide to Raising Sexually Healthy Teens—from middle school to high school and beyond* (New Market Press 2001) recommends these sites to teens: goaskalice.com, positive.org, gURL.com, sexetc.org, teenwire.org (now Teen Talk)).

27. This is not to say girls should not be vaccinated.

28. (Statistics based on 9 million new infections a year in persons between the ages of 15 and 24.) Guttmacher Institute, "Facts on Sexually Transmitted

Diseases in the United States," August 2006; available online at: www. guttmacher.org/pubs/fb_sti.html.

29.   "State of the Nation 2005: Challenges Facing STD Prevention in Youth," American Social Health Association; available online at: www.ashastd. org/pdfs/ASHA_05.final.pdf.

30.   Laura T. Coffey, "Survey: Unprotected sex common among teens," msnbc.com Today, November 14, 2008; available online at: http://today. msnbc.msn.com/id/27706917/from/ET/.pdf.

31.   "State of the Nation 2005: Challenges Facing STD Prevention in Youth," American Social Health Association; available online at: www. ashastd.org/pdfs/ASHA_05.final.pdf.

Chapter 1

1.   Clearly these sites fill a need, but I had a mixed reaction to the discovery of online "advice" for adolescents. As a child and adolescent psychiatrist, I've spent years helping kids like these. While there are benefits to quick and confidential access to an informed adult, there are also hazards.

2.   This question appeared at www.gURL.com

3.   Question and answer posted on Scarleteen: Sex ed for the real world; http://www.scarleteen.com/article/advice/is_it_normal_for_girls_to_experi ment_with_sex_together_when_theyre_not_lesbian.

4.   "Working the Kinks Out," www.scarleteen.com/article/sexuality/working_the_kinks_out.

5.   According to the homepage of www.scarleteen.com.

6.   Heather also provides teens with objectionable material: "Want to learn how to flirt? Or talk dirty? Or go Tantric? The Society for Human Sexuality includes exercises to teach you how, as well as a concise guide to safer sex, a comprehensive and fully up-to-date annotated bibliography of books relevant to sexuality and/or sex-positive culture, and a guide to finding local sex-positive community resources. www.sexuality.org (the site warns that it is intended for adults).

7.   www.sexuality.org (the site warns that it is intended for adults).

8.   See "DASH Funded Nongovernmental Organization (NGO) Activities," http://www.cdc.gov/DASH/program_mgt/docs_pdfs/ngo_activity_matrix.doc.

9.   SIECUS Leadership and Staff, http://www.siecus.org/index.cfm?fuseaction= Page.viewPage&pageId=490&parentID=472.

10.   "Frequently Asked Questions," available at: http://www.siecus.org/index.cfm? fuseaction=Page.ViewPage&PageID=529

11.   "This Is Planned Parenthood," http://www.ppaction.org/ppvotes/08_ issues.html.

12.   Report available at: http://www.plannedparenthood.org/ppcw/files/ ColumbiaWillamette/AR_07-08_web.pdf.

13.   "Human Sexuality—What Children Need to Know and When," Planned Parenthood, October 29, 2008; available online at: http://www.planned-

parenthood.org/parents/human-sexuality-what-children-need-know-when-they-need-know-it-4421.htm.

14. "Advocates for Youth: Historical Overview," http://www.advocatesforyouth. org/index.php?option=com_content&task=view&id=15&Itemid=44

15. "Sexual Development through the Life Cycle," The Media Project (adapted from Advocates for Youth, *Life Planning Education*, 1995), http://www.the-mediaproject.com/facts/development/lifecycle.htm.

Every parent knows that babies and young children explore their bodies, and are capable of some response to genital stimulation. At the same time, they are cognitively, emotionally, and physically immature and therefore incapable of understanding, on any level whatsoever, what we adults call sexuality. Erections are a physiological response to various conditions, and children may touch their genitals for a number of reasons, not only to experience pleasurable sensations. In fact frequent touching of genitals in childhood is often a sign of anxiety. –MG

16. Planned Parenthood and Columbia University have placed their sites, Teen Talk and Go Ask Alice, on sites like Facebook, MySpace, and Twitter, where even the youngest teens spend large chunks of their time.

17. James H. Jones, *Alfred C. Kinsey: A Public/Private Life* (New York: W. W. Norton & Co., 1997), 512 and 519.

18. "Kinsey Report, 50 Years Later," NPR Politics and Society, November 9, 2004; available online at: http://www.npr.org/templates/story/story. php?storyId=4161159

19. James H. Jones, *Alfred C. Kinsey*, 610.

20. Ibid., 610, reference: "Author's interview with Anon.A, Dec 15, 1987, 83; author's interview with Anon B, Feb 17, 1988, 95."

21. James H. Jones, *Alfred C. Kinsey*, 739.

22. Ibid., 603.

23. Ibid., 609.

24. Why is there no consideration of his mental illness in recent books on the sex ed conflict, like Moran's and Irvine's?

25. Anything outside of sexual intercourse within marriage.

26. "5,940 Women," *TIME* Magazine, August 24, 1953; available online at: http://www.time.com/time/magazine/article/0,9171,818752,00.html.

27. Margaret Mead, "An Anthropologist Looks at the Report," in *Problems of Sexual Behavior* (New York: American Social Hygiene Association, 1948), from James H. Jones, *Alfred C. Kinsey*, 579.

28. Lawrence S. Kubie, M.D., "Psychiatric Implications of the Kinsey Report," *Psychosomatic Medicine* 10, no.2 (1948): 97; available online at: http://www.psychosomaticmedicine.org/cgi/content/abstract/10/2/95.

29. "Manners & Morals", *TIME*, March 1, 1948. 16.

30. Pomeroy admitted under oath to seeking funds from the sex industry to produce his own child pornography (Campbell District Court, *Commonwealth of Kentucky vs. Happy Day, Inc., et al* 1980, 803).

31. SIECUS Report, May–July 1982, 6: the Kinsey Institute omitted one
     major field: sex ed. "[I]t seemed appropriate, not only to the Institute but
     to its major funding source, the NIMH, to leave this area for SIECUS to
     fulfill."

32. Hefner continued to fund it and other programs that would develop cur-
     ricula for changing the sexual attitudes of young men and women.

33. Christie Hefner, introduction to Earl E. Shelp, ed., *Sex, Medicine, Ethics*, Vol.
     2, *Ethical Viewpoints in Transition*, (Boston: D. Reidel Publishing Co., 1987).

34. Janice M. Irvine, *Talk About Sex: The Battles over Sex Education in the United
     States* (CA: University of California Press, 2002), 31.

35. Jeffrey P. Moran, *Teaching Sex: The Shaping of Adolescence in the 2oth Cen-
     tury* (Boston: Harvard University Press, 2000), 161.

36. Richard Stiller, *The Love Bugs: A National History of the Venereal Diseases*
     (New York: Thomas Nelson, 1974).

37. Larry Brilliant, "The Age of Pandemics," *Wall Street Journal*, May 2–3,
     2009, W1; available online at: http://online.wsj.com/article/
     SB124121965740478983.html.

38. Genital herpes and warts existed, but their incidence was low. Chlamydia
     was not reportable until 1984. HIV was not yet on the scene.

39. Roger W. Libby, introduction to a volume in which Kirkendall was inter-
     viewed: *Alternative Lifestyles* 2, no.1 (February 1979): 5.

40. Lester Kirkendall, *A New Bill of Sexual Rights and Responsibilities* (New
     York: Prometheus Books, 1976).

41. Janice M. Irvine, *Talk About Sex*, 26.

42. "Happy Birthday, Dr. Kinsey," Planned Parenthood, http://www.planned-
     parenthood.org/issues-action/other/articles/happy-birthday-dr-kinsey-
     21171.htm.

43. "Who We Are," Planned Parenthood, http://www.plannedparenthood.
     org/about-us/who-we-are-4648.htm.

44. In high school, the same rationale can be used to justify including explicit
     porn on the required reading list. See for example: Pete Winn, "High
     School Offers Homosexual Porn, Parents Complain," CNSNews.com,
     March 10, 2008.

45. Evonne Hedgepeth and Joan Helmich, *Teaching About Sexuality and HIV:
     Principles and Methods for Effective Education* (New York: New York Uni-
     versity Press, 1996), 31.

46. Barbara Defoe Whitehead, "The Failure of Sex Education," *The Atlantic
     Monthly*, 274.n4 (Oct 1994)

47. SIECUS, *Families Are Talking* 2, no.2 (2003).

48. Ibid.

49. "How to Talk with Your Children About Sex," http://www.plannedparent-
     hood.org/parents/how-talk-your-child-about-sex-4422.htm.

50. Ibid.

51. "Human Sexuality—What Children Need to Know and When," http://www.plannedparenthood.org/health-topics/parents/human-sexuality-what-children-need-know-when-they-need-know-it-4421.htm.

52. Barbara Huberman, RN, Med, "Growth and Development, Ages Six to Eight—What You Need to Know," Advocates for Youth, 2002; at The Media Project, http://www.themediaproject.com/facts/development/6_8.htm.

53. "Human Sexuality—What Children Need to Know and When," http://www.plannedparenthood.org/parents/human-sexuality-what-children-need-know-when-they-need-know-it-4421.htm.

54. "Growth and Development, Ages Six to Eight—What Parents Need to Know," http://www.advocatesforyouth.org/index.php?option=com_content&task=view&id=154&Itemid=206.

55. "How to Talk With Your Children About Sex," http://www.plannedparenthood.org/parents/how-talk-your-child-about-sex-4422.htm.

56. Selma H. Fraiberg, *The Magic Years: Understanding and Handling the Problems of Early Childhood* (New York: Charles Scribner's Sons, 1959).

57. Calvin A. Colarusso, *Child and Adult Development: A Psychoanalytic Introduction for Clinicians* (New York: Plenum Press, 1992).

58. See Anne C. Bernstein, *Flight of the Stork: What Children Think (and When) about Sex and Family Building* (Indianapolis, IN: Perspectives Press, 1994).

59. Ibid., 29

60. "How to Talk with Your Children About Sex," http://www.plannedparenthood.org/parents/how-talk-your-child-about-sex-4422.htm.

61. Ronald F. Moglia and Jon Knowles, *A Family Resource on Sex and Sexuality* (New York: Three Rivers Press, 1997), 12–15.

62. "Wardell Pomeroy: Kinsey Coauthor Speaks Out" *Chic Magazine*, February 1981.

63. George Leonard (1983) *The End of Sex*, JP Tarcher, Inc. Los Angeles, p 89.

64. *SIECUS Newsletter* Vol 7, No 4, April 1972

65. Online program for 2008 Annual Meeting of The Society for the Scientific Study of Sexuality (SSSS), San Juan, Peurto Rico November 5-9, 2008, available at http://www.sexscience.org.

66. Barbara Defoe Whitehead, "The Failure of Sex Education," *The Atlantic Monthly*, 274.n4 (Oct 1994)

Chapter 2

1. All the stories in this book are true. In order to protect the confidentiality of my patients, I've changed their names and some details about their lives.

2. Sexuality Information and Education Council for the United States (SIECUS), *Guidelines for Comprehensive Sexuality Education* (2004), http://www.siecus.org/pubs/guidelines/guidelines.pdf.

3. Some readers might ask why I focus only on Kayla. What about David? I focus on Kayla because in over twenty years of psychiatric work, I have yet

to see a man hurting or confused from casual sexual encounters. When a boy or man experiences pain within a relationship, he describes a serious situation in which he has invested time and emotion.

4.   Sexuality Information and Education Council for the United States (SIECUS), *Guidelines for Comprehensive Sexuality Education* (2004), http://www.siecus.org/pubs/guidelines/guidelines.pdf.

5.   Ibid., 50.

6.   Ibid., 20.

7.   Ibid., 71.

8.   A belief is not a stereotype.

9.   Estrogen, progesterone, and oxytocin.

10. All except her mature red blood cells.

11. Louann Brizendine, *The Female Brain* (New York: Random House, 2006), 3.

12. George Preti, Charles J. Wysocki, Kurt T. Barnhart, Steven J. Sondheimer, James J. Leyden, "Male Axillary Extracts Contain Pheromones that Affect Pulsatile Secretion of Luteinizing Hormone and Mood in Women Recipients," *Biology of Reproduction* 68 (2003): 2107–13.

13. Personal communication with George Preti, Ph.D. of the Monell Chemical Senses Center and the Department of Dermatology, University of Pennsylvania School of Medicine, April 7, 2008.

14. Menstrual synchrony between women living in close quarters is thought to occur via a similar mechanism. The original study was by M. J. Russell, et al, "Olfactory Influences on the human menstrual cycle," *Pharmacology, biochemistry, and behavior* 13, no.5 (November 1980): 737–38.

15. Starting in adolescence, female sensitivity to this male pheromone is much higher than male. See Thomas Hummel, Franziska Krone, Johan N. Lundstrom, Oliver Bartsch, "Androstadienone odor thresholds in adolescents," *Hormones and Behavior* 47, no.3 (March 2005): 306–10.

16. Suma Jacob and Martha K. McClintock, "Psychological state and mood effects of steroidal chemosignals in women and men," *Hormones and Behavior* 37, no.1 (February 2000): 57–78.

17. Brizendine, *The Female Brain*, 13–16.

18. J. Cameron, "Interrelationships between hormones, behavior and affect during adolescence: understanding hormonal, physical, and brain changes occurring in association with pubertal activation of the reproductive axis," *Annals New York Academy of Sciences* 1021 (2004):1-22.

19. Brizendine, *The Female Brain*, 38.

20. Ibid., 39.

21. Ibid., 48.

22. Ibid., 38.

23. Ibid., 68.

24. Ibid., 3.

25. Ibid., 2.

26. Ibid., preface.

27.   Carol Milano, "The physiological and the psychological: how women and men are different," *Yale Medicine* 42, no.2 (Winter 2008): 41–42.

28.   I have often been asked why I focus on the actions of oxytocin in young women. This hormone exists in men too, in addition to the hormone vasopressin, which differs by only one amino acid in its structure, and plays a role in the formation of social bonds in males. These are the reasons: estrogen is critical to oxytocin control, and it increases production and the number of receptors in the brain. In certain areas, the increase can be rapid (72 hours) and profound (300 percent increase in binding). See Thomas R. Insel, "A Neurobiological Basis of Social Attachment," *American Journal of Psychiatry* 154, no.6 (June 1997): 731.   Women appear to be more sensitive to oxytocin, (see Grewen, 2005, 537) and they have more of it. Men have more vasopressin, but young men also have raging levels of testosterone, which Drives lust, not attachment. The saturation of the female brain with estrogen and oxytocin, especially at mid-cycle, creates a neurochemical environment ripe for intense interpersonal bonding. There does not appear to be a corresponding situation for men. Everyday observations and common sense also support this position; in fact, a study of 16,288 people across ten major world regions, examining the desire for sexual variety and the likelihood of consenting to sex quickly, demonstrated "universal sex differences" (David P. Schmitt, "Universal Sex Differences in the Desire for Sexual Variety: Tests from 52 Nations, 6 Continents, and 13 Islands," *Journal of Personality and Social Psychology* 85, no.1 (2003): 85–104).

29.   Thomas R. Insel, "A Neurobiological Basis of Social Attachment," *American Journal of Psychiatry* 154, no.6 (June 1997): 726–35.

30.   Ibid., 727.

31.   Ibid., 728.

32.   Our knowledge of the actions of vasopressin in the brains of human males is limited. In both humans and voles, there is a gene that controls the number and type of vasopressin receptors in the brain. Having more of a particular receptor means higher sensitivity to the pair-bonding effects of the hormone. So scientists speculate that where a human male's behaviors fall on the spectrum of totally polygamist to totally monogamous may be somewhat predetermined and passed down genetically (Louann Brizendine, *The Female Brain*, 73–74).

33.   Meissner corpuscles.

34.   John P. Aggleton and Andrew W. Young, "The enigma of the amygdala: on its contribution to human emotion." In R. D. Lane and L. Nadel, eds., *Cognitive Neuroscience of Emotion* (New York: Oxford University Press, 2000); R. Adolps, Peter Kirsch, et al, "Oxytocin Modulates Neural Circuitry for Social Cognition and Fear in Humans," *The Journal of Neuroscience* 24, no.49 (December 2005): 11489–493; R. Adolphs, D. Tranel, A. R. Damasio, "The human amygdala in social judgment," *Nature* 393 (4 June 1998): 470–74.

35.   Adam J. Guastella, Philip B. Mitchell, and Mark R. Dadds, "Oxytocin Increases Gaze to the Eye Region of Human Faces," *Biological Psychiatry* 63, no.1 (January 2008): 3–5.

36.   The same thing happens in maternal love. See Andreas Bartels and Semir Zeki, "The neural correlates of maternal and romantic love," *NeuroImage* 21, no.3 (March 2004): 1155–66.

37.   Michael Kosfeld, Marcus Heinrichs, Paul J. Zac, Urs Fischbacher, and Ernest Fehr, "Oxytocin increases trust in humans," *Nature* 435 (2 June 2005): 673.

38.   Science has confirmed the existence of "beer goggles"—when a person seems more attractive to you after you've had a few drinks. In a British study, eighty college students rated photos of unfamiliar faces of men and women their age; alcohol consumption significantly raised the scores given to photos of the opposite sex. Drinking affects the nucleus accumbens, the area of the brain used to determine facial attractiveness. (Barry T. Jones et al, "Alcohol consumption increases attractiveness ratings of opposite-sex faces: a possible third route to risky sex," *Addiction* 98 (2003): 1069–75.

39.   Reuters, "'Trust me' says cuddle hormone," ABC News Online (2 June 2005), http://www.abc.net.au/news/newsitems/200506/s1382513.htm.

40.   Associated Press, "Scientists study 'trust in a bottle,'" MSNBC Mental Health, June 1, 2005; available at: http://www.msnbc.msn.com/id/8059069/.

41.   Planned Parenthood, SIECUS, Advocates for Youth.

42.   Ruth Bell's book mentions it in context of abortion.

43.   "The question of 'What does it mean?'—in other words what does a particular sex act signify and communicate—is centrally important to the female sexual experience, before, during, and after. For men, by contrast, the different possible meanings matter less, and sex might often be a perfectly fine experience even if it hardly means anything at all." (R. F. Baumeister, "Gender Differences in Erotic Plasticity: The Female Sex Drive as Socially Flexible and Responsive," *Psychological Bulletin* 126, no.3 (2000): 371).

44.   A phrase borrowed from Institute for American Values' *Hardwired to Connect: The New Scientific Case for Authoritative Communities*, 2003.

45.   SIECUS, *Guidelines*, 54; available at: http://www.siecus.org/pubs/guidelines/guidelines.pdf.

46.   David P. Schmitt, "Universal Sex Differences in the Desire for Sexual Variety: Tests from 52 Nations, 6 Continents, and 13 Islands," *Journal of Personality and Social Psychology* 85, no.1 (July 2003): 85-104.

47.   Johan N. Lundstrom, Miguel Goncalves, Francisco Esteves, and Mats J. Olsson, "Psychological effects of subthreshold exposure to the putative human pheromone 416-androstadien-3-one," *Hormones and Behavior* 44, no.5 (December 2003): 395–401.

48.   Aron Weller, "Human pheromones: Communication through body odour," *Nature* 392 (12 March 1998): 126–27.

49.   The vomero-nasal organ.

50. Caroline M. Larsen, Ilona C. Kokay, and David R. Grattan, "Male pheromones initiate prolactin-induced neurogenesis and advance maternal behavior in female mice," *Hormones and Behavior* 53, no.4 (April 2008): 509–17.

51. H. Gelez and C. Fabre-Nys, "The 'male effect' in sheep and goats: a review of the respective roles of the two olfactory systems," *Hormones and Behavior* 46, no.3 (September 2004): 257-71.

52. M. T. Mendonca and D. Crews, "Control of Attractivity and Receptivity in Female Red-Sided Garter Snakes," *Hormones and Behavior* 40, no.1 (August 2001): 43–50.

53. Peter W. Sorensen, Norman E. Stacey, and Katherine J. Chamberlain, "Differing behavioral and endocrinological effects of two female sex pheromones on male goldfish," *Hormones and Behavior* 23, no.3 (1989): 317–32.

54. Christopher A. Pearl, Misty Cervantes, Monica Chan, Uyen Ho, Rane Shoji, and Eric O. Thomas, "Evidence for a Mate-Attracting Chemosignal in the Dwarf African Clawed Frog Hymenochirus," *Hormones and Behavior* 38, no.1 (August 2000): 67–74.

55. Bruce Alexander Schulte, Elizabeth Watson Freeman, Thomas Elton Goodwin, Julie Hollister-Smith, and L. Elizabeth Little Rasmussen, "Honest signaling through chemicals by elephants with applications for care and conservation," *Applied Animal Behaviour Science* 102, nos.3-4 (February 2007): 344–63.

56. Kathleen Stern and Martha K. McClintock, "Regulation of ovulation by human pheromones," *Nature* 392 (12 March 1998): 177–79.

57. Martha K. McClintock, Susan Bullivant, Suma Jacob, Natasha Spencer, Bethanne Zelano, and Carole Ober, "Human Body Scents: Conscious Perceptions and Biological Effects," *Chemical Senses* 30, suppl. 1 (2005): I135–I137.

58. Martha K. McClintock, "Pheromones, Odors, and Vanna: The Neuroendocrinology of Social Chemosignals in Humans and Animals," in *Hormones, Brain and Behavior*, Vol.1, ed. D. W. Pfaff (Academic Press, 2002), 797–870.

59. H. Varendi and R. H. Porter, "Breast odour as the only maternal stimulus elicits crawling towards the odour source," *Acta Paediaticar* 90, no.4 (2001): 372–75.

60. Bruce J. Ellis, "Timing of Pubertal Maturation in Girls: An Integrated Life History Approach," *Psychological Bulletin* 130, no.6 (Nov 2004): 920–58.

61. Kerstin Uvnas Moberg, *The Oxytocin Factor: Tapping the Hormone of Calm, Love, and Healing* (New York: Da Capo Press, 2003).

Chapter 3

1. Zogby International, "2004 Survey on Parental Opinions of Character or Relationship-based Abstinence Education vs. Comprehensive (or Abstinence-First, Then Condoms) Sex Education," January 28, 2004. Retrieved on 4/28/2008 from www.citizenlink.org.

2.   Margo Adler, Wade F. Horn, and James Wagoner, "Abstinence-Only Edu-
      cation," Justice Talking, July 9, 2007. Downloaded from http://www.
      justicetalking.org/ShowPage.aspx?ShowID=426.

3.   Perhaps the interviewer thought she was being balanced by also having on
      the executive director of the National Abstinence Education Association,
      Valerie Huber.

4.   "Young people explore their sexuality as part of a process of achieving sex-
      ual maturity; adolescents are capable of expressing their sexuality in
      healthy, responsible ways." See for example: "We Believe," Planned Par-
      enthood of Indiana, http://www.ppin.org/values.aspx.

5.   Debra W. Haffner, "Sexual Health for America's Adolescents," Journal of
      School Health 66, no. 4 (1998): 151–2.   This report was a statement of
      the National Commission on Adolescent Sexual Health, consisting of 21 of
      the nation's leading medical, psychological, education, and youth-serving
      professionals. The Commission's report was based on a Consensus State-
      ment on Adolescent Sexual Health, "endorsed by more than 50 national
      organizations."

6.   "The Commission felt strongly that intercourse is developmentally disad-
      vantageous for the youngest adolescents because they do not have the cog-
      nitive or emotional maturity for involvement in intimate sexual behaviors,
      especially intercourse."

7.   "Health Education: Sex—safer and satisfying," Planned Parenthood, avail-
      able at: http://www.pposbc.org/education/safeSex.asp.

8.   "Pro sex," available at: http://www.positive.org/JustSayYes/prosex.html.

9.   Similar guidance is found on www.GoAskAlice.com, www.positive.org,
      www.iwannaknow.org, www.scarleteen.com, and many other resources.

10.   Elisa Klein, "Am I Ready?" Planned Parenthood; available at:
      http://www.plannedparenthood.org/teen-talk/sex-masturbation/teens-vir-
      ginity/am-ready-25396.htm

11.   Most girls feel they were too young at time of first intercourse (see Susan
      Rosenthal et al, "Heterosexual Romantic Relationships and Sexual Behav-
      iors of Young Adolescent Girls," Journal of Adolescent Health 21
      (1997):238–43.)

12.   In a Planned Parenthood classroom activity for young adults, students
      examine the ways they would feel comfortable being intimate, and where
      they would draw the line. Possible activities to suggest to students include:
      skinny dipping, sleeping together without sex, showering, and massage
      (www.plannedparenthood.org/resources/lesson-plans/wheres-your-
      line.htm).

13.   "Q & A with Dr. Cullins," available at http://www.plannedparenthood.
      org/health-topics/ask-dr-cullins-6602.htm

14.   "Ask Dr. Cullins: Birth Control," http://www.plannedparenthood.
      org/health-topics/ask-dr-cullins/ask-dr-cullins-birth-control-5472.htm.

Q: My daughter is 12. I've talked with her about menstruation and sex. She hasn't started her period yet. Should I take her to my gynecologist for an exam when she starts? If not, what age should she go? Is it appropriate for me to start her on some type of birth control when she starts having her period? I had her at the age of 16, and I'm scared to death of her going through the same thing!

A: Gynecological exams are not necessary as soon as a young woman starts having her period. We now recommend that young women start having pelvic exams with Pap tests within three years of starting vaginal intercourse. If a young woman has not had first vaginal intercourse by age 21, then she should have a pelvic exam when she becomes 21—even though she has not had vaginal intercourse. Of course, gynecologic visits are a very good idea if sexual or reproductive health concerns or problems arise earlier than within three years of starting vaginal intercourse or age 21.

Young women should be counseled about their birth control options before they become sexually active. They may want to consider taking regular, ongoing, highly effective hormonal prescription methods before beginning vaginal intercourse because of the health benefits of some methods. After they have been used for a few months, combined hormone methods such as the pill and the patch offer health benefits, including lighter periods, less bleeding during periods, less pain with periods, more regular periods, and reduced acne. Combined hormone methods also offer advanced protection against pregnancy as a woman reaches the point in her life when she decides to have vaginal intercourse.

When it comes to sexual and reproductive health, young women are often more comfortable with health care providers who are not also their parent's providers. Even young women who talk with their parents about sex and sexuality may be more trusting and confident with their own providers. Ask your daughter whether she wants her own personal clinician—a clinician different from her pediatrician, your family-medicine doctor or nurse practitioner, or your gynecologist—to take care of her now that she is older. Respect whatever decision she makes, and help her to find a caring provider if she chooses to change providers. Regardless of the provider they choose, young people should be encouraged to have their visits in private—by themselves. They should also be given every assurance that their confidences will be respected.

15. Stedman's Online Medical Dictionary, http://www.stedmans.com/section.cfm/45.

16. Society for Adolescent Medicine, "Guidelines for Adolescent Health Research: A Position Paper of the Society for Adolescent Medicine," *Journal of Adolescent Health* 33 (2003): 396–409. Available from http://www.adolescenthealth.org/PositionPaper_Guidelines_for_Adolescent_Health_Research.pdf.

17. World Health Organization, "Approach to adolescents," http://www.un. org.in/Jinit/who.pdf.

18. Robert E. Rector and Kirk A. Johnson, Ph.D., "Teenage Sexual Abstinence and Academic Achievement"; available online at: http://www.heritage.org/Research/Welfare/upload/84576_1.pdf.

19. Robert E. Rector, Kirk A. Johnson, Ph.D., Lauren R. Noyes, and Shannan Martin, "The Harmful Effects of Early Sexual Activity and Multiple Sexual Partners Among Women: A Book of Charts"; available online at: http://www.heritage.org/Research/Family/upload/44695_2.pdf.

20. In adult women using hormonal contraceptives, the probability of failure in the first 12 months is 7 percent (injectable) and 9 percent (oral). (Kathryn Kost et al, "Estimates of contraceptive failure from the 2002 National Survey of Family Growth," *Contraception* 77 (2008): 10–21); typical use by *adult* women of oral contraceptives results in pregnancy in 8 percent of them within the first year (www.guttmacher.org/in-the-know/prevention.html).

21. Planned Parenthood, "About Us," http://www.plannedparenthood.org/about-us/about-us-90.htm.

22. Planned Parenthood, "Who We Are," http://www.plannedparenthood.org/about-us/who-we-are-4648.htm.

23. Elise DeVore and Kenneth R. Ginsburg, "The protective effects of good parenting on adolescents," *Current Opinion in Pediatrics* 17, no.4 (August 2005): 460–65.

24. Most of this material is from DeVore and Ginsburg, 2005.

25. If the girl is out of control and nothing adults do has any impact, the answer is still not birth control; it's crisis intervention by a team of mental health professionals.

26. Laurence Steinberg, Susie D. Lamborn, Sanford M. Dornbusch, and Nancy Darling, "Impact of Parenting Practices on Adolescent Achievement: Authoritative Parenting, School Involvement, and Encouragement to Succeed," *Child Development* 63 (1992):1266–81; Laurence Steinberg, "We Know Some Things: Parent-Adolescent Relationships in Retrospect and Prospect," *Journal of Research on Adolescence* 11, no.1 (2001): 1–19.

27. While this is unlikely to be the case for this girl, the information may be relevant for siblings. This is general information that every parent should have.

28. Under the age of 17.

29. Before she turned 5. Bruce J. Ellis, John E. Bates, Kenneth A. Dodge, David M. Fergusson, L. John Horwood, Gregory S. Pettit, and Lianne Woodward, "Does Father Absence Place Daughters at Special Risk for Early Sexual Activity and Teenage Pregnancy?" *Child Development* 74, no.3 (May/June 2003): 801–821.

30. "Having an unrelated male in the home is also associated with earlier puberty." In Bruce J. Ellis, "Timing of Pubertal Maturation in Girls: An Integrated Life History Approach," *Psychological Bulletin* 130, no.6 (November 2004): 920–58; Bruce J. Ellis and Judy Garber, "Psychosocial antecedents

of variation in girls' pubertal timing: Maternal depression, stepfather presence, and marital and family stress," *Child Development* 71, no.2 (March/April 2000): 485–501; Terry E. Moffitt, Avshalom Caspi, Jay Belsky, and Phil A. Silva, "Childhood Experience and the Onset of Menarche: A Test of a Sociobiological Model," *Child Development* 63, no.1 (February 1992): 47–58; Bruce J. Ellis, John E. Bates, Kenneth A. Dodge, David M. Fergusson, L. John Horwood, Gregory S. Pettit, and Lianne Woodward, "Does Father Absence Place Daughters at Special Risk for Early Sexual Activity and Teenage Pregnancy?" *Child Development* 74, no.3 (May/June 2003): 801–21. Regarding the increased risk to early-maturing girls, see Laurence Steinberg and Amanda S. Morris, "Adolescent Development," *Annual Review of Psychology* 1, no.52 (February 2001): 83–110; also see Ronald Rohner and Robert Veneziano, "The Importance of Father Love: History and Contemporary Evidence," *Review of General Psychology* 5, no.4 (2001): 382–405; Mark D. Regnerus and Laura B. Luchies, "The Parent-Child Relationship and Opportunities for Adolescents' First Sex," *Journal of Family Issues* 27, no.2 (2006): 159–83.

31. P. Donovan, "Mother's Attitudes Toward Adolescent Sex, Family's Dating Rules Influence Teenagers' Sexual Behavior," *Family Planning Perspectives* 27, no.4 (1995): 177–78; Renee Sieving, Clea S. McNeely, and Robert Wm. Blum, "Maternal Expectations, Mother-Child Connectedness, and Adolescent Sexual Debut," *Archives of Pediatrics and Adolescent Medicine* 154 (2000): 809–16; Melina Bersamin, Michael Todd, Deborah A. Fisher, Douglas L. Hill, Joel W. Grube, and Samantha Walker, "Parenting Practices and Adolescent Sexual Behavior: A Longitudinal Study," *Journal of Marriage and the Family* 70, no.1 (February 2008): 97–112.

32. Michael Ungar, "The importance of parents and other caregivers to the resilience of high-risk adolescents," *Family Process* 43, no.1 (February 2004): 23–41; M. Resnick, P. Bearman, R. W. Blum, et al, "Protecting Adolescents from Harm: Findings from the National Longitudinal Study on Adolescent Health," *JAMA* 278 (1997): 823–32; Renee Sieving, et al, "Maternal Expectations."

33. Allowing a teen to make health decisions in a closed room with her provider undermines and weakens the parent-child relationship. Planned Parenthood does that with this approach.

34. C. Lammers, M. Ireland, and M. Resnick, "Influences on adolescents' decision to postpone onset of sexual intercourse: a survival analysis of virginity among youths aged 13 to 18 years," *Journal of Adolescent Health* 26, no.1 (January 2000): 42–48; M. Resnick, et al, "Protecting Adolescents from Harm."

35. Between the ages of 15 and 18.

36. Laura Fingerson, "Do Mothers' Opinions Matter in Teens' Sexual Activity?" *Journal of Family Issues* 26, no.7 (2005): 947.

37. Kimberly K. Usher-Seriki , Mia Smith Bynum, and Tamora A. Callands, "Mother–Daughter Communication About Sex and Sexual Intercourse

Among Middle- to Upper-Class African American Girls," *Journal of Family Issues* 29, no.7 (2008): 901–17; P. J. Dittus and J. Jaccard, "Adolescents' perceptions of maternal disapproval of sex: relationship to sexual outcomes," *Journal of Adolescent Health* 26, no.4 (April 2000): 268–78.

38. One study of Asian and Pacific Islander teens concludes, "[This] highlights how powerful and simple an intervention can be between mothers and adolescents." (Hyeouk Hahm et al, "Longitudinal Effects of Perceived Maternal Approval on Sexual Behaviors of Asian and Pacific Islander (API) Young Adults," *Journal Youth Adolescence* 37 (2008): 74–84.)

39. V. Minichiello, S. Paxton, and V. Cowling, "Religiosity, sexual behavior and safe sex practices: Further evidence," *Australian and New Zealand Journal of Public Health* 20, no.3 (June 1996):321–22; M. Resnick, et al, "Protecting Adolescents from Harm"; Michael J. Donahue and Peter L. Benson, "Religion and the Well-Being of Adolescents," *Journal of Social Issues* 51, no. 2 (Summer 1995): 145–60.

40. Laura Fingerson, "Do Mothers' Opinions Matter in Teens' Sexual Activity?" *Journal of Family Issues* 26, no. 7 (2005): 947–74.

41. X. Li, S. Feigelman, and B. Stanton, "Perceived parental monitoring and health risk behaviors among urban low-income African-American children and adolescents," *Journal of Adolescent Health* 27 (2000): 43–48; A.A. Rai, B. Stanton, Y. Wu, et al, "Relative influences of perceived parental monitoring and perceived peer involvement on adolescent risk behaviors: an analysis of six cross-sectional data sets," *Journal of Adolescent Health* 33 (2003):108–18.

42. Richard A. Crosby, Ph.D.; Ralph J. DiClemente, Ph.D.; Gina M. Wingood, ScD, MPH; Delia L. Lang, MPH, Ph.D.; and Kathy Harrington, MPH, MAEd, "Infrequent Parental Monitoring Predicts Sexually Transmitted Infections Among Low-Income African American Female Adolescents," *Archives of Pediatrics & Adolescent Medicine* 157 (2003):169–73.

43. Cohen D. A., Farley T. A., Taylor S. N., et al, "When and where do youths have sex? The potential role of adult supervision," *Pediatrics* 110 (2002): 66; Elaine A. Borawski et al, "Parental Monitoring: Negotiated Unsupervised Time, and Parental Trust: The Role of Perceived Parenting Practices in Adolescent Health Risk Behaviors," *Journal of Adolescent Health* 33 (2003): 60–70; Colleen DiIorio et al, "Sexual Possibility Situations and Sexual Behaviors Among Young Adolescents: The Moderating Role of Protective Factors Journal of Adolescent Health 35 (2004):528.e11-528.e20.

44. Ibid.

45. Debra W. Haffner, *Beyond the Big Talk: Every Parent's Guide to Raising Sexually Healthy teens—from middle school to high school and beyond* (New York: Newmarket Press, 2001).

46. Ibid., 113.

47. See "Sex and the Anticultural Teenager" in Kay S. Hymowitz, *Ready or Not: Why Treating Children as Small Adults Endangers Their Future—and Ours* (New York: Free Press, 1999).

48. New York Academy of Sciences, Sept 18-20, 2003

49. B. J. Casey, Jay N. Giedd, and Kathleen M. Thomas, "Structural and functional brain development and its relation to cognitive development," *Biological Psychiatry* 54 (2000): 241–57.

50. Rhoshel K. Lenroot and Jay N. Giedd, "Brain development in children and adolescents: Insights from anatomical magnetic resonance imaging," *Neuroscience and Biobehavioral Reviews* 30 (2006): 718–29.

51. Claudia Wallis, "What Makes Teens Tick?" *TIME Magazine*, May 10, 2004; available online at: http://www.time.com/time/magazine/article/0,9171,994126,00.html?internalid=ACA.

52. Roshel K. Lenroot and Jay N. Giedd, "Brain development in children and adolescents."

53. Linda Patia Spear, "The psychobiology of adolescence," in Kathleen Kovner Kline, *Authoritative Communities: The Scientific Case for Nurturing the Whole Child* (New York: Springer-Verlag, 2007).

54. Daniel Weinberger, "Brain Development, Culpability and the Death Penalty: The International Justice Project"; available online at: www.scribd.com/doc/2169002.

55. Claudia Wallis, "What Makes Teens Tick?" *Time*, September 26, 2008.

56. "Growth and Development, Ages 13 to 17—What Parents Need to Know," http://www.advocatesforyouth.org/index.php?option=com_content&task=view&id=156&Itemid=206

57. Daniel Weinberger, "Brain Development, Culpability and the Death Penalty: The International Justice Project"; available online at: www.scribd.com/doc/2169002.

58. Greg Muirhead, "Early Puberty Tied to Risky Behavior," *Clinical Psychiatry News* 36, no. 4 (2008): 3.

59. Of course there are wide variations among individual adolescents, and not everything here will apply to every teen.

60. Monique Ernst and Martin P. Paulus, "Neurobiology of Decision Making: A Selective Review from a Neurocognitive and Clinical Perspective," *Biological Psychiatry* 58 (2005): 597–604.

61. Ibid.

62. Adriana Galvan et al, "Earlier Development of the Accumbens Relative to Orbitofrontal Cortex Might Underlie Risk-Taking Behavior in Adolescents," *Journal of Neuroscience* 26, no.25 (2006): 6885–92.

63. Laurence Steinberg, "Cognitive and affective development in adolescence," *Trends in Cognitive Sciences* 9, no. 2 (February 2005).

64. Of course, alcohol increases the likelihood of risky behavior. But even while sober, teens are susceptible to lapses in judgment.

65.   Ibid.; K. Kersting, "Brain research advances help elucidate teen behavior,"
        Monitor on Psychology (July/August 2004): 80; John Merriman, "Linking
        Risk-Taking Behavior and Peer Influence in Adolescents," *NeuroPsychiatry
        Reviews* 9, no.1 (2008).

66.   Ronald E. Dahl, "Adolescent Brain Development; A Period of Vulnerabili-
        ties and Opportunities," *Annals of the New York Academy of Sciences* 1021
        (2004).

67.   Yurgelin-Todd, www.sosparents.org/flash10.html

68.   Laurence Steinberg, "Cognitive and affective development in adolescence."

69.   Ibid.

70.   Linda Patia Spear, "The psychobiology of adolescence," 272.

71.   Ronald E. Dahl, "Adolescent Brain Development"; Professor of Psychiatry
        and Pediatrics at the University of Pittsburgh and organizer of the 2003
        conference on adolescent brain development.

72.   Linda Patia Spear, "The Adolescent Brain and Age-related Behavioral Man-
        ifestations," *Neuroscience and Biobehavioral Reviews* 24 (2000): 424–25.

73.   Laurence Steinberg, "Risk Taking in Adolescence: What Changes, and
        Why?" *Annals New York Academy of Sciences* 1021 (June 2004): 54–57.

74.   Claudia Wallis, "What Makes Teens Tick?"

75.   Richard L. Wiener and Monica K. Miller, "Determining the death penalty
        for juveniles," *Monitor on Psychology* 35, no. 1 (January 2004).

76.   Planned Parenthood of the Southern Finger Lakes newsletter, "SEX: Talk
        About It," Fall 2005, 1; available online at: http://www.
        plannedparenthood.org/ppsfl/newsletter-sex-talk-about-it-2486.htm.

77.   Stats for 2007: Chlamydia: 324, 548 cases in females under twenty, higher
        than any other age group and almost 5 times the reported cases in males
        (http://www.cdc.gov/std/stats07/tables/10.htm).
            HPV: this infection does not need to be reported; estimated prevalence
        for 03-04 among sexually active females was approximately 40 percent in
        those aged 14–19 years and 50 percent in those aged 20–24 years
        (http://www.cdc.gov/nchs/about/major/nhanes/nhanes2003-
        2004/nhanes03_04.htm).

78.   "Sexually Transmitted Disease Surveillance 2007 Supplement," Department
        of Health and Human Services, Centers for Disease Control and Preven-
        tion, http://www.cdc.gov/std/Chlamydia2007/CTSurvSupp2007Short.pdf;
        and "Quick Stats: Prevalence of HPV Infection Among Sexually Active
        Females, Aged 14–59 Years, by Age Group," National Health and Nutrition
        Examination Survey, United States, 2003–2004, http://www.cdc.
        gov/mmwr/preview/mmwrhtml/mm5633a5.htm?s_cid=mm5633a5_e

79.   Amanda Dempsey, Sharon Humiston, and Anna-Barbara Moscicki, "Panel
        Discussion: Practical Pediatrics: Effective Communication Strategies for
        Cervical Cancer Prevention" (part of symposium held October 8, 2006,
        called Pediatricians at the Forefront of Preventing Cervical Cancer: What
        You Need to Know About HPV), http://www.medscape.com/
        viewprogram/6281.

80.   The size of the T-zone can be affected by other factors besides age.
81.   There is wide individual variation in the size of transformation zones.
82.   To be more accurate, it moves up through the uterine os, or opening, toward
      the uterus. But for the purposes of this discussion, it's fair to describe this
      as "shrinking," because the area available for infection gets smaller.
83.   Franck Remoue et al, "High intraepithelial expression of estrogen and
      progesterone receptors in the transformation zone of the uterine cervix,"
      American Journal of Obstetrics and Gynecology 189 (2003): 1660–5.
84.   I.e., the immune system.
85.   Sun Kuie Tay and Albert Singer, "The effects of oral contraceptive steroids,
      menopause and hormone replacement therapy on the cervical epithelium,"
      in Jordan, Singer, Jones, and Shafi, eds.S, *The Cervix*, 2nd edition (Black-
      well Publishing, 2006), 132.
86.   I.e., a lymph node.
87.   Margaret A. Stanley, "Immunochemistry and Immunology of the Cervix,"
      in Jordan, Singer, Jones, and Shafi, eds., *The Cervix*, 57.
88.   Smoking can also inhibit these cells functioning.
89.   Sandra L. Giannini et al, "Influence of the Mucosal Epithelium Microenvi-
      ronment on Langerhans Cells: Implications for the Development of Squa-
      mous Intraepithelial Lesions of the Cervix," *International Journal of Cancer*,
      97 (2002): 654–59.
90.   Szarewski (2001); also see *Cervix*, 57
91.   Franck Remoue et al, "High intraepithelial expression of estrogen and
      progesterone receptors in the transformation zone of the uterine cervix."
92.   Sun Kuie Tay and Albert Singer, "The effects of oral contraceptive steroids,
      menopause and hormone replacement therapy on the cervical epithelium,"
      135.
93.   From discussion with Anna Barbara Moscicki, MD, October 2007; and Jor-
      dan, Singer, Jones, and Shafi, eds., *The Cervix*, 135. With the average age
      of sexual debut at age fifteen, and the postponement of childbearing for ten
      years or more, this is something to keep in mind.
94.   Anna-Barbara Moscicki et al,"Cervical Ectopy in Adolescent Girls with and
      without Human Immunodeficiency Virus Infection," *Journal of Infectious
      Diseases* 183 (March 15, 2001).
95.   Jordan, Singer, Jones, and Shafi, eds., *The Cervix*, 91.
96.   R. L. Winer, "Risk of female human papillomavirus acquisition associated
      with first male sex partner," *Journal of Infectious Disease* 197, no.2 (Janu-
      ary 15, 2008): 279–82.
97.   Anna-Barbara Moscicki et al, "Differences in biologic maturation, sexual
      behavior, and sexually transmitted disease between adolescents with and
      without cervical intraepithelial neoplasia," *Journal of Pediatrics* 115 (1989):
      487–93.
98.   I found the immature cervix mentioned by Alice one time, in her explana-
      tion of why it's important for sexually active young women to go for regu-
      lar gynecologic check-ups.

99.   For example, see: "Ready or Not? The Scarleteen Sex Readiness Checklist," http://www.scarleteen.com/article/boyfriend/ready_or_not_the_scarleteen_ sex_readiness_checklist; "Trying to decide when to have first intercourse," http://www.goaskalice.columbia.edu/1970.html; and Robie H. Harris, *It's Perfectly Normal: Changing Bodies, Growing Up, Sex & Sexual Health* (Cambridge, MA: Candlewick Press, 2004).

100. K. Kersting, "Brain research advances help elucidate teen behavior," *Monitor on Psychology* (July/August 2004): 80; Claudia Wallis, "What Makes Teens Tick?"

101. Ronald E. Dahl, "Adolescent Brain Development," referring to the work of Ann Masten, Ph.D., op cit.

102. Dr. Mary S. Calderone, Dr. James Ramey, *Talking with your Child About Sex*, Ballantine Books (1982).

Chapter 4

1.   They are in conflict over other issues too, but my focus is risky sexual behaviors.

2.   The video had been developed by MCPS staff.

3.   James Trussell, "Contraceptive failure in the US," Contraception 70, no.2 (August 2004): 89–96.

4.   Citizens for Community Values, "Workshop Summary: Scientific Evidence on Condom Effectiveness for Sexually Transmitted Disease (STD) Prevention" (12–13 June 2000), http://www.ccv.org/downloads/pdf/CDC_ Condom_Study.pdf.

5.   King K. Holmes, Ruth Levine, and Marcia Weaver, "Effectiveness of condoms in preventing sexually transmitted infections," *Bulletin of the World Health Organization* 82, no.6 (June 2004): 454–61.

6.   This was an analysis of many studies. The range of risk reduction was 35–94 percent.

7.   Susan Weller and Karen Davis, "Condom effectiveness in reducing heterosexual HIV transmission," *Family Planning Perspectives* 31, no.6 (November–December, 1999): 272–79.

8.   Jorge Sanchez, Pablo Campos, Barry Courtois, Lourdes Gutierrez, Carlos Carrillo, et al, "Prevention of sexually transmitted diseases in female sex workers: prospective evaluation of condom promotion and strengthened STD services," *Sexually Transmitted Diseases* 30, no.4 (April 2003): 273–79; Richard Crosby, Ralph DiClemente, Gina Wingood, Delia Lang, and Kathy Harrington, "Value of Consistent Condom Use: a study of sexually transmitted disease prevention among African American adolescent females," *American Journal of Public Health* 93, no.6 (June 2003): 901–2.

9.   The study only examined three STDs and therefore does not reflect the possible acquisition of other STDs including HIV, herpes, syphilis and the human papillomavirus (HPV); see Richard Crosby et al, "Value of Consistent Condom Use," *American Journal of Public Health* 93, no.6 (June 2003): 901–902.

10.   Judith Shlay, Melissa McClung, Jennifer Patnaik, and John Douglas, Jr., "Comparison of sexually transmitted disease prevalence by reported level of condom use among patients attending an urban sexually transmitted disease clinic," *Sexually Transmitted Diseases* 31, no.3 (March 2004): 154-160; Anna Wald, Andria G.M. Langenberg, Elizabeth Krantz, John M. Douglas Jr., H. Hunter Handsfield, Richard P. DiCarlo, Adaora A. Adimora, Allen E. Izu, Rhoda Ashley Morrow, and Lawrence Corey, "The relationship between condom use and herpes simplex virus acquisition," *Annals of Internal Medicine* 143, no.10 (15 November 2005):707–13.

11.   When the public is informed about condom effectiveness by the CDC and other authorities, terms such as "highly effective," "very good," and "significant" are used. While there is no doubt that proper use of condoms prevents some infections to some degree, it would be ethical to remind people this refers only to vaginal intercourse and to provide the actual statistics so they can make informed decisions about their behavior. From what I could gather, "significant" sometimes refers to "statistically significant," a level of protection many people would consider unacceptable.

12.   Ruth M. Jacobs, MD, letter to *The Gazette*, March 28, 2005.

13.   She teamed up with Citizens for Responsible Curriculum (CRC) to challenge the video. CRC was also concerned about the lack of warning about the risks of multiple partners, oral sex; the partial protection against herpes, HPV, and other organisms; and subsequently about transgenderism and issues related to homosexuality.

14.   Pertaining to HIV, for the receptive individual, compared to receptive vaginal intercourse.

15.   Barbara G. Silverman and Thomas P. Gross, "Use and Effectiveness of Condoms During Anal Intercourse: A Review," *Sexually Transmitted Diseases* 24, no.1 (January 1997):11–17.

16.   In Holland, concern about condom failure during anal sex was so serious that a new type was designed and marketed specific to this use. It appears that the FDA considered the possibility but was concerned about ethical issues involved in testing a new device.

17.   Ruth M. Jacobs, MD, letter to *The Gazette*, March 28, 2005.

18.   Jami S. Leichliter, Anjani Chandra, Nicole Lidden, Kevin A. Fenton, and Sevgi O. Aral, "Prevalence and Correlates of Heterosexual Anal and Oral Sex in Adolescents and Adults in the United States," *The Journal of Infectious Diseases* 196, no.12 (15 December 2007): 1852–59.

19.   Bradley O. Boekeloo and Donna E. Howard, "Oral Sexual Experience Among Young Adolescents Receiving General Health Examinations," *American Journal of Health Behavior* 26, no.4 (August 2002): 306–14.

20.   Stephanie A. Sanders and June Machover Reinisch, "Would You Say You 'Had Sex' If . . . ?" *JAMA* 281, no.3 (20 January 1999): 275-277; M. Keith Rawlings, Robert J. Graff, Rodrigo Calderon, Shelisa Casey-Bailey, and Mary V. Palsey, "Differences in Perceptions of What Constitutes Having

'Had Sex' in a Population of People Living with HIV/AIDS," *JAMA* 98, no.6 (June 2006): 845–50.

21. The legal action was based on the curriculum's exclusion of ex-gays and its discriminatory religious references. The judge found that it violated the establishment clause.

22. And PFOX (Parents and Friends of Ex-Gays).

23. Getting two minutes before the MCPS Board was not easy. The Board office only accepts calls from interested parties on the Monday before they meet, and only for two, thirty-minute periods—one for speakers who wish to address issues relating to the day's agenda, and the other for speakers wishing to address other issues. At the time Jacobs was trying to present, the number was usually busy. She succeeded in getting through by using the redial button on two separate phones. See Montgomery County Public Schools, "Public Participation," http://www.montgomeryschoolsmd.org/boe/community/participation.shtm.

24. Usually males are asymptomatic and may only learn of their infection when symptoms develop in a female partner and she is diagnosed.

25. "HIV Services for a New Generation," January 1, 2001; available at: http://www.marketingpower.com/ResourceLibrary/MarketingHealthServices/Pages/2001/21/4/6131134.aspx?sq=hiv 1 aids 1 epidemic.

26. Discussed as a variation of sexual behavior on GoAskAlice and other sites for teens.

27. This is the email my assistant got when she wrote MCPS to ask if their current (as of March 2009) curriculum specifies that:

   1. Anal sex is the most dangerous type of intercourse and
   2. Condoms may be more likely to fail during non-vaginal use:

   Date: Mon, Mar 30, 2009 at 2:49 PM
   Subject: sex ed curricula question
   Dear Ms. ****:

   Thank you for your March 16, 2009, e-mail message to Dr. — —, superintendent of schools, in which you request information regarding the Montgomery County Public Schools Health Curriculum, specifically: "does the current sex ed curricula specify that anal sex is the most dangerous type of intercourse, i.e., the easiest way to transmit infection?" and, "does the curricula provide the same or a similar warning to that on condom wrappers (regarding the possible breakage of a condom for non-vaginal use)?"

   A 45-minute condom use demonstration lesson for Grade 10 health education students is designed to address the following concept and objectives:

   Abstinence is the only 100 percent effective way to prevent unwanted pregnancy and sexually transmitted infections. Individuals who engage in sexual activity are responsible for protecting themselves and their partners from unwanted pregnancy and sexually transmitted infections.

   Describe how a condom works to help prevent contracting a sexually transmitted disease.

List in order the proper steps for correctly examining a condom, putting on a condom, and removing/disposing of a condom.

Anal sex and condom use warnings are not the focus of the condom demonstration lesson or the Montgomery County Public Schools Curriculum Framework for Pre-K-12 Health Education.

[name redacted], Associate Superintendent for Curriculum and Instructional Programs Montgomery County Public Schools

28. Mark Jacobs, "Due warning in a 'risky' world," *The Washington Times*, May 8, 2005.

29. Citizens for Community Values, "Workshop Summary: Scientific Evidence on Condom Effectiveness for Sexually Transmitted Disease (STD) Prevention."

30. U.S. Food and Drug Administration, "Condoms and Sexually Transmitted Diseases, Brochure" (December 1990), http://www.fda.gov/oashi/aids/condom.html#strong.

31. Ibid.

32. Surgeon General C. Everett Koop, "To MCPS Board of Education and Superintendent Weast," available at: http://www.mcpscurriculum.com/pdf/Ruthanalsexpetition.pdf.

33. HPV-related anal cancer is on the rise and has striking similarities to cervical cancer. It most commonly occurs in the anal transition zone, an area of immature cells very like the cervical transformation zone. Having receptive anal sex causes trauma and repair of the anal transition zone, a process that accelerates the turnover of cells and makes the area more vulnerable to malignant change. Teresa M. Darragh, "Anal Cytology for Anal Cancer Screening: Is It Time Yet?" Diagnostic *Cytopathology* 30, no.6 (May 2004): 371–73. This is the reason some physicians are performing anal Pap tests on men who have sex with men. Also, a 2008 Robinson article indicates that the sexual revolution is a major contributor to HPV-related cancers. See D. Robinson, et al, "An analysis of temporal and generational trends in the incidence of anal and other HPV-related cancers in Southeast England," *British Journal of Cancer* 100, no.3 (January 2009): 527–31.

34. SIECUS, "Prevalence of Unprotected Anal Sex Among Teens Requires New Education Strategies," http://www.siecus.org/index.cfm?fuseaction=feature.showFeature&FeatureID=1036&varuniqueuserid=20986960210.

35. Martha Kempner and Monica Rodriguez, "Talk About Sex" (SIECUS, 2005), 46, 68, 76, 79. Accessed at http://siecus.org/_data/global/images/TalkAboutSex.pdf .

36. Stephen Joseph, MD, personal communication, December 1, 2005.

37. American Lung Association, www.lungusa.org.

38. "Anal Sex Basic Facts," http://www.gURL.com/findout/fastfacts/articles/0,,605386_671456-5,00.html.

39. Remember, Planned Parenthood says, "Parents know that the best foundation for their children's success is a good education. When it comes to sexual health, Planned Parenthood provides what parents want for their children—medically accurate, comprehensive, and age-appropriate information to guide them through a lifetime of choices." From Planned Parenthood, "About Us," http://www.plannedparenthood.org/about-us/about-us-90.htm. Also, "Planned Parenthood is proud of its vital role in providing young people with honest sexuality and relationship information in classrooms and online."

40. Planned Parenthood, "Vaginal, Oral & Anal Sex," http://www.plannedparenthood.org/teen-talk/ask/sex-masturbation/vaginal-oral-anal-sex-26056.htm.

41. Answer, "Medical Advisory Board," http://answer.rutgers.edu/page/medical_advisory_board/.

42. Sex, Etc., "The Truth About Anal Sex," http://www.sexetc.org/story/sex/2226.

43. Heather Corinna, *S.E.X: The All-You-Need-to-Know progressive sexuality guide to get you through High School and College* (New York: Marlowe and Co., 2007), 156.

44. Ibid., 159.

45. "Why is anal sex so wrong?" http://www.scarleteen.com/article/advice/why_is_anal_sex_so_wrong.

46. "Receiving anal sex: What does it mean?" http://www.goaskalice.columbia.edu/0847.html.

47. Norman Sohn, Michael Weinstein, and Joel Gonchar, "Social Injuries of the Rectum," *American Journal of Surgery* 134, no.5 (November 1977): 611–12.

48. Go Ask Alice! "What's fisting?" http://www.goaskalice.columbia.edu/1429.html.

49. Heather Corinna, *S.E.X.*, 147.

50. Miriam Grossman, *Unprotected: A Campus Psychiatrist Reveals How Political Correctness Endangers Every Student* (New York: Sentinel, 2006), 68–70.

51. *Merck Manual*, available at: www.merckmanual.com.

52. Ibid.

53. Luis Carlos Junqueira and Jose Carneiro, *Basic Histology: Text and Atlas*, 10th ed. (New York: McGraw-Hill, 2003).

54. Peter Greenhead, Peter Hayes, Patricia S. Watts, Ken G. Laing, George E. Griffin, and Robin J. Shattock, "Parameters of Human Immunodeficiency Virus Infection of Human Cervical Tissue and Inhibition by Vaginal Virucides," *Journal of Virology* 74, no.12 (June 2000): 5577–86.

55. B. Voeller and D. J. Anderson, letter to the *Journal of the American Medical Association* 267 (October 2003): 1917–18.   (from Brody, *Sex at Risk*, 216)

56. A. Moriyama, K. Shimoya, I. Ogata, T. Kimura, T. Nakamura, H. Wada, K. Ohashi, C. Azuma, F. Saji and Y. Murata, "Secretory leukocyte protease inhibitor (SLPI) concentrations in cervical mucus of women with normal menstrual cycle," *Molecular Human Reproduction* 5, no.7 (July 1999): 656–61.

57. Lot de Witte, Alexey Nabatov, Marjorie Pion, et al, "Langerin is a natural barrier to HIV-1 transmission by Langerhans cells," *Nature Medicine*, 13, no. 3 (2007): 367-371.

58. S. J. Robboy, M. Prade and G. Cunha, in Steven S. Sternberg, ed., *Histology for Pathologists*, (North Holland, New York: Raven Press, 1992), 881–92.

59. Peter Greenhead et al, "Parameters of Human Immunodeficiency," *Journal of Virology* 74, no.12 (June 2000): 5577–86. The cervix may be more vulnerable, especially the transformation zone.

60. Reuters, "HIV infects women through healthy tissue: U.S. Study," 18 December 2008, http://www.reuters.com/article/newsOne/idUS-TRE4BF7FF20081216.

61. M cells were actually first identified by Dr. Kenzaburo Kumagai of Osaka Tuberculosis Institute in 1922. See Robert L. Owen, "Uptake and transport of intestinal macromolecules and microorganisms by M cells in Peyer's patches—a personal and historical perspective," *Seminars in Immunology* 11, no.3 (June 1999): 157–63.

62. A. D. O'Leary and E. C. Sweeney, "Lymphoglandular Complexes of the Colon: Structure and Distribution," *Histopathology* 10 (1986): 267–83.

63. Marian R. Neutra, Nicholas J. Mantis, Andreas Frey, and Paul J. Giannasca, "The composition and function of M cell apical membranes: Implications for microbial pathogenesis," *Seminars in Immunology* 11, no.3 (June 1999). 171–81; Harvey Miller, Jianbing Zhang, Rhonda KuoLee, Girishchandra B. Patel, and Wangxue Chen, "Intestinal M Cells: The fallible sentinels?" *World Journal of Gastroenterology* 13, no.10 (14 March 2007):1477–86.

64. Robert L. Owen, "Uptake and transport," *Seminars in Immunology*.

65. J. P. Kraehenbuhl and M. R. Neutra, "Mollecular and cellular basis of immune protection of mucosal surfaces," *Physiological Review* 72, no.4 (1 October 1992): 853–79.

66. This has been demonstrated in vitro but not in vivo.

67. William B. Whitman, David C. Coleman, and William J. Wiebe, "Prokaryotes: The unseen majority," *Proceedings of the National Academy of Sciences USA* 95, no.12 (9 June 1998): 6578–83.

68. Harvey Miller et al "Intestinal M cells: The fallible sentinels?" *World Journal of Gastroenterology*.

69. Sinead C. Corr, Cormac C.G.M. Gahan, and Colin Hill, "M-Cells: origin, morphology and role in mucosal immunity and microbial pathogenesis," *FEMS Immunology and Medical Microbiology* 52, no.1 (January 2008): 2–12.

70. See Malcom Gladwell, *The Tipping Point* (New York: Little, Brown & Company, 2002).

71. John Potterat, personal communication with author, May 29, 2008.

Chapter 5

1. Herpes Homepage Discussion Forum, http://racoon.com/cgi-bin/dcforum/dcboard.cgi.

2. Cynthia A. Taylor, Mary L. Keller, Judith J. Egan (1997), "Advice from Affected Persons about Living with Human Papillomavirus Infection," *Image: Journal of Nursing Scholarship* 29, no. 1 (1997):27–32; J. Waller, L. A. V. Marlow, J. Wardle, "The association between knowledge of HPV and feelings of stigma, shame and anxiety," *Sexually Transmitted Infections* 83 (2007): 155–59.

3. Michael Reitano, "Counseling Patients with Genital Warts," *American Journal of Medicine* 102, 5A (1997): 38–43

4. H. M. Conaglen, R. Hughes, J. V. Conaglen, J. Morgan, "A prospective study of the psychological impact on patients of first diagnosis of human papillomavirus," *International Journal of STD&AIDS*, 12 (2001): 651–58.

5. The frequency of outbreaks may eventually diminish after several years.

6. R. Patel et al, "Patients' perspectives on the burden of recurrent genital herpes," *International Journal of STD & AIDS* 12 (2001): 640–45.

7. "HPV and You," Teen Talk, Planned Parenthood, http://www.plannedparenthood.org/teen-talk/watch/hpv-you-26817.htm.

8. "Teaching about Sexually Transmitted Infections," http://www.etr.org/recapp/freebies/freebie200008.htm; http://www.teenwire.com/education/activity-019.pdf.

9. www.ashastd.org: "Just remember that almost everyone gets HPV at some time . . . the virus is so common that having only a single lifetime partner does not assure protection . . . anyone who has ever had sexual relations has a high chance of being exposed to this virus"; www.GoAskAlice.com: "As you probably realize, the only way to be 100% percent certain you don't get any infections is to not have any oral, vaginal, or anal sex. Most people eventually decide to take the plunge and explore the joys of sex." www.scarleteen.com: "What's the answer? There isn't an easy one. In most cases, if you simply chose to abstain from all sexual activities, forever, you could like avoid HPV and HSV-2. But very few people are going to do that. . . . "

10. Margaret R. H. Nusbaum et al, "Sexually Transmitted Infections and Increased Risk of Co-Infection with Human Immunodeficiency Virus," *Journal of the American Osteopathic Association* 104, no.12 (2004): 527.

11. Kate Pavao, "Gay Couples Say "I DO!" available at: www.teenwire.com.

12. "Take Action," http://www.sexetc.org/page/take_action/.

13. Susan Rosenthal et al, "Heterosexual Romantic Relationships and Sexual Behaviors of Young Adolescent Girls," *Journal of Adolescent Health* 21 (1997):238–43.

14. "The Sex Mission: Accomplished," Comment on comic by Martina Fugazzotto. http://gurl.typepad.com/gurl_comix/2007/11/the-sex-missi-3.html.

15. "Survey Indicates Nearly 1 in 10 US Adolescents Had Major Depressive Episode in 2004," *CNS Spectrum* 11, no.2 (February 2006): 83; "Suicide Rates Increasing in Girls," *Psychiatric Annals* 37, no.10 (2007): 663.

16. Diana Mahoney, "Educate Patients about Asymptomatic Herpes," *Clinical Psychiatry News*, May 22, 2008, 54.

17. Graph: "Fifty-Five Percent of Teens Aged 15-17 Say Depression Is a Big Concern," source: The Henry J Kaiser Foundation; from *Clinical Psychiatry News*, February 2004, 61.

18. Darron R. Brown, "A Longitudinal Study of Genital Human Papillomavirus Infection in a Cohort of Closely Followed Adolescent Women," *Journal of Infectious Diseases* 191 (2005): 182–92.

19. Rachel L. Winer et al, "Genital Human Papillomavirus Infection: Incidence and Risk Factors in a Cohort of Female University Students," *American Journal of Epidemiology* 157 (2003): 218–26; Rachel L. Winer, Qinghua Feng, James P. Hughes, Sandra O'Reilly, Nancy B. Kiviat, and Laura A. Koutsky, "Risk of female human papillomavirus acquisition associated with first male sex partner," *Journal of Infectious Diseases* 197, no.2 (2008): 279–82.

20. Fact Sheet. "Human Papillomavirus and Genital Warts," National Institute of Allergy and Infectious Diseases. Available at: www.niaid. nih.gov/factsheets/stdhpv.htm.

21. Charles J. N. Lacey , "Therapy for genital human papillomavirus-related disease," *Journal of Clinical Virology* 32S (2005): S82–S90

22. This study was done prior to the HPV vaccine.

23. Rachel Winer et al, "Condom Use and the Risk of Genital Human Papillomavirus Infection in Young Women," *New England Journal of Medicine* 354 (2006): 25.

24. Rachel L. Winer et al, "Genital Human Papillomavirus Infection: Incidence and Risk Factors in a Cohort of Female University Students," *American Journal of Epidemiology* 157 (2003): 218–26.

25. "Safer Sex (Safe Sex)," Planned Parenthood. http://www.plannedparenthood. org/health-topics/stds-hiv safer-sex/safer-sex-4263.htm

26. Cumulative incidence.

27. Cumulative incidence.

28. Jeffrey M. Partridge et al, "Genital Human Papillomavirus Infection in Men: Incidence and Risk Factors in a Cohort of University Students," *Journal of Infectious Diseases*, 196 (October 2007): 1128–36;

     The same finding had been reported eight years earlier: C. Sonnex, S. Strauss, J. J. Gray, "Detection of human papillomavirus DNA on the fingers of patients with genital warts," *Sexually Transmitted Infections*, 75 (1999):317–19.

29. Tom Paulson, "New risks discovered for HPV," *Seattle Post Intelligencer*, July 31, 2007.

30. "Safer Sex (Safe Sex)," Planned Parenthood. http://www.plannedparenthood. org/health-topics/stds-hiv-safer-sex/safer-sex-4263.htm and "Birth Control," Planned Parenthood. http://www.plannedparenthood.org/teen-talk/birth-control-25029.htm.

31. "HPV (Human Papillomavirus): What Women Should Know," American Social Health Association. http://www.ashastd.org/learn/learn_hpv_women.cfm.

32. Unless parents can be certain that their daughter will delay sexual behavior until entering into a faithful relationship with a man who also waited, parents should have their daughters vaccinated, but I don't support state laws mandating such vaccinations.

33. Gypsyamber D'Souza et al, "Case-Control Study of Human Papillomavirus and Oropharyngeal Cancer," *The New England Journal of Medicine*, 356 (2007): 1944–56.

34. Dagney Stuart, "HPV's Link to Head and Neck Cancer Investigated," *Reporter*, September 14, 2007; available at: http://www.mc.vanderbilt.edu/reporter/index.html?ID=5808 at Vanderbilt-Ingram.

35. Oral cancers due to HPV are more prevalent in men.

36. Bonnie Halpern-Felsher et al, "Oral Versus Vaginal Sex Among Adolescents: Perceptions, Attitiudes, and Behavior," *Pediatrics* 115, no.4 (2005): 845.

37. Site recommended to teens by SIECUS.

38. "Sea men: a hero's tale," comic by Martina Fugazzotto, http://www.gURL.com/showoff/comix/pages/0,,605672_716692-12,00.html.

39. "Vaginal, Oral, and Anal Sex: Examining Oral Sex," Planned Parenthood. http://www.plannedparenthood.org/teen-talk/sex-masturbation/vaginal-oral-anal-sex/examining-oral-sex-25409.htm.

40. Mike Stobbe, "US sets record in sexual disease cases," AP News, November 13, 2007; available at: http://b1104w.blu104.mail.live.com.

41. Miriam Grossman, *Unprotected: A Campus Psychiatrist Reveals How Political Correctness in Her Profession Endangers Every Student* (New York: Penguin Sentinel, 2007).

42. Steven S. Witkin, personal communication with author, May 14, 2005.

43. D. Patton et al, "Significant Reduction in the Macaque model of Chlamydial Pelvic Inflammatory Disease with Azithromycin Treatment," *Journal of Infectious Diseases*, 192 (July 2005): 129–35.

44. Steven S. Witkin et al, "Unsuspected Chlamydia trachomatis infection and in vitro fertilization outcome," *American Journal of Obstetrics and Gynecology* 171, no.5: 1213; www.specialtylabs.com.

45. Joseph Debattista et al (2003), "Immunopathogenesis of Chlamydia trachomis infections in women," *Fertility and Sterility* 79, no. 6 (2003): 1273–87.

46. S. Faro, D. E. Soper, eds., *Infectious Diseases in Women* (Philadelphia: WB Saunders, 2001), 261–2.

47. D. L. Sipkin, A. Gillam, L. B. Grady, "Risk Factors for Chlamydia Trachomatis Infection in a California Collegiate Population," *Journal of American College Health* 52, no.2: 65–71.

48. Ibid.

49. Stuart N. Seidman and Sevgi Oketn Aral, "Behavioral Aspects of Pelvic Inflammatory disease," in *Pelvic Inflammatory Disease*, Daniel Landers and Richard Sweet, eds. (New York: Springer, 1997), 181.

50. Steven S. Witkin et al, "Unsuspected Chlamydia trachomatis infection and in vitro fertilization outcome," *American Journal of Obstetrics and Gynecology* 171, no. 5 (1994): 1213.

51. A. Neuer et al, "Heat Shock Protein Expression during Gametogenesis and Embryogenesis," *Infectious Diseases in Ob Gyn* 7, i1-2 (1999): 10–16; A. Neuer et al, "Humoral Immune Response to membrane components of Chlamydia trachomatis and expression of human 60 kDa heat shock protein in follicular fluid of in-vitro fertilization patients," *Human Reproduction* 12, no.5 (1997): 925.

52. Under age 25.

53. "Up in Smoke: Anti-Smoking Campaign Targets Teens," Sexetc.org. Available at http://www.sexetc.org/story/Drugs/2158.

54. "Ice, Ice Baby," *Elle Magazine*, April 2004; available at http://www.extendfertility.com/downloads/documents/elle-200404-ice_ice_baby.pdf: "Most of the women who come in here are healthy," said the director of the largest fertility clinic in San Francisco. "They're here because they're forty." Also see *Chronicle of Higher Education*, January 26, 2007, "This year's freshman at 4 year colleges: a statistical profile."

55. Miriam Grossman, *Unprotected*, 122.

56. Ibid., 135.

57. Ibid., 89.

58. Claudia Kalb, "Should You Have Your Baby Now?" *Newsweek*, August 13, 2001.

59. As reported by Anne Newman, "The Risks of Racing the Reproductive Clock," *Business Week*, 1997; available at http://www.businessweek.com/1997/18/b352592.htm.

60. "Age and Fertility, a Guide for Patients," (American Society for Reproductive Medicine, 2003) 3: "If you are a healthy thirty-year-old woman, you have about a 20 percent chance per month to get pregnant. By age 40 however, your chance is only about 5 percent per month."

61. Sylvia Ann Hewlett, *Creating a Life: Professional Women and the Quest for Children*, (Miramax: 2002), 33.

62. Ibid., 86.

63. Harrell W. Chesson, John M. Blandford, Thomas L. Gift, Guoyu Tao, Kathleen L. Irwin, "The estimated direct medical cost of sexually transmitted diseases among American youth, 2000." *Perspectives on Sexual and Reproductive Health* Jan–Feb, 2004.

Chapter 6

1. Lesbians who have never had sexual contact with a male have lower rates of STIs than straight women, but this group constitutes a small minority.

In a study of 1,400 women who have sex with women, only 7 percent reported never having had sexual contact with a male (Fethers 2000).

2.   I include books, too.

3.   Mitchel L. Zoler, "Syphilis Rising in Men Who Have Sex with Men," *Clinical Psychiatry News* (April 2005): 30.

4.   Esther Drill, Heather McDonald, and Rebecca Odes, *Deal With It! A Whole New Approach to Your Body, Brain, and Life as a gURL* (New York: Pocket Books, 1999), 141.

5.   Miranda Elliot, "Soulforce Q on the Bus for Equality," www.sexetc.org/story/glbtq/4160/.

6.   "Common" does not mean "normal."

7.   "F@SB:* * * with your head, maintaining your sanity," http://www.girl2girl.info/cms/index.php?page=hints_for_maintaining_your_sanity&images=on.

8.   AACAP, "Facts for Families: Normal Adolescent Development Part II," http://www.aacap.org/cs/root/facts_for_families/normal_adolescent_development_part_ii.

9.   Esther Drill, Heather McDonald, and Rebecca Odes, *Deal With It!*, 139.

10.   (With the usual admonition to practice safe sex.)

11.   SIECUS, "Sexual Orientation," http://www.siecus.org/index.cfm?fuseaction=Page.viewPage&pageId=591&parentID=477.

12.   SIECUS, http://www.siecus.org/index.cfm?fuseaction=Page.viewPage&pageId=502&grandparentID=472&parentID=494.

13.   Ellen Bass and Kate Kaufman, *Free Your Mind: The Book for Gay, Lesbian, and Bisexual Youth—and Their Allies* (New York: Harper Perennial, 1996), 13.Recommended by gURL.com, Planned Parenthood, and SIECUS.

14.   But at outproud.com (recommended on teenwire), it's like being short or tall (www.outproud.org/brochure_be_yourself.html), and at PFLAG (SIECUS link) it's like being left- or right-handed (community.pflag.org/Page.aspx?pid=290)—rather insignificant.

15.   Robert E. Rector, Kirk A. Johnson, Ph.D., Lauren R. Noyes, and Shannan Martin, "The Harmful Effects of Early Sexual Activity and Multiple Sexual Partners Among Women: A Book of Charts"; available online at: http://www.heritage.org/Research/Family/upload/44695_2.pdf.

16.   "Why do nice guys always finish last?" GoAskAlice!, http://www.goaskalice.columbia.edu/1698.html.

17.   This is based on the famous Kinsey scale.

18.   Planned Parenthood, "Sexual Orientation & Gender," http://www.plannedparenthood.org/health-topics/sexual-orientation-gender-4329.htm.

19.   "Be Yourself: Questions and Answers for Gay, Lesbian and Bisexual Youth," http://www.outproud.org/brochure_be_yourself.html.

20.   "Fantasizing in the wrong direction?" GoAskAlice!, www.goaskalice-cms.org/scripts/printerfriendly.cfm?questionid=5919.

21.   "Sexual orientation: continuum," http://www.gURL.com/react/think/pages/0,,672040,00.html.

22. Very hazardous, when it comes to sexual behavior!
23. "Is it natural to be confused or question your sexuality at a young age?" http://www.plannedparenthood.org/teen-talk/ask/lesbian-gay-bisexual-trans/questioning/Is-it-natural-be-confused-question-sexuality-at-young-age-25737.htm.
24. Coalition for Positive Sexuality, http://www.positive.org.
25. Recommended to teens by SIECUS.
26. Advocates for Youth, http://www.advocatesforyouth.org/publications/safe-space/faq.htm.
27. GoAskAlice!, www.goaskalice.com.
28. "Should I explore my sexuality?" GoAskAlice!, http://www.goaskalice.columbia.edu/1093.html.
29. "I'm 15 and bisexual, but how do I know for sure?" http://www.scarleteen.com/article/advice/im_15_and_bisexual_but_how_do_i_know_for_sure.
30. Before it became "Teen Talk."
31. "In fact, 'normal' may not exist . . . 'sexually normal' is a subjective term, and defined by a certain culture at a certain time." www.goaskalice-cms.org/scripts/printerfriendly.cfm?questionid=5919.
32. "You can say to yourself every day, 'I'm a lesbian and I'm okay.'" (In Advocates for Youth's "I Think I Might Be Lesbian, Now What Do I Do?: A Brochure by and for Young Women," 9.)
33. "Your e-mail will also be read by the peer education supervisor." This individual is not identified.
34. "Peer Support," http://www.youthresource.com/peer/index.htm.
35. "Peer Educator: Devin," http://www.youthresource.com/peer/devin.htm.
36. Theodora writes in a later installment of her diagnosis with Polycystic Ovary Syndrome. Due to this potentially serious condition, she has an excess of male hormones. The treatment, however, will make her body more female. That's the last thing she wants, since she feels that she is male. Theodora's situation is a mess. Can't Advocates for Youth do a better job finding help for confused teens?
37. Site recommended to teens by SIECUS.
38. "A Girl Kisses a Girl . . . Is She Lesbian? Straight? Bi?" http://www.sexetc.org/story/glbtq/2163.
39. This organization also recommends gURL.com's Deal With It!—containing explicit and vulgar material—to teens ages 14 and above, and to parents, Planned Parenthood's All About Sex (mentioned earlier).
40. "Congratulations to Elizabeth Schroeder," http://findarticles.com/p/articles/mi_m0LFL/is_2006_Summer-Fall/ai_n17215455.
41. "A Girl Kisses a Girl . . . Is She Lesbian? Straight? Bi?" http://www.sexetc.org/story/glbtq/2163.
42. Come to think of it, Pomeroy was also chairman of SIECUS's board of directors; is urging teens to explore sexuality a requirement of that position?
43. Since 1998. See www.cdc.gov/hiv/topics/surveillance/resources/slides/adolescents/slides/adolescents_4.pdf.

44.   Especially racial/ethnic minority young people.

45.   And many health providers.

46.   Again, this indicates the reliance on condoms, which—as has been dis-
      cussed—do not provide adequate "protection."

47.   "HIV infection and AIDS in adolescents: An update of the position of the
      Society for Adolescent Medicine" (position paper), *Journal of Adolescent
      Health* 38 (2006): 88; National Office of AIDS Policy. *Youth and HIV/AIDS
      2000: A New American Agenda.*

48.   A majority in young people of color.

49.   "Communities at Risk: Youth," www.cdcnpin.org/scripts/population/
      youth.asp.

50.   GLB youth are more likely to have been sexually abused or victimized; this
      partially explains their higher risk behaviors.

51.   Robert Garofalo, R. Cameron Wolf, Shari Kessel, Judith Palfrey, and Robert
      H. DuRant, "The Association between Health Risk Behaviors and Sexual
      Orientation among a School-Based Sample of Adolescents," *Pediatrics* 101
      (1998): 895–902; Elizabeth M. Saewyc, Linda H. Bearinger, Robert Wm.
      Blum, and Michael D. Resnick, "Sexual Intercourse, Abuse and Pregnancy
      among Adolescent Women: Does Sexual Orientation Make a Difference?"
      Family Planning Perspectives 31, no. 3 (May/June 1999): 127–31; Goode-
      now C., Netherland], Szalacha L. "Aids related risk among adolescent
      males who have sex with males, females, or both: evidence from a
      statewide survey *American Journal of Public Health*, 92 (2002): 203–10;
      Bryan N. Cochran, MS, Angela J. Stewart, BA, Joshua A. Ginzler, Ph.D., and
      Ana Mari Cauce, Ph.D., "Challenges faced by homeless sexual minorities:
      comparison of gay, lesbian, bisexual, and transgender homeless adolescents
      with their heterosexual counterparts," *American Journal of Public Health* 92
      (2002): 773–77; S. M. Blake, R. Ledsky, T. Lehman, C. Goodenow, R.
      Sawyer, and T. Hack, "Preventing sexual risk behaviors among gay, lesbian,
      and bisexual adolescents: the benefits of gay-sensitive HIV instruction in
      schools," *American Journal of Public Health* 91 (2001): 940–46; E. M.
      Saewyce, C. L. Skay, L. H. Bearinger, R. W. M. Blum, and M. D. Resnick,
      "Sexual orientation, sexual behaviors, and pregnancy among American
      Indian adolescents," *Journal of Adolescent Health* 23, no. 4 (1998): 238–47.

52.   Robert Garofalo, R. Cameron Wolf, Shari Kessel, Judith Palfrey, and Robert
      H. DuRant, "The Association between Health Risk Behaviors and Sexual
      Orientation among a School-Based Sample of Adolescents"; Bryan N.
      Cochran, MS, Angela J. Stewart, BA, Joshua A. Ginzler, Ph.D., and Ana
      Mari Cauce, Ph.D., "Challenges faced by homeless sexual minorities: com-
      parison of gay, lesbian, bisexual, and transgender homeless adolescents
      with their heterosexual counterparts"; and S. M. Blake, R. Ledsky, T.
      Lehman, G. Goodnew, R. Sawyer, and T. Hack, "Preventing sexual risk
      behaviors among gay, lesbian, and bisexual adolescents: the benefits of gay-
      sensitive HIV instruction in schools."

53.   Elizabeth M. Saewyc, Linda H. Bearinger, Robert Wm. Blum, and Michael
      D. Resnick, "Sexual Intercourse, Abuse and Pregnancy among Adolescent
      Women: Does Sexual Orientation Make a Difference?"; Goodenow C.,
      Netherland, Szalacha L. "Aids related risk among adolescent males who
      have sex with males, females, or both: evidence from a statewide survey";
      Bryan N. Cochran, MS, Angela J. Stewart, BA, Joshua A. Ginzler, Ph.D., and
      Ana Mari Cauce, Ph.D., "Challenges faced by homeless sexual minorities:
      comparison of gay, lesbian, bisexual, and transgender homeless adolescents
      with their heterosexual counterparts"; Rotheram-Borus MJ, Marelich WD,
      Srinivasan S. HIV risk among homosexual, bisexual, and heterosexual male
      and female youths," *Arch Sex Behavior*28 (1999):159–77.
54.   Robert Garofalo, R. Cameron Wolf, Shari Kessel, Judith Palfrey, and Robert
      H. DuRant, "The Association between Health Risk Behaviors and Sexual
      Orientation among a School-Based Sample of Adolescents"; Goodenow C.,
      and Netherland, Szalacha L. "Aids related risk among adolescent males
      who have sex with males, females, or both: evidence from a statewide sur-
      vey." Note also that GLBTQ youth are twice as likely to use alcohol, three
      times more likely to use marijuana, and eight times more likely to use
      crack/cocaine; http://youthresource.com/health/lives/mental.htm.
55.   Duncan MacKellar et al, "Unrecognized HIV infection, Risk Behaviors, and
      Perceptions of Risk Among Young Men Who Have Sex with Men: Oppor-
      tunities for Advancing HIV Prevention in the Third Decade of HIV/AIDS,"
      Journal of Acquired Immune Deficiency Syndromes 38 no.5 (2005).
56.   Elizabeth M. Saewyc, Linda H. Bearinger, Robert Wm. Blum, and Michael
      D. Resnick, "Sexual Intercourse, Abuse and Pregnancy among Adolescent
      Women: Does Sexual Orientation Make a Difference?"; Robin L, Brener
      ND, Donahue SF, Hack T, Hale K, and Goodenow C, "Associations between
      health risk behaviors and opposite-, same-, and both sex sexual partners
      in representative samples of Vermont and Massachusetts high school stu-
      dents," *Arch Pediatr Adolesc Med.* 156, no. 4 (2002): 349–55; Rotheram-
      Borus MJ, Marelich WD, and Srinivasan S., "HIV risk among homosexual,
      bisexual, and heterosexual male and female youths."
57.   Katherine Fethers, Caron Marks, Adrian Mindel, and Claudia S Estcourt,
      (2000) "Sexually Transmitted Infections and risk behaviors in women who
      have sex with women," *Sexually Transmitted Infections* 76 (2000): 345–49.
58.   "Lesbians are twice as likely as their heterosexual peers to experience
      unwanted pregnancy," http://youthresource.com/health/women/index.htm.
59.   Teresa M. Darragh, "Anal Cytology for Anal Cancer Screening: Is it Time
      Yet?" *Diagnostic Cytopathology* 30, no. 6 (2004).
60.   "Anal Cytology for Anal Cancer Screening," 2004.
61.   "Syphilis and MSM (Men Who Have Sex with Men)—CDC Fact Sheet,"
      www.cdc.gov/std/syphilis/STDFact-MSM&Syphilis.htm#concern.
62.   Michele G. Sullivan, "Bisexual College Women at Greatest Risk for STDs,"
      Clinical Psychiatry News, May 2008, 55.

63.   Interesting that with sex education teaching kids how common SSA and SS behavior are, only 3 percent in this large sample of women are self-described as bisexual, 1 percent as lesbian, and 1 percent as unsure.

64.   Surveys of almost 40,000 people in Massachusetts on overall health status indicated poorer health was observed most often for bisexuals. Regarding mental health alone, 21 percent of straight/heterosexual, 25 percent of gay/lesbian/homosexual, and 45 percent of bisexual adults reported feeling tense or worried for more than 14 of the last 30 days. 16 percent of straight/heterosexual and gay/lesbian/homosexual and 29 percent of bisexual adults reported feeling sad or blue for more than 14 of the last 30 days. 3 percent of straight/heterosexual, 4 percent of gay/lesbian/homosexual, and 29 percent of bisexual adults reported that they seriously considered suicide in the prior 12 months. 8 percent of straight/heterosexual, 17 percent of gay/lesbian/homosexual, and 34 percent of bisexual adults reported illicit Drug use at some point in the last 30 days. See Anthony F. Jorm et al, "Sexual Orientation and Mental Health: results from a community survey of young and middle-aged adults", *British Journal of Psychiatry* 180 (2002): 423–27, and http://www.mass.gov/Eeohhs2/docs/dph/health_equity/sexual_orientation_disparities_report.pdf.

65.   "Gay Marriage Goes Dutch," CBS News Online, http://www.cbsnews.com/stories/2001/04/01/world/main283071.shtml.

66.   Eric D. Widmer, Judith Treas, and Robert Newcomb, "Attitudes Toward Nonmarital Sex in 24 Countries," *The Journal of Sex Research* 35, no. 4 (1998): 349–58.

67.   G. Stolte, N. H. Dukers, J. B. de Wit, H. Fennema, R. A. Coutinho, "A summary report from Amsterdam: increase in sexually transmitted diseases and risky sexual behavior among homosexual men in relation to the introduction of new anti-HIV Drugs," *European Surveillance* 7, no.2 (February 2002):19–22; A. K. Van der Bij, I. G. Stolte, R. A. Coutinho, N. H. Dukers, "Increase of sexually transmitted infections, but not HIV, among young homosexual men in Amsterdam: are STIs still reliable markers for HIV transmission?" *Sex Transm Infect* 81, no.1 (February 2005):34–37; J. S. Fennema, I. Cairo, and R. A. Coutinho, "Substantial increase in gonorrhea and syphilis among clients of Amsterdam Sexually Transmitted Diseases Clinic," *Ned Tijdschr Geneeskd* 144, no.13 (March 2000): 602–3; Ineke G. Stolte et al, "Low HIV-testing rates among younger high-risk homosexual men in Amsterdam," *Sex Transm Infect* 83 (2007): 387–91; E. M. van der Snoek et al, "Prevalence of STD and HIV infections among attendees of the Erasmus MC STD clinic, Rotterdam, The Netherlands, during the years 1996 to 2000," *International Journal of STD&AIDS* 14 (2003): 119–24.

68.   Ron de Graaf et al, "Suicidality and Sexual Orientation: Differences Between Men and Women in a General Population-Based Sample From The Netherlands," *Archives of Sexual Behavior* 35, no. 3 (June 2006): 253–62; Theo G. M. Sandfort, "Same-Sex Sexual Behavior and Psychiatric Disorders," *Arch Gen Psychiatry* 58 (2001): 85–91.

69. "Why do nice guys always finish last?" GoAskAlice!, www.goaskalice. columbia.edu/1698.html.

70. Unless you're a girl who is exclusively with girls—in that case the risk of STDs is very low, and HIV virtually impossible.

71. Esther Drill et al, *Deal With It!*, 162; and Don Romesburg, *Young Gay & Proud* (Alyson Books, 1995), 76 (book suggested by Sex etc from Rutgers).

72. Op cit. 88-89; *YG&P*, 77.

73. *YG&P*, 81-83.

74. "Menage a Trois?" GoAskAlice!, http://goaskalice.com/0673.html.

75. "The pill—where do I get it and do my parents have to know?" GoAskAlice!, http://www.goaskalice.columbia.edu/1703.html; "Parental Consent for Abortion?" GoAskAlice!, http://www.goaskalice.columbia. edu/2060.html.

76. "S/M role playing," GoAskAlice!, http://goaskalice.com/0646.html.

77. Anna Montrose, "Brain Candy: Meow meow meow mix," *The McGill Daily* 40, March 10, 2005.

78. Dennis Prager, "College taught her not to be a heterosexual," Town-Hall.com, April 19, 2005.

79. Lisa M. Diamond, "What Does Sexual Orientation Orient? A Biobehavioral Model Distinguishing Romantic Love and Sexual Desire," *Psychological Review* 110, no. 1 (2003): 173-92.

80. Lisa M. Diamond, *Sexual Fluidity: Understanding Women's Love and Desire* (MA: Harvard University Press, 2008).

81. These women were non-heterosexual, but declined to attach a label to their sexual identity.

82. Lisa M. Diamond, *Sexual Fluidity*, 10.

83. Ibid., 82.

84. Lisa M. Diamond, "Development of Sexual Orientation Among Adolescent and Young Adult Women," *Developmental Psychology* 34, no.5 (1998): 1085.

85. Pagan Kennedy, "Q&A with Lisa Diamond: A scholar finds women's sexual orientation to be surprisingly fluid," *The Boston Globe*, December 30, 2007.

86. Lisa M. Diamond, "Female Bisexuality from Adolescence to Adulthood: Results From a 10-Year Longitudinal Study," *Developmental Psychology* 44, no. 1 (2008): 5.

87. Lisa M. Diamond, *Sexual Fluidity*, 89.

88. Ibid., 83, 105.

89. An earlier study of 7,000 lesbians revealed 77.3 percent had a history of one or more male partners. [Allison L Diamant et al, "Lesbians' Sexual History with Men," *Archives of Internal Medicine* 159 (December 1999)].

90. Lisa M. Diamond, *Sexual Fluidity*, 110.

91. Craig Hoffman, "A class apart," *Financial Times*, April 15, 2005.

92. E. O. Laumann et al, *The social organization of sexuality: Sexual practices in the United States* (Chicago: University of Chicago Press, 1994), 309.

93. The question of "What does it mean?"—in other words what does a particular sex act signify and communicate—is centrally important to the female sexual experience, before, during, and after. For men, in contrast, the different possible meanings matter less, and sex might often be a perfectly fine experience even if it hardly means anything at all." (R. F. Baumeister, "Gender Differences in Erotic Plasticity: The Female Sex Drive as Socially Flexible and Responsive," *Psychological Bulletin* 126, no. 3 (2000): 371)

94. "Teen Talk," http://www.teenwire.com/infocus/1998/if-19981201p052.php.

95. This might be correct when it comes to boys, but we know that boys and girls are different. And the scientific evidence backs that up. In 2000, the eminent psychologist Roy F. Baumeister wrote a scholarly review of the subject, using data from nearly 200 references to support his proposal that the female sex drive is "more malleable" than the male. From his conclusion: "The relatively low plasticity of the male sex drive suggests that biochemical factors such as hormones, age, general health, and genetic predispositions may often be the driving forces. . . . For women, in contrast, sex is driven by sociocultural factors, interpretations, context, expectations, and the like."

    Meredith L. Chivers is an eminent psychologist and research fellow at the Canadian Institutes of Health (Canada's NIH?). She also sits on the Board of Directors, *Sex Information and Education Council of Canada (SIEC-CAN)*—Canada's SIECUS. She was awarded $100,000 to study female sexual arousal. She reported in 2004 that "Female sexuality, in general, may be more motivated by extrinsic factors, such as the desire to initiate or maintain a romantic than by intrinsic factors, such as genital sexual arousal. Also, "a self identified heterosexual woman would be mistaken to question her sexual identity because she became aroused watching female-female erotica; most heterosexual women experience such arousal." For girls, research indicates that over time, their emotional and physical attraction will be liable to shift, depending on the nature and context of relationships, and that it is more likely to shift toward heterosexuality.

96. Victoria A. Veter, "The Role of Friendship in the Development and Maintenance of Lesbian Love Relationships," *Journal of Homosexuality* 8, no.2 (1982): 51.

97. "A Girl Kisses a Girl . . . Is She Lesbian? Straight? Bi?" http://www.sexetc.org/story/glbtq/2163.

98. According to teenwire, sexual orientation "*may change* over the course of a lifetime." SIECUS explains in a newsletter for parents: the understanding and identification of one's sexual orientation *may change* over the course of a lifetime. But elsewhere SIECUS declares: sexual orientation *cannot be changed*, a view shared by AFY: ". . . like right or left handedness . . . sexual orientation cannot be changed."

99. Pagan Kennedy, "Q&A with Lisa Diamond: A scholar finds women's sexual orientation to be surprisingly fluid."

100. Commonly called reparative therapy.

101. Dr. Spitzer spearheaded the effort to have homosexuality officially removed from the APA's list of mental disorders, which was accomplished in 1973.

102. Robert L. Spitzer, "Can Some Gay Men and Lesbians Change Their Sexual Orientation? 200 Participants Reporting a Change from Homosexual to Heterosexual Orientation," *Archives of Sexual Behavior* 32, no. 5 (October 2003), 403–17.

103. National Association for Research and Therapy of Homosexuality (www.narth.com).

104. Debra W. Haffner, *Beyond the Big Talk* (New York: Newmarket Press, 2001), 183.

105. Not a sex ed site, but frequently referred to by sex educators' sites.

106. "How Can I Get My Parents to Understand That I Can't Change My Sexual Orientation?" www.hrc.org/issues/4121.htm.

107. "Young Gay America Magazine," http://www.ygamag.com/.

108. Lydia Malmedie, "Gay journalist claims to be straight," July 3, 2007, http://www.pinknews.co.uk/news/articles/2005-4837.html; "Michael Glatze Falls Prey to Ex-Gay Indoctrination," gayrepublic.org/print.php?sid= 1488&lead=1—4k; Gay City News, gaycitynews.com/site/news.cfm? newsid=18576571&BRD=2729&PAG=461&dept_id=568864&rfi=6—53k; "'Ex-Gay' Editor Still Talking," http://www.queerty.com/ex-gay-editor-still talking-20070712/; "Gay Activist Leaves Homosexuality," http://www.gay.eu/ article/10371//Gay_activist_leaves_homosexuality.

109. F. O. Laumann, J. H. Gagnon, R. T. Michael, and F. Michaels, *The Social Organization of Sexuality: Sexual Practices in the United States* (Chicago: University of Chicago Press, 1994).

110. Robert Garofalo, R. Cameron Wolf, Shari Kessel, Judith Palfrey, and Robert H. DuRant, "The Association between Health Risk Behaviors and Sexual Orientation among a School-Based Sample of Adolescents," *Pediatrics* 101, no 5 (May 1998): 895–902; Milton Wainberg et al, *Crystal Meth and Men Who Have Sex with Men: What Mental Health Care Professionals Need to Know* (New York: Haworth Medical Press, 2006); Perry Halkitis, Leo Wilton, and Jack Drescher, eds., *Barebacking: Psychosocial and Public Health Approaches* (New York: Haworth Medical Press, 2005); Sean Esteban McCabe et al, "Assessment of Difference in Dimensions of Sexual Orientation: Implications for Substance Use Research in a College-Age Population," *Journal of Studies on Alcohol* 66 (2005): 602–29.

111. Centers for Disease Control, "Trends in HIV/AIDS Diagnoses among men who have sex with men—33 States, 2001-2006," *MMWR* Weekly 57, no. 25 (June 2008): 681–86.

112. "Parents and Friends of Ex-Gays and Gays," www.pfox.org.

113. Rogers H. Wright and Nicholas A. Cummings, op cit., xv.

Chapter 7

1. Lewis Carroll, *Alice in Wonderland*.

2. From a book recommended to teens: "a system of dividing people into one of two impossible-to-live-up-to standards: male or female," Kate Bornstein, *My Gender Workbook: How to Become a Real Man, a Real Woman, the Real You, or Something Else Entirely* (New York: Routledge, 1997), 25.

3. He defined the word's new meaning as "the overall degree of masculinity and/or femininity that is privately experienced and publicly manifested . . . and that usually though not invariably correlates with the anatomy of the organs of reproduction." John Money, *Gendermaps: Social Constructionism, Feminism, and Sexosophical History* (New York: Continuum International Publishing Group, 1995), 19.

4. Ibid., 52.

5. Money gave the example of pedophilia, which is usually seen as child molestation, a crime, and is "never called 'a love-affair between an age-discrepant couple,' which it sometimes is." Marsha Pomerantz, "Sexual Congress," *Jerusalem Post*, June 24, 1981, 6; and Theo Sandfort, *Boys on Their Contacts with Men: A study of Sexually Expressed Friendships* (New York: Global Academic Publishers, 1987), 5–7.

6. "If I were to see the case of a boy aged ten or eleven who's intensely erotically attracted toward a man in his twenties or thirties, if the relationship is totally mutual, and the bonding is genuinely totally mutual . . . then I would not call it pathological in any way."

7. "A childhood sexual experience, such as being the partner of a relative or of an older person, need not necessarily affect the child adversely."

8. John Colapinto, *As Nature Made Him: The Boy Who was Raised as a Girl* (New York: HarperCollins, 2000), 26–27.

9. As well as other intersex conditions.

10. Christine Gorman, "A Boy Without a Penis," *TIME* magazine, March 24, 1997; Peggy T. Cohen-Kettenis, "As Nature Made Him: The boy who was raised as a girl," book review in *The New England Journal of Medicine* 342, no.19: 1457–8.

11. "It reminded me of the guy with the odds stacked against him," David said of his choice of a name two decades later, "the guy who was facing up to a giant eight feet tall. It reminded me of courage."

12. Paul R. McHugh, *The Mind Has Mountains: Reflections on Society and Psychiatry* (Johns Hopkins University Press, 2006), 227.

13. John Colapinto, *As Nature Made Him*, 55–60.

14. John Colapinto and Natalie Angier, "X 1 Y=Z," *New York Times* Book Review, February 20, 2000; available online at: http://www.nytimes.com/books/00/02/20/reviews/000220.20angiert.html.

15. David Reimer on the Diane Rehm Show: http://www.wamu.org/programs/Dr./00/02/22.php.

16. His mother required hospitalization for depression and a suicide attempt; his dad became an alcoholic. Brian descended into drug use and petty crime. Aside from the horrible circumstances into which they'd been thrown, there was most likely a genetic component to the family's depres-

sion and substance abuse. (John Colapinto, "Gender Gap," *Slate*, posted June 3, 2004).

17.   John Colapinto, *As Nature Made Him*, 180, 182.

18.   Natalie Angier, "X 1 Y=Z," *New York Times* Book Review, February 20, 2000.

19.   "Advocates for Youth," http://www.advocatesforyouth.org/publications/safespace/faq.htm

20.   "Genderpalooza! A Sex & Gender Primer," http://www.scarleteen.com/article/body/genderpalooza_a_sex_gender_primer.

21.   "I hate being a girl: is that wrong?" http://www.scarleteen.com/article/advice/i_hate_being_a_girl_is_that_wrong.

22.   Planned Parenthood program content guidelines I, 5.

23.   Ibid., 71.

24.   On the other hand, males are expected to be "tough, muscular, strong, unemotional, rational, not stylish, better at math and science, athletic, more sexual, powerful, not domestic, build things (sic)."

25.   This was a heinous crime, and the murderers deserved their sentences (death and life imprisonment). However, it's highly unlikely Teena was targeted solely because of failure to conform to a female gender stereotype—emotional, delicate, domestic, etc. Teena had a history of unlawful behavior and had associated with her murderers, violent ex-convicts, for some time. The two individuals murdered with her also knew the killers. In short, there's much more to the story of Brandon Teena than gender issues, which gURL.com should not leave out.

26.   Each person normally has one pair of sex chromosomes in each cell. The Y chromosome is present in males, who have one X and one Y chromosome, while females have two X chromosomes.

27.   Helen Skaletsky et al, "The male-specific region of the human Y chromosome is a mosaic of discrete sequence classes," *Nature* 423, no 6942 (2003): 825–38.

28.   Larry Cahill, "Why Sex Matters for Neuroscience," *Nature Reviews Neuroscience* 7 (June 2006): 477–84.

29.   Jill B. Becker et al, eds., *Sex Differences in the Brain: From Genes to Behavior* (Oxford University Press, 2006), xviii; see also Daniel D. Federman, "The Biology of Human Sex Differences," The *New England Journal of Medicine* 354 (2006): 1507–14.

30.   Clearly this is a complex subject; childhood experiences may be important too, depending on the individual. Still, it is accurate to conclude that there *are* typical boy and girl behaviors, due primarily to differences in how the embryonic brain develops and secondarily to psychosocial factors. The fact that there are many exceptions among individuals does not contradict the finding that, as a group and across cultures, certain behaviors are expressed more frequently. (see Richard C Friedman and Jennifer I Downey (2008) Sexual Differentiation of Behavior: The Foundation of a Developmental Model of Psychosexuality, *Journal of the American Psychoanalytic Association* 56).

31. Other genes influence the process as well.

32. Louann Brizendine, *The Female Brain* (New York: Random House, 2006), 5.

33. Differences in fetal hormone levels can sometimes be discerned as early as day 16 post-fertilization.

34. Richard C. Friedman and Jennifer I. Downey, "Sexual Differentiation of Behavior: The Foundation of a Developmental Model of Psychosexuality," Journal of the American Psychoanalytic Association 56 (2008): 147.

35. Jennifer Connellan, Simon Baron-Cohen, Sally Wheelwright, Anna Batki, and Jag Ahluwalia, "Sex differences in human neonatal social perception," *Infant Behavior and Development* 23 (2000): 113–18.

36. Svetlana Lutchmaya and Simon Baron-Cohen, "Human Sex Differences in social and non-social looking preferences, at 12 months of age," *Infant Behavior and Development* 25 (2002): 319–25.

37. Svetlana Lutchmaya, Simon Baron-Cohen, and Peter Raggatt, (2002) "Foetal testosterone and eye contact in 12-month-old human infants," *Infant Behavior & Development* 25 (2000): 327–35.

38. "When my granddaughter was born, I noticed her little knit cap and blanket was pink and blue. Another victory."

39. "FYI: Gender at gURL.com," http://www.gURL.com/findout/guides/articles/0,,702673-5,00.html.

40. Megumi Iijima, Osamu Arisaka, Fumie Minamoto, and Yasumasa Arai, "Sex Differences in Children's Free Dr.awings: A Study on Girls with Congenital Adrenal Hyperplasia," *Hormones and Behavior* 40 (2001): 99–104.

41. David Reimer on The Diane Rehm Show, February 22, 2000; http://www.wamu.org/programs/Dr./00/02/22.php.

42. Jill B. Becker et al, eds., *Sex Differences in the Brain: From Genes to Behavior* (Oxford University Press, 2008).

43. D. N. Ruble, C. L. Martin, and S. A. Berenbaum, "Gender Development," in N. Eisenberg, ed., *Handbook of Child Psychology 3: social, emotional, and personality development*, 6th edition, 858–32 (New York: Wiley, 2006).

44. Lisa A. Serbin, et al, "Gender Stereotyping in Infancy: Visual preferences for and knowledge of gender-sterotyped toys in the second year," *International Journal of Behavioral Development*, 25, no.1 (2001), 7–15.

45. Anne Campbell, Louisa Shirley, Charles Heywood , and Charles Cook, "Infants' visual preference for sex-congruent babies, children, toys and activities: A longitudinal study," *British Journal of Developmental Psychology* 18 (2000): 494.

46. Lisa A. Serbin, et al, "Gender Stereotyping in Infancy: Visual preferences for and knowledge of gender-sterotyped toys in the second year."

47. Anne Campbell, et al, "Infants' visual preference for sex-congruent babies, children, toys and activities: A longitudinal study"; Lisa A. Serbin, et al, "Gender Stereotyping in Infancy: Visual preferences for and knowledge of gender-sterotyped toys in the second year."

48. S.A. Berenbaum and M. Hines, "Early androgens are related to childhood sex-typed toy preferences," *Psychological Science* 3 (1992): 203–06; M. Hines and F.R. Kaufman, "Androgen and the development of human sex-

typical behavior: rough-and tumble play and sex of preferred playmates in children with congenital adrenal hyperplasia (CAH)," *Child Development* 65 (1994): 1042–53.

49. Gerianne M. Alexander and Melissa Hines, "Sex differences in response to children's toys in nonhuman primates (Cercopithecus aethiops sabaeus)," *Evolution and Human Behavior* 23 (2002): 467–79; Janice M. Hassett, Erin R. Siebert, and Kim Wallen, "Sexually Differentiated Toy Preferences in Rhesus Monkeys," *Hormones and Behavior* 46 (2004): 91 (abstract only).

50. Ewen Callaway, "Male monkeys prefer boys' toys," April 4, 2008, http://www.newscientist.com/article/dn13596-male-monkeys-prefer-boys-toys.html.

51. "I think I might be transgender, now what do I do?" Found on www.AdvocatesforYouth.org; see also Jessie Gilliam, "I'm coming out . . . I want the world to know. . . (Or do I?)" *Transitions* 14, no. 4 (June 2002), available online at: http://www.lgbthealth.net/downloads/research/AdvocatesforYouth.pdf.

52. "Ask the Experts," www.teenwire.com/ask/2005/as-20050623p1056-gender.php?print=yes.

53. Jesse Ellison, "BIID: Why Sufferers Amputate Their Own Limbs," Newsweek Health, May 28, 2000, http://www.newsweek.com/id/138932.

54. David Brang, Paul McGeoch, Vilayanur Ramachandran, "Apotemnophilia: a neurological disorder," *NeuroReport* 19, no.13 (August 2008).

55. "Genderpalooza! A Sex & Gender Primer," http://www.scarleteen.com/article/body/genderpalooza_a_sex_gender_primer.

56. Harold I. Kaplan, Alfred M. Freedman, and Benjamin J. Sadock, *Comprehensive Textbook of Psychiatry Vol. 2*, 3rd edition (Williams and Wilkins, 1980), 1697; Mollie S. Smart and Russell C. Smart, *Children: Development and Relationships*, 4th edition (New York: Macmillan Publishing, 1982), 280–81; see also Diane M. Ruble, Carol Lynn Martin, and Sheri A. Berenbaum, "Gender Development," in Vol. 3 of Nancy Eisenberg, ed , *Handbook of Child Psychology*, 6th Edition, (John Wiley, 2006), 861–62; Ross Vasta, Marshall H. Haith, and Scott A. Miller, *Child Psychology: The Modern Science*, 2nd edition (John Wiley, 1992), 561.

57. A diagnosis that is being challenged by gender activists in the mental health profession.

58. "Your understanding of who you are [regarding gender identity] may change over the course of your lifetime." http://www.siecus.org/_data/global/images/TalkAboutSex.pdf.

59. "Many of us question our gender at various points in our lives," says Planned Parenthood's site for teens. "And our gender identity may shift and evolve over time." http://www.teenwire.com/infocus/2007/if-20070717p495-trans.php.

60. "Advocates for Youth," www.advocatesforyouth.org/publications/safespace/faq.htm.

61. "LGBTQ 101," http://www.plannedparenthood.org/teen-talk/lesbian-gay-bisexual-trans/questioning/lgbtq-101-25421.htm.

62.   It's important to note that in many instances "atypical gender expression" includes tomboys and sensitive males as well as individuals who insist they were born in the wrong body. The MCPS refused to change their curriculum to explain that being a tomboy or a sensitive male does not mean you are transgender.

63.   "From Sexuality and Society"—Powerpoint of sex educator Judy Chaission.

64.   Samuel Lurie, "Overview of Transgender Issues for College Health Centers," *Action: The Official Newsletter of the American College Health Organization* 45, no.4 (2006): 1.

65.   Fred A. Bernstein, "On Campus, Rethinking Biology 101," *New York Times*, March 7, 2004.

66.   Regret after sex reassignment surgery has been documented; see Stig-Eric Olsson and Anders Moller, "Regret after Sex Reassignment Surgery in a Male to Female Transsexual: A Long Term Follow-Up," *Archives of Sexual Behavior* 35, no. 4 (2006): 501–06.

67.   "I hate being a girl: is that wrong?" http://www.scarleteen.com/ article/advice/i_hate_being_a_girl_is_that_wrong.

68.   American Psychiatric Publishing, Inc, *Diagnostic and Statistical Manual— Text Revision* (DSM-IV-TR™, 2000).

69.   One notes how often the term "transgender folks" is used to get us to believe these are people just like you and I—they just want to be castrated, that's all.

70.   "The prevalence of gender dysphoria among patients aged over 15 years was calculated as 8.18 per 100 000, with an approximate sex ratio of 4:1 in favour of male-to-female patients," Wilson P., Sharp C., and Carr S., "The prevalence of gender dysphoria in Scotland: a primary care study," *British Journal of General Practice* 49, no.449 (December 1999): 991–92; "There are no recent epidemiological studies to provide data on prevalence of Gender Identity Disorder. Data from smaller countries in Europe with access to total population statistics and referrals suggest that roughly 1 per 30,000 adult males and 1 per 100,000 adult females seek sex-reassignment surgery." *Diagnostic and Statistical Manual*, 4th edition (American Psychiatric Publishing); "Gender confusion . . . affects about 1:20,000 males and 1:50,000 females," Bonnie R. Strickland, exec ed., *Gale Encyclopedia of Psychology*, 2nd edition, (Gale Group, 2001). Even more liberal estimates fail to support Heather's claim: in a study of non-referred children ages 12–13, 2.7 percent of girls and 0 percent of boys wished to be the opposite sex; this included transient events, therefore not truly representing gender dysphoria. From Melvin Lewis, ed., *Child and Adolescent Psychiatry* (Williams & Wilkens, 1991), 605. While there are limitations to all the data, I cannot find any study supporting the notion that gender dysphoria is "especially common" at any age.

71.   "Genderpalooza! A Sex & Gender Primer," http://www.scarleteen. com/article/body/genderpalooza_a_sex_gender_primer.

72. SIECUS, "Talk About Sex," http://www.siecus.org/_data/global/images/ TalkAboutSex.pdf, 24.

73. Kay Clark, "Transgender: Understanding Gender Differences", *ETR Associates*, 2005.

74. Consider themselves beyond or between genders.

75. "Advocates for Youth," http://www.advocatesforyouth.org/publications/ safespace/faq.htm.

76. "FYI: Gender at gURL.com," http://www.gURL.com/findout/guides/ articles/0,,702673-6,00.html.

77. "My Gender Workbook: How to Become a Real Man, a Real Woman, the Real You, or Something Else Entirely," http://www.scarleteen.com/node/ 502; here, Heather calls the book "awesome"; "Start Your Sexuality Canon,"
http://www.scarleteen.com/article/read/start_your_sexuality_canon; and "I hate being a girl: is that wrong?" http://www.scarleteen.com/article/advice/ i_hate_being_a_girl_is_that_wrong.

78. Kate Bornstein, *My Gender Workbook*, 7.

79. Susan Brindle, "Gender Outlaw: An interview with Kate Borstein," *EnlightenNext* magazine, http://www.enlightennext.org/magazine/j16/ kate.asp.

80. Terry Vanderheyden "Harvard Applicants May Now Declare Third 'Gender,'" LifeSiteNews.com, July 26, 2006.

81. Joanne Creighton, president of Smith College: "Our policy is to admit women and to support them in their intellectual and personal development. We expect that students will explore a wide range of issues of identity." (Allison Metz, "Do transgender students adhere to the mission of a women's college?" May 3, 2007, www.themhnews.com).

82. Fred A. Bernstein, "On Campus, Rethinking Biology 101," *New York Times*, March 7, 2004.

83. Also at Emerson College, University of Michigan , University of Vermont, and Washington University.

84. "UCLGBTIA: Transgender Health," http://www.uclgbtia.org/transhealth.html.

85. "Creative_yayas: Mail Art Call—We All Bleed (Period)," LiveJournal post by user violetanger, http://community.livejournal.com/creative_yayas/ 16094.html.

86. "Another reason not to send your kids to UMass Amherst...," www.massresistance.org/docs/gen/08b/tranny_parade/part3/trans_flyer.html.

87. Event sponsored in part by the Department of Psychology, Department of American Studies, and the College of Education and Human Development, http://www.glbta.umn.edu/trans/kate.html.

88. Kate Bornstein, *My Gender Workbook*, 21, 35.

89. Ibid., 30–31.

90. Ibid.

91. Consider this email exchange between Kate and her transgender friend, Riki:

Riki: "What is it that makes you so sad, Kate? What is 'sad and frightening' all the time? Ever since I've known you, you wear sadness like a chemise under whatever garb is on top."

Kate: "I think it's the combined sorrow of all those good-byes, that's the essence of the sorrow. As to fear. . . . It's little kid fears that are always there. Monsters in the attic, mom won't be there when I get home, nobody loves me, someone's gonna hurt me, no one's gonna rescue me, I'm gonna be all alone and lonely to the bone."

Riki: "I can't believe how many transpeople are 'lonely to the bone,' and I can't believe how little we talk about it, even amongst each other." (from Bornstein, *My Gender Workbook*, 248–49)

92.   Paul R. McHugh, *The Mind Has Mountains: Reflections on Society and Psychiatry* (Johns Hopkins University Press, 2006).

Conclusion

1.   MSNBC, "Maine middle school to offer birth control," (18 October 2007) http://www.msnbc.msn.com/id/21358971/.

Index